Mussolini:

The Secrets of His Death

Luciano Garibaldi

Mussolini:

The Secrets of His Death

Enigma Books

Translated by Robert L. Miller

Original Italian title:
La pista inglese

Copyright © 2004 Enigma Books

ISBN 1-929631-23-5

Printed in the United States of America

Library of Congress Cataloging-in-Publication Data

Garibaldi, Luciano.
 [La pista inglese. English]
 Mussolini : the secrets of his death / Luciano Garibaldi ; translated by Robert L. Miller.

 p : ill. ; cm.
 Originally published in Italian: La pista inglese : chi uccise Mussolini e la Petacci? Milano : Ares, c2002.
 Includes bibliographical references and index.
 ISBN: 1-929631-23-5

1. Mussolini, Benito, 1883-1945—Death and burial. 2. Petacci, Clara, 1912-1945—Death and burial. 3. Heads of state—Italy—Death. 4. Mistresses—Italy—Death. 5. Treasure-trove—Italy—Dongo. 6. Dongo (Italy)—History. I. Miller, Robert L. (Robert Lawrence), 1945- II. Title. III. Title: La pista inglese.

DG575.M8 G29 2004
945.091/092/4 B

TABLE OF CONTENTS

INTRODUCTION TO THIS EDITION

MUSSOLINI was shot on April 28, 1945. This much is certain and no one disputes the date of his death. The bodies—that of Mussolini, of his mistress Claretta Petacci and the other fascist leaders—were put on display and photographed hanging by the feet in Milan's Piazzale Loreto during the early morning of April 29, 1945, in full view of a large crowd. Those brutal images remain to this day, some sixty years later, as one of the many symbols of closure to the Second World War for Italy and the world.

The key question investigative journalist and historian Luciano Garibaldi is asking in this book is a startling one. Was Mussolini's death in fact a summary execution by Italian partisans acting on behalf of a British Special Force (SOE)?

A very recent documentary produced by Peter Tompkins a former OSS officer in Italy in 1943–1944 was aired on Italy's RAI-3 channel on August 28 and September 4, 2004. The documentary goes over much of the same material contained in this book with very convincing interviews of the main protagonists in the matter of Mussolini's death and the documents he was carrying with him at the time of his arrest. There are several versions of Mussolini's execution by partisans and many Italian researchers and historians have spent years trying to unravel the truth. An article in the London *Times* written by Richard Owen and published on August 28,

2004, quotes SOE historian and researcher Christopher Woods as disputing "the suggestion that a British spy had led the assassination mission "It's just love of conspiracy-making. The leaders of the Resistance in Milan, particularly the left-wing parties, decided that Mussolini should be killed before the Allies arrived."" We believe this book by reviewing the various claims gets closer to what actually happened on April 28, 1945, in the village of Giulino di Mezzegra on Lake Como where Mussolini and his mistress Claretta Petacci spent their final night and met their violent end.

After a quarter of a century of research with a number of archives still out of reach or closed to historians, and other documents either missing or destroyed, much of the available evidence is necessarily circumstantial. To date there is no "smoking gun." The winding path leading to the theory of SOE involvement however is studded with disturbing clues. In intelligence matters when dealing with espionage and covert operations at a very sensitive level every element, however elusive, acquires of necessity extraordinary importance. One background issue appears to be well documented, namely that Winston Churchill in his determination to destroy Nazism and fascism and eradicate their political existence was not averse to resort to assassination when necessary.[1] The execution of Nazis and their collaborators from SS Obergruppenführer Reinhard Heydrich in Prague to Admiral Darlan in Algiers, both taking place in 1942, carried the imprint of SOE operations and were not at all out of character with the Prime Minister's words and decisions.

The lingering questions in the elimination of Benito Mussolini and his mistress must therefore concentrate on the motive for the execution. The issue of getting to the facts, beyond archival problems, is compounded by the peculiarities of Italian politics. Almost sixty years after the bloody events of 1943–1945 the entire period is still perceived by many Italians as being taboo. Most academic Italian historians—with a few notable exceptions—have kept their distance from any real scientific gathering and analysis of the facts, let alone venturing into any interpretations. The years 1943–1945 thus became the exclusive domain of investigative journalists, many of them politically on the right but not all of them necessarily neo-fascists, who labored relentlessly in their search for the facts. Of course there were and are a number of neo-fascist writers also working on this subject, seeking to rehabilitate the fascist regime in general and even the RSI period, which given the record, becomes a rather difficult enterprise by any standard.

Several books by authors politically on the Left have now appeared on the subject of the collaborationist period of 1943–1945 and the retribution that took place after Liberation. The most noteworthy and popular being the work by Giampaolo Pansa *Il Sangue dei Vinti* (Milan: Sperling Kupfer, 2003). The first complete historical reconstruction of the political career of Benito Mussolini was published in Renzo De Felice's eight volume unfinished biography ending in mid-1944. De Felice began working on this monumental endeavor while still influenced by Marxist ideology—he was a member of the Italian Communist Party until 1956—but by the time he came close to finishing the work and was no longer a Marxist he had graduated into the *bête noire* of the left. De Felice had consulted, among many others, the works of many investigative journalists, including, in particular, those of Luciano Garibaldi, the author of this book.[2] At the end of 1995 in various interviews De Felice announced that his final volume of the Mussolini biography would include documents supporting the theory of British involvement in the Duce's execution. This prompted famed Oxford historian Denis Mack Smith to accuse De Felice of being "an anti-British historian" and demanding that he (De Felice) produce any new documents he may have. However, De Felice's sudden death from pancreatic cancer in 1996 prevented him from completing the final key volume of the Mussolini biography and the documents he referred to many times were nowhere to be found among his papers.[3] The biography does not therefore discuss the facts surrounding Mussolini's execution and any related notes in preparation for that book have not been found according to historians who knew De Felice and his widow. It is important however to examine the exact words used by De Felice in his declarations to the press: at a meeting of historians De Felice stated to the *Corriere della Sera* on November 19, 1995: "If I had to say that I did have a hard document in my hand I would not be telling the truth. However, I have assembled a vast body of documents that clearly indicate British involvement in the death of Mussolini." And he added: "The documentation in my possession leads to one conclusion: Benito Mussolini was killed by a group of partisans from Milan at the request of the British intelligence services." "For the British it was best for Mussolini to be dead. Their national interest was at stake because of the explosive compromises that were proposed in the correspondence that Prime Minister Churchill had with Mussolini before and during the war." And De Felice firmly stated that the correspondence did in fact exist: "There are the statements of the persons who saw the documents and a major Italian political figure who told me 'We have returned it.'" The action itself was ordered by a British officer in Milan, close to the partisans in the area, two or three groups supported either by the British or the Americans, all looking to seize Mussolini. The Americans wanted the former Duce alive to bring him to trial according to the clauses of the armistice between Italy and the Allies, while the British according to De Felice had their own agenda, as events would show.

Isolated reports began to surface in Italy in 1945–1947 hinting at differences in the accounts regarding Mussolini's execution and focusing on the sensational disappearance of large amounts of money and valuables that were part of the convoy of automobiles and trucks traveling with the Duce as he left Milan in the early evening of April 25, 1945. The total value of that "treasure" is estimated in the billions of today's dollars. With a few exceptions, such as *Life* magazine, most of the articles and interviews on the subject did not reach the international press at the time. The turning point came in March 1947 at a Communist party rally in Rome when Walter Audisio, also known by his nom de guerre as Colonel Valerio,* gave a well-publicized speech taking credit for the execution of the Duce. Audisio de-

---

* Several participants in the events at Dongo on April 28, 1945, have declared that they did not recognize Walter Audisio as the person referred to as Colonel Valerio. Some even stated that Colonel Valerio was actually Luigi Longo, a top partisan leader. [NDT]

scribed in graphic detail how Mussolini was gunned down along with Claretta Petacci. This account, with some subsequent variations became the "vulgate" according to the Italian Communist Party and appeared to satisfy most of Italian public opinion at the time. Audisio was quickly elected to Parliament as a communist deputy. Accounts by various eyewitnesses and others familiar with the final days of the Duce and his entourage began appearing several years later in a number of books and magazine articles. While most Mussolini biographers have obviously described the Duce's demise in some detail, they tend to treat it as a final, almost grotesque episode in the life of a dictator.

Dongo, the quaint little town perched on the banks of beautiful Lake Como, is more suited as the setting of romantic nineteenth century novels than the scene of bloody retribution against fleeing fascist leaders. Various members of the RSI government, along with some unfortunate people traveling with them, were lined up along the lakefront in the early afternoon and shot in the back like traitors. Mussolini and Claretta Petacci, however, were being held at a separate location and according to one version were already dead at that time, or in another version, were about to be shot shortly thereafter. Many questions remained unanswered and several theories began to surface.

In this remarkably well-researched work of historical detection, Luciano Garibaldi provides a fascinating description of the more noteworthy theories surrounding Mussolini's death. He centers on some very elusive material commenting upon the scenarios offered by other investigators and focusing on the forensic aspects that contradict the time and place of death in the official version. It should be said at the outset that, from the time the "official" version of Walter Audisio was made public in 1947, no serious investigation by the Italian government or magistrates of the courts was ever initiated into the specific matter of Mussolini's death. It is also surprising that Allied Military Government, the organization that was in charge of administering occupied Italy in 1945–1946, relied on the reports from the CLNAI in this case. Apart from eyewitness accounts of the bodies hanging from the feet at the Piazzale Loreto by Colonel Charles Poletti, the head of AMG in occupied Italy there are very few descriptions by non-Italian observers of the events of April 29-30, 1945 in Milan.

As Winston Churchill noted in the closing volume of his *Second World War*: "But at least the world was spared an Italian Nuremberg."[4]

Perhaps the absence of a serious official inquiry into the facts, and a broad public assessment of the fascist regime, is precisely what prompted the endless research into what is still viewed by many as an elusive truth. A form of "political correctness" was at play for many years after the war, whereby anyone questioning the official version exposed himself to being labeled a "fascist," a description that could end many a career and stifle historical investigation. Our purpose here is not to engage in any such debate but only to examine the facts as they are described by various sources and attempt to provide an explanation.

One of the provisions of the armistice between Italy and the Allies signed in Sicily on September 3, 1943, was that the Italian government would physically surrender Benito Mussolini to the Allied forces. Official U.S. and British policy therefore was to secure the Duce alive and in person for the purpose of bringing him along with a number of fascist party leaders to trial as war criminals, the "Italian Nuremberg" that Churchill was alluding to. The first key question is therefore: Why was Mussolini killed? From a legal standpoint the Italian government headed by Premier Ivanoe Bonomi at the time, was bound by the armistice clause and had authority over the actions and policies of the CLNAI. The summary executions were therefore carried out in spite of government policy and the Allied forces occupying Italy. The "official" version relies on the account by Walter Audisio, who explained the execution as simple retribution "in the name of the Italian people."

The many attempts to initiate contacts and feelers leading to a separate peace or at least an armistice remain among the more obscure mysteries of the Second World War. One example will demonstrate the complexity of the issue. Mussolini, supported and encouraged by the Japanese, attempted in 1943 right after the defeat of the Axis at Stalingrad, to persuade Hitler to seek a separate peace with Stalin. There are various credible traces of Axis-Soviet contacts in 1943, several reports surfaced in the US press in 1947 about such secret negotiations. In fact those attempts intensified up to the very day of Mussolini's overthrow on July 25, 1943. Earlier that week, on July 19, what was to be the last Axis military conference between Hitler and Mussolini took place at the Villa Gaggia in Feltre near Venice. The meeting lasted from 11 a.m. to 3 p.m. but the original plans called for a much longer three-day visit by the Führer. In a previous book[5] containing the edited diaries and notations of fascist minister and close Mussolini confidant Carlo Alberto Biggini, Luciano Garibaldi reports a rumor that Soviet foreign minister Vyacheslav Molotov was expected to secretly attend the Feltre conference. Hence the three-day schedule. This could tie into a secret meeting between Molotov and von Ribbentrop that reportedly did take place in June 1943 behind German lines on the Eastern front that is mentioned among others by B. H. Liddell Hart in his *History of the Second World War,* by Renzo De Felice in his Mussolini biography and by William Stephenson in his book, *A Man Called Intrepid.*[6] Molotov in his memoirs, on the other hand, denied all such rumors and statements.

Among other indications, attempts at serious talks between the Germans and the Soviets were reported in Turkey and Sweden through Soviet Ambassador Alexandra Kollontai.[7] There is also an assertion of a major effort by Stalin in February 1942 showing a willingness to make major concessions to Nazi Germany in exchange for a separate peace agreement. None of these initiatives got very far but they did operate as a very powerful deterrent among the Allies against any idea of deviating from the doctrine of "unconditional surrender." Roosevelt and Churchill were acutely sensitive to the potentially catastrophic consequences of freeing up some 185 German divisions from the Eastern front that would then be redeployed elsewhere as in 1918, following the treaty of Brest-Litovsk, in the West. The conclusion, for our purposes, given the circumstances, is that the Duce may have been carrying some sensitive papers relating to those and other contacts when he was seized by the partisans at Dongo on April 27th.

Garibaldi examines a second important question: How did Mussolini's execution actually take place? The answer triggers a chain-reaction of consequences with a host of other issues coming into play, for example the exact time of death. Garibaldi argues that Mussolini and Claretta Petacci were killed in the morning of April 28 and not in the afternoon. This is a potentially crucial point because if the executions took place in the morning then the official version becomes obsolete and other scenarios necessarily come into play. If Mussolini was killed in the morning then the identity of the executioners could lead anywhere, including back to SOE and British intelligence. According to the best sources there are no traces of such an operation in the British archives, in the various books on SOE operations in the Second World War, nor in the Churchill papers to support any of these theories, and Churchill steadfastly denied any such occurrence. Here there are many differing and sometimes contradictory versions including two that are explored in detail during the RAI-3 documentary by Peter Tompkins: the assertion by former partisan leader Bruno Giovanni Lonati of having been the trigger man who shot Mussolini with a burst of his Sten submachine gun acting under orders from a mysterious "Captain John," whom he could not positively identify but was the son of Italian immigrants to Great Britain and an officer of the SOE Special Force. Lonati indicates specifically how the shooting took place and how Claretta was shot by "Captain John" almost simultaneously. The second is an eyewitness named Dorina Mazzola who said she saw Mussolini being executed much the same way Lonati described it but contradicting many key details.

A further disturbing assertion concerns the sixty-five kilos of gold bullion that Mussolini was said to be transporting in his convoy a total value of almost five billion U.S. dollars in 2004. Garibaldi citing many sources states that this gold originated in the valuables seized from Italian and foreign Jews who had been arrested and deported to concentration camps in Italy and Germany. That gold also disappeared when the fascist leaders were arrested and Garibaldi traces its final startling destination as none other than the coffers of the Italian Communist Party!

Other Italian Communists, besides Walter Audisio, played a key role in the events at Dongo and Milan in April 1945. Many of the protagonists in the arrest of Mussolini and his entourage were card-carrying Party members and rank-and-file militants, several of them later becoming involved in intra-party struggles leading to a long list of victims assassinated shortly after the war and well into the 1950s. Anyone connected to the "Dongo treasure" and the events around Lake Como of April 27–29, 1945 was at risk and over five hundred people in northern Italy were known to have met a violent end because of some knowledge they may have had. It was a time, prior to the Marshall Plan, when Italy was viewed in the West as being on the verge of turning into a Soviet satellite. In the words of Churchill to Anthony Eden in early 1945: "I hope we may still save Italy from the Bolshevik pestilence."[8]

Garibaldi also deals with a number of other mysteries, and in particular the fact that Claretta Petacci could have saved her own life simply by taking advantage of the military plane with Croatian markings the Germans provided to fly her parents and sister Myriam to Barcelona and safety on April 23. She refused, wanting to remain next to her lover Benito Mussolini until the bitter end. It would also have been possible for Mussolini himself to have easily escaped by plane as late as April 24 to either Spain or Turkey as suggested by several members of his entourage. The Duce's son Vittorio also proposed that his father hide in a safe apartment in Milan and wait for the arrival of the Allies. He refused, attempting instead to enter into negotiations with the CLNAI (Committee of National Liberation of Northern Italy) through Cardinal Schuster the Archbishop of Milan. Once it became clear to him that he would be required to surrender, he decided to leave immediately for Como and precisely the left bank road along the lakefront that was closest to Switzerland but also very vulnerable to partisan attacks. What prompted that choice? Garibaldi provides the possible explanations, the most important ones being linked to the documents that the Duce was known to be carrying.

Politically and historically fascism had ended in Italy with the Duce's arrest on orders of the King of Italy on July 25, 1943.

Mussolini knew that his own career coincided with the fortunes of the political movement he had created. "The infallible voice of the blood tells me that my star has set forever." He wrote in August 1943 while a prisoner of King Victor Emmanuel III on the island of Ponza off the coast of Sardinia.[9] He sensed that his active political life was now behind him, even after he was liberated by Otto Skorzeny on September 12, 1943 and placed by Hitler at the head of what was by any description a satellite collaborationist government. Mussolini appears to have been for the most part politically passive during the new regime known as the RSI (Italian Social Republic) or Republic of Salò.

The sense of fatalism one gathers from reading Mussolini's notations during his captivity and from the various eyewitness descriptions of his behavior during the closing months of the RSI could also be deceptive. If true it would tend to confirm many descriptions of what took place at the end, a kind of fateful rendezvous with death that the Duce and the fascist diehards who followed him to Lake Como were seeking one way or the other. However, his final actions and decisions, to leave Milan in a convoy of cars ostensibly headed either towards an Alpine redoubt for a final battle or to some other destination, do not appear to fit in with the fatalism that has been described. The question that Garibaldi ultimately asks remains open: Was there another agenda? Was there a plan, even a desperate one that at some point went wrong? This book attempts to provide some possible if unproven explanations. True to his character, Mussolini did always see himself as something of a revolutionary adventurer who was ready to attempt the ultimate gamble. At the same time his past history demonstrated that he was careful to stack the deck of cards heavily in his own favor before taking action.

Did Mussolini have a final card to play on April 25, 1945?

The pages that follow will trace some of the clues.

Robert L. Miller

AUTHOR'S PREFACE

THE PURPOSE of this book is to shed light on the most dramatic chapter in twentieth century Italian history.

It is also a reply to the judgment of libel issued against me in 1998 for having written that Mussolini's death certificate was a forgery because it does not state the real time of his death. The book is an investigative report divided into twelve chapters, based in part on material that I have assembled (documents, interviews, and research) and a critical examination of the vast literature published in Italy and abroad regarding the death of Mussolini and his mistress. It should be viewed as the result of eight years of research, study, comparisons, and analysis on the subject.

The research begins with a famous document: the cable sent by the CLNAI* to the Allied Headquarters on April 28, 1945, following the news of Mussolini's arrest and requesting that he be turned over immediately in accordance with the clauses of the armistice. The answer provided was itself a lie: "CVL to AGH sorry could not deliver Mussolini who judged by popular tribunal was executed same place where fifteen patriots previously executed by Nazifascists."

---

* See Glossary for all terms, abbreviations, and acronyms.

Actually, this was not true. At that very moment Mussolini was still being held as a prisoner at Dongo. What the cable did prove was that the leadership of the Resistance had decided to take Mussolini to Milan and execute him by firing squad in the Piazzale Loreto in the presence of the crowds during a solemn execution similar to the decapitation of Louis XVI. Fifteen other fascist leaders were to have been dealt "justice" together with Mussolini: a number equal to the partisan fighters that had been shot during reprisals at the Piazzale Loreto in August 1944.

Why wasn't the plan carried out? What happened that made it fail? Colonel Valerio, dispatched from Milan to Dongo unexpectedly, discovered that someone else had preceded him and had killed Mussolini and Claretta Petacci during the morning of April 28. At that point the plan had to be changed to bring not fifteen live men plus their leader to the Piazzale Loreto but sixteen dead bodies. These changes were made by the firing squad executions during the afternoon of April 28 on the boardwalk on the Dongo lakefront.

A second *coup de théâtre* then took place because no one had decided on the execution of Claretta Petacci. It was neither expected nor desired by anyone. In fact, her name was not among the list of prisoners that the partisan commander Pedro provided to Colonel Valerio. However, as Colonel Valerio said—or rather exclaimed—when checking off the names on the list (as others were to relate): "Mussolini: to death! Clara Petacci: to death!" Why? Because just like the Duce he had found her dead that morning, but most of all because he "had to" assume the responsibility for an execution that its true perpetrators—the British secret services—did not wish to be associated with.

This is where the arresting story of the "British thread" begins, as described by many historians, including Renzo De Felice, to which I have added many new facts that are revealed in this book for the first time. One unknown element appears to confirm the version provided by Bruno Giovanni Lonati, the former partisan commander, who revealed in 1994—without being believed by anyone—that he was the one who had killed Mussolini, following orders from the British secret services, while a second British agent permanently silenced Claretta Petacci. What was the motive? The fear that either of them, Mussolini or Petacci, if questioned by American newsmen, would reveal the ongoing secret contacts between Mussolini and Churchill, up to the last moments, to persuade Hitler to end the fighting in the west and turn the entire German army against the Red Army.

On this specific topic I have assembled for the first time many accounts, totally ignored until now regarding secret contacts between Mussolini and the British. These are recounted by Dino Campini, secretary to Cabinet Minister C. A. Biggini; Sergio Nesi, an officer of the "Decima Mas"; Pietro Carradori, who was Mussolini's orderly; Filippo Anfuso, the RSI's ambassador to Berlin; Ermanno Amicucci, editor of the *Corriere della Sera*; Alfredo Cucco, undersecretary for popular culture; Ruggero Bonomi, undersecretary of the air force; Edmondo Cione, founder of the "Raggruppamento repubblicano socialista"; Nino D'Aroma, director of the "Istituto Luce"; Georg Zachariae, the Duce's German doctor; Drew Pearson, the American columnist; and Umberto Alberici, a notary in Milan.

Most important are the accounts—which I have assembled and excerpted from various publications—of eyewitnesses, such as Quinto Navarra, Mussolini's valet; Raffaele La Greca, the head cashier of the police force at Salò; Pietro Carradori, Mussolini's orderly; and Urbano Lazzaro, the partisan known as Bill, who arrested Mussolini while he was dressed in a German uniform—all are in agreement that the so-called "Dongo gold" that the partisans found in the "Mussolini convoy" and that was appropriated by the PCI [Italian Communist party] did not originate with the "State treasury" of the RSI [Italian Social Republic], but was rather made up of the valuables belonging to Jewish families that had been arrested and sent to the camps under the racial laws. Mussolini intended to hand over these valuables to the Americans following his surrender in the Valtellina so that they could be returned to those who had been persecuted and survived, thus "proving" that those confiscations had not been made by harming the victims to enrich the RSI, but were instead a heavy obligation attached to the alliance with the Third Reich. As everyone knows by now, that treasure ended up in the coffers of the Communist party. Did the Party know where those valuables came from? If the Italian Communist party still existed today, it would obviously deny it strenuously.

The greatest mystery I ran into in the course of my research came from the brave and unyielding support of Massimo Caprara, who was Palmiro Togliatti's secretary for twenty years (since 1944) and is today one of Communism's great *repentants*. Caprara told me how the "Audisio version" (namely the execution of Mussolini and Claretta Petacci during the afternoon of 28 April in front of the gates of the villa Belmonte) was a "deliberate fabrication." Above all, Caprara told me about the totally secret meetings that took place immediately following the war between Togliatti, who was at the time the most authoritative representative of Soviet communism in the west, and Winston Churchill, who following his Fulton, Missouri, speech (when he coined the phrase "iron curtain"), had become the foremost enemy of Stalin's Russia. It is hard to imagine such meetings even taking place—in fact, basically announcing a secret choice by the Italian Communist leader in favor of the West long before the official and by now "historical" one made by Enrico Berlinguer. Togliatti was well aware of what would have happened—primarily to the Party's leadership—had Italy fallen into Stalin's clutches: everyone would have been thrown into the Gulag, starting with the leaders of the PCI.

I am therefore pleased to see that my book has rekindled interest in historical research regarding the final moments of fascism by successfully rejecting once and for all the simplistic statement that the hour of Mussolini's and Claretta Petacci's death was unimportant, as some judges have written in their oversimplified and hurried opinions. My work shows, rather, that the hour of death is key to our understanding. If the two tragic lovers had really been killed during the afternoon, then the "vulgate" could become credible even after having been demolished by many historians. If, on the other hand, they were killed in the morning, then everything makes sense, and the British thread becomes credible.

Luciano Garibaldi

Chapter I

THE MYSTERY OF C. A. BIGGINI

The strange death at age 43 of Carlo Alberto Biggini, one of the two recipients of the Mussolini-Churchill correspondence.

Milan in the autumn of 1945: with yellowing skin, shortness of breath, sudden hair loss, the man not yet 43 years old and just a few short months before one of the youngest, most personable and influential of Benito Mussolini's ministers, was bedridden at the San Camillo clinic in via Boscovich, close to the central railway station. He had been hospitalized under the name of Professor Mario De Carli, but he was really Carlo Alberto Biggini, minister of national education of the defeated Italian Social Republic. Most of all he was Mussolini's confidant and the keeper of the Duce's secret papers. However, Biggini had lost those papers and he was unable to forgive himself. It became his daily source of worry, as Dino Campini, his private secretary and the only true friend Biggini had in those dramatic autumn days, would attest. Using various stratagems and disguises Campini was able to visit with him on several occasions.[1]

When I saw him again I almost failed to recognize him. Just a few months earlier he was an energetic young man. Now, in the hospital bed, lay a thin old man with a graying beard. On the evening of the insurrection, on April 25 in Padova, he had left the ministry's headquarters at the Palazzo Diena to take cover at Saint Anthony's Basilica. He had always been and remained on friendly terms with the religious authorities. There had even been negotiations at the start of the Republic of Salò to obtain Vatican recognition of the regime. The Church was interested in continuing the "status" of the Concordat. As usual it succeeded in obtaining what it wanted without conceding anything in return. The negotiations were conducted by Biggini, according to Mussolini's instructions.[2]

Biggini had been admitted to the San Camillo clinic thanks to Father Agostino Gemelli, the founder and regent of Milan's Catholic University. Gemelli felt obligated to the young minister for having protected and saved the lives of many university professors closely linked to the Resistance, which included Father Gemelli himself. According to Dino Campini:

After telling me about his problems he asked if I knew anything about the moroccan red leather briefcase containing the secret documents that the Duce had given him for safekeeping. He told me that he had left it at the Villa Gemma, his residence on Lake Garda. I explained that I had not traveled to Villa Gemma because I assumed he kept those papers at Padua. He was distraught: "If they find those documents it will be a big problem. No one yet knows that there were negotiations between Italy and England!" and waved his hands unhappily. Every time I went to see him later on we would always discuss the fate of those documents. We wondered where they could be. As the days went by Biggini's condition worsened. The last time

I went to the San Camillo clinic I was told that the professor had died. The man who held the secret that took Mussolini to the Piazzale Loreto was dead.[3]

What had caused the death of the young intellectual and politician remains a mystery to this day. His family (his wife, sister-in-law, and mother-in-law were hiding in their hometown of La Spezia, in order to avoid leading the police to arrest the former minister during their travels) never received a statement from the clinic. After the funeral they were told that Biggini died of pancreatic cancer. But no autopsy was performed and, as we shall show, there are serious doubts regarding the accuracy of that diagnosis.

Who was Biggini and how did he manage to gain the confidence and affection of the leader of fascism? What stands out about him to any researcher and historian is the generosity of the man. A telling point is that partisan fighters were told not to shoot at his Lancia Aprilia automobile that was constantly traveling between Padua, where the minister had his headquarters, and Lake Garda, where Mussolini was working. The partisans were well aware that most of the time Biggini carried with him a list of people to be saved: students, professors, and personalities who were the targets of the most intransigent fascists or of the Germans themselves. Biggini was almost always successful because the Duce never denied the young minister anything. Biggini can furthermore be credited with saving Italy's artworks from many Nazi depredations, with doing away with the obligation to swear allegiance to fascism by university professors, high school and elementary school teachers, and introducing a less rhetorical style to the school system inspired more by the thoughts of Mazzini (the principle of duties and rights). As a constitutional law expert he was the author of the planned constitution of the RSI. In 1983, when that document was published for the first time, it drew considerable interest on the part of political scientists and constitutional law experts.[4] The workers, rather than the political parties (whose full freedom of action was taken into account), were to become the source of sovereignty in the constitution as conceived by Carlo Alberto Biggini. Before examining the document in the light of its originality, we should first place it in historical context. The forty-year-old Biggini, minister of national education, had followed the Duce to northern Italy, not out of allegiance to neo-fascism, but rather because of personal loyalty to Mussolini himself, who in turn asked him at the council of ministers of the RSI of November 24, 1943, to draft the Republic's constitution. Mussolini had been liberated by the Germans on the Gran Sasso on the preceding September 12. The first RSI government had been formed in Rome on September 23. The constituent assembly was announced on the 27th, and on November 14 it approved the "Eighteen Points of Verona" that actually made up the "Social Charter" of the new State.

It was during that meeting of the Council of Ministers of November 24 that the "Fascist Republican State of Italy" (as it was called up to that time) took the name Repubblica Sociale Italiana [Italian Social Republic], with Biggini having the task of writing the constitution to be delivered to the Duce "by December 15." The young but already famous jurist (he had contributed significantly to the drafting of the civil code that is being used in Italy to this day) had only about two weeks to draft the document. He worked night and day uninterruptedly, filling the 142 articles that make the text with his passion for public service and above all his culture, which was inspired by the social doctrine of the Church, as well as his liberal-democratic roots, inherited from his masters, Gioele Solari and Francesco Ruffini.

History tells us that the analysis of the document was postponed when, on December 18, 1943, the council of ministers decided that the Constituent Assembly was to be convened after the end of the war. At the time, there were no hints as to the catastrophic end that the Axis forces were to face. Mussolini, however, packed the fifty-two typed pages in his briefcase (these were to resurface over forty years later thanks to Biggini's family—his widow, Maria Bianca, and his son, Carlo—and their passion for history and culture) and took them to the Villa Feltrinelli where he resided. Mussolini read and reread those pages, making occasional changes in blue pencil, and finally handed them back to their author, along with his letter of approval.[5] The historian may therefore say that the document reflects the vision of the State that Benito Mussolini had in mind, having recently and quite bitterly ended a twenty-year totalitarian experience. In short, it was to be a presidential Republic similar to what many in Italy are calling for at this time. The president of the Republic, however, was not to be elected directly by the people as in the United States or in France, but rather by a constituent assembly that would be renewed every seven years (precisely in order to elect the head of State). The people would elect the assembly itself, with one elected member for every fifty thousand citizens (actually one thousand constituents) as the "expression of all the living forces of the Nation."

The constituents were not to be represented by political parties, but rather by "the representatives of workers (entrepreneurs, laborers, employees, technicians, and management) of industry, agriculture, commerce, credit, and insurance, the professions, the arts, artisans, and cooperatives." Along with them could be elected "war veterans, and especially those who had been decorated and volunteers," the "kin of the war dead," and "Italians living overseas." This was Biggini's idea of the nation's elite, differing greatly from what Italy has known for the past half century.

There are many other surprisingly modern aspects in the Biggini Charter. A note to the document explains how he sought "to create a system that could cancel out privilege and free the masses from the problem of finding work that is the real form of servitude of the proletariat to the bourgeoisie." Biggini felt that

> to provide freedom for the masses does not just mean, as the old liberals believed or pretended to believe, handing to the masses the same rights of freedom as the bourgeoisie, but to agree that a preliminary assumption of any other form of freedom is the right to work and the equality of the initial positions in the struggle for life. Such an assumption implies a whole series of other assumptions, such as a planned economy, the nation's economic independence, the guarantee to private en-

terprise, a change in the right to property ownership, and on the international level a redistribution of the world's riches.[6]

Article 105 proclaimed the sacred nature of private property, "the fruit of individual work and savings, the extension and exercise of the human personality, the efficient tool for the development and multiplication of wealth to be at the nation's disposal." The section dedicated to the "right to work" is also very explicit. The current constitution of the Republic of Italy states in Article 4 that: "The Republic recognizes the right to work for all its citizens." Therefore, we now have (and it is the current law) a text that says "the Republic recognizes the right to work to all its citizens." On the other hand, Biggini's Charter "guarantees the right to work to each citizen." It may seem a small difference and yet it is enormous. "Recognizes" means nothing, while "guarantees" means everything. To "recognize" belongs to the realm of good intentions and positive wishes. To "guarantee" is an actual fact. "Recognizes" is a mystification, a disinformation of sorts, actually a fraud for a Republic that is "based upon work." It means: I recognize your right to work but I just take note of the fact that you are unemployed. On the other hand, to "guarantee" is a commitment by the Republic that was to be founded upon the "conquest and preservation of Italy's freedom in the world," to the point that Biggini recommended stamping on the Italian flag the words "freedom" and "work" to replace the republican eagle.

Was Biggini's vision on the Right or on the Left? It is fashionable to have idle and superficial discussions on the meaning of those terms today. Without a doubt, if on the Right means making progress while respecting man and erasing—without violence—the injustice in economic relations (meaning that which is tipped in favor of one party in the social contract) then Biggini's constitution is most certainly not at all on the Left but rather accurately and in practical terms is the precursor of the ideas of a "Social Right." Yet it cannot be referred to as being right wing if it remains identified with the stereotypes that equate the Right with the stubborn defense of privilege and sinecures that were obtained without merit, but through graft and corruption. It often happens that everyone, based upon his militancy or even his feelings, has a tendency to demonize his opponents, equating them with evil and giving them a label. In Biggini's case the drive towards fairness and the attempt to promote human values appear so obvious that we can ignore the traditional and in many ways outdated split among two opposing world views.

It is not surprising that another, more obscure draft of a constitution existed—on the opposite side—written by Duccio Galimberti, the anti-fascist intellectual founder of "Giustizia e Libertà," who was to die in combat. That project also called for a presidential Republic with sovereignty emanating from work and not from the political parties.[7]

Who then was Biggini? He was born in Sarzana, in Liguria, on December 9, 1902, and obtained a law degree from the University of Genoa and another in political science from the University of Turin, with mentors such as Gioele Solari, Giuseppe Rensi, Francesco Ruffini, Guido De Ruggiero, and Benedetto Croce. These were not simply teachers handing him top grades and honors in both his university degrees with the right to publish his doctoral dissertation. They are in fact his true masters, his friends who held him in high esteem and whom he admired as their grateful and devoted student, ready to learn and to give. The moment to be generous was soon to come, when the theory of the Corporate State convinced Biggini that fascist Italy was writing a new revolutionary page in the conflict of socio-economic ideas, which for two centuries had been tearing away at the best minds of European universities.

Biggini's conversion to corporatism came as the result of serious investigation and comparative study. It can be said that Biggini, who had deep democratic roots in the philosophy of Giuseppe Mazzini, became a fascist because he found in fascism the blend of two views, Communist and capitalist, which were otherwise inevitably meant to clash and which, being above all else a man of peace, was unacceptable to him. He was elected to Parliament from Sarzana in 1934; in 1937 he was appointed to teach corporate law at the University of Sassari. From that point on his career took off. Writer, historian, author of pamphlets, charismatic speaker, he served as a volunteer in East Africa during the Ethiopian war and was promoted to the rank of captain in the infantry on the basis of merit. He was a member of the Commission to Reform the Civil Code, the Commercial Code and the Maritime Code, President of the Labor Committee of the Chamber of Deputies, director of the Higher School of Corporate Sciences at the University of Pisa and finally, at age 39, Chancellor of the University of Pisa with the recommendation and backing of Giovanni Gentile, who considered Biggini to be one of the best young minds of "a-fascist" fascism.

He became minister of national education for the first time on February 6, 1943, when he replaced Giuseppe Bottai. On July 25, 1943, he voted against Dino Grandi's Agenda at the meeting of the fascist Grand Council.[8] Following the "40 days" of the Badoglio government, Biggini joined the RSI and was appointed to the same position even though he was convinced that civil war was now inevitable. He accepted "purely out of personal loyalty towards the Duce," not because he felt himself a fascist and even less a republican fascist. Such a stance was to become the source of many problems but also provided some advantages.[9] He was faced with problems, such as being denounced to the party's disciplinary commission and subjected to persecution by the Germans on various occasions. One advantage was that he had a blank check from the Duce, who used Biggini to save hundreds of people (military men, intellectuals, Resistance leaders, and, mostly, Jews).[10]

He constantly went to great lengths—always in agreement with Giovanni Gentile—to protect his colleagues, other academics, and writers, first by preventing their being sent into internal exile and later from being deported to Germany; to provide them with work and food, and helping to avoid the destruction of their careers. Most of all Biggini tried to avoid the bloody outcome of civil war in a contest of noble efforts that placed his old friend Corrado Bonfantini on the opposite side of the political fence. Bonfantini would always be reluctant to discuss this after the war, "otherwise Sandro Pertini might get angry,"[11] as he was to tell the author of this book. On the fascist side were Giorgio Pini, Edmondo Cione, Carlo Silvestri, and

Benito Mussolini himself, who described Biggini with the following image: "Sometimes a flower can blossom even in a pile of mud."[12]

Biggini died at age 43 in a Milan cancer clinic (this was what his widow was told) on November 19, 1945. As mentioned earlier, no autopsy was performed and the family was not provided with a medical report following his death. Such serious omissions would be bad enough where any patient is concerned, but they take on a more ominous light with such an important figure.

Biggini was one of the persons entrusted with a copy of the Mussolini-Churchill correspondence. Unfortunately, the minister was unable to take the file with him to the Basilica of Saint Anthony in Padua, where he went into hiding on the evening of April 25, 1945. He kept those papers at the private home that had been assigned to his family, called Villa Gemma, on Lake Garda and he hoped that his wife and sister-in-law had taken them. But the two women were terrified by their predicament and abandoned the villa to seek refuge with the bishop of Brescia—taking nothing from the minister's study.

When I published *Mussolini e il Professore*, the biography of Biggini, in 1983, I made a first attempt to discover who had taken possession of "the red moroccan leather briefcase." The owner of Villa Gemma, Aldo Triboldi, an antiques dealer from Brescia, told me: "I gave the papers in two or three small boxes to Professor Michele Tumminelli, who came to me immediately following the liberation as a friend of the minister." Tumminelli (he had been, after the war, a Christian Democrat member of Parliament and a friend of Alcide De Gasperi, the top leader of the Christian Democratic party) was still alive in 1983; he was 90 years old and living in Milan. I made an attempt to approach him but his son, Professor Mario Tumminelli, who at the time was the director of the private school bearing his name, did not allow me to proceed: "Could it be possible," I asked him, "that your father had handed everything over to the British?" He answered: "Knowing my father's national pride, I don't think so. But I would not be surprised, on the other hand, if he gave those papers to some official Italian entity, possibly the commander of the Carabinieri."

Michele Tumminelli was the minister's next-door neighbor and right after the war he was elected to the Senate from the Christian Democratic party, with close ties to the head of the government, Alcide De Gasperi. It may not be so far-fetched to imagine that through that channel—meaning De Gasperi—the copy that Biggini was holding found its way back to Churchill. With no offense intended towards the officers of the Carabinieri, De Gasperi certainly wielded more authority than any ordinary commander.

My inquiry did not end in a single meeting, however. Biggini became ill when he was at the Basilica of Saint Anthony of Padua—it possessed at the time (and still does today) an extraterritorial status as part of the Vatican City State. He had a tumor of the pancreas, according to the doctors who had been called in by the friars. It appeared in a flash. He was transferred to a clinic in Milan under a false name. Father Agostino Gemelli, the founder of the Catholic University, organized everything as we said previously, since he felt deeply indebted to the former minister of national education for many past favors.

Anna Tolentino, secretary to the famous friar, was also still alive in 1983. I tried to get her to recall the matter, but, hard as nails, she kept on repeating: "I never met Minister Biggini nor did I ever speak to him." Yet I had—and still have—written proof that the lady was lying. She had actually been helping the minister up until the end that took place on November 15, 1945, while Biggini's family remained secluded at La Spezia due to the Communist-inspired terror. Anna Tolentino died in 1992, taking to her grave the echo of that repeated, insistent cry that Biggini never stopped invoking even in his physical agony: "The papers! My papers! Where have they gone?"

Young historian Fabio Andriola became intrigued by the matter and paid a visit to Anna Tolentino at her residence in Rome in 1991, the year before her death. This is how he relates that attempt:

> Father Gemelli's secretary refused to make any kind of statement and even denied to me ever having met Biggini or having heard any confidential information from him that every other

person who paid a visit to his bedside heard him repeat. Among the possible reasons, there may be her desire to follow Father Gemelli's instructions to the end. In any case, the secret of Anna Tolentino's stubborn silence is part of the mysteries of the Mussolini-Churchill papers.[13]

The mystery surrounding the circumstances of Biggini's death appears to be even more intricate: a sudden and strange death that was not supported by any detailed medical post mortem and that certainly must have come as a welcome surprise to all those interested in hushing up any talk about the correspondence.

The "cancer of the pancreas" remains a diagnosis unsupported by any x-ray or biopsy. The Basilica's prior at the time, Father Lino Brentari, was extremely reticent with this writer, as if he were the bearer of an incredible burden. The attitude of Father Agostino Gemelli appears to be even more mysterious—if not incomprehensible. At first, having helped admit his friend, the former minister, under the assumed name of "Professor De Carli," to the San Camillo Clinic in Milan, Father Gemelli wrote to defense attorney Paolo Toffanin, who was to represent the minister at his trial at the special session of the Supreme Court and who was insistently asking about his illustrious client: "Professor De Carli, whom we have seen, has no form of cancer." Later on, when the lawyer kept insisting on meeting Biggini, the priest replied as follows: "Professor De Carli could not be seen by anyone. I did not know the reasons why."[14]

It is obvious that the persons who were preventing anyone from approaching Biggini, in agony in his hospital room, knew full well that in the past Mussolini had used him to reveal important historical secrets as in 1940, for example, when the Duce handed Biggini the confidential correspondence between himself and Pope Pius XI, which resulted in the famous book *Storia Segreta della Conciliazione* [The Secret History of the Concordat]. Without a doubt Biggini's sudden and obscure death must have come as a welcome surprise to anyone interested in seeing the whole story of the correspondence permanently buried. A final mysterious stroke in this dramatic and unresolved matter is the initial disappearance and partial reappearance of the minister's diaries, which were returned to the family by a priest. Only those parts that were not compromising to anyone were returned, either to the British or to the Italians in charge of Biggini up to the day he died.

Was Biggini a Freemason? If so, how significant could this be to his demise? There is no dearth of historical references. "They mentioned to Mussolini that Biggini was a Freemason. 'Eighteen,' answered the Duce. Eighteen is a Masonic degree."[15] And again: "Mussolini made another attempt to ensure that his documents would be known to the world and become part of history. He gave a copy to his young minister of national education, Carlo Alberto Biggini, a Freemason he greatly respected, asking him to make sure he survived in order to be able to publish them when the time came."[16]

If Biggini's freemasonic connection were true, one may imagine a careful calculation on Mussolini's part based on the respect that the London Great Masonic Lodge would extend to one of its affiliates even though he was Italian. They would certainly slam the door in Mussolini's face as a persecutor of Freemasons, but would not do so to Biggini. Actually the only doors that were open to the young minister and the Duce's confidant were those to the netherworld. "The 'British path' went through Florence (actually the Masonic Lodges in Florence). There exists—and we know where—a photo of Churchill in Como in the company of a man who is directly connected to those Masonic circles who managed the entire matter, starting with the Duce's capture in that area, which was no coincidence."[17]

Chapter II

THE DISAPPEARING
PAPERS OF BARON HIDAKA

*The surprising political "resurrection" of the Japanese ambassador to
Italy, Baron Shinrokuro Hidaka, the other recipient of the copies of
the correspondence (and also of Mussolini's Diaries).*

There is no doubt that after Biggini the second recipient of the documents relating the secret contacts between Mussolini and
Churchill was the Japanese ambassador (first to Rome and then later
to Salò), Shinrokuro Hidaka. The first statement to that effect comes
once more from Dino Campini, Minister Biggini's private secretary:

> Once the outcome of the war was no longer in doubt
> Mussolini worried about the future and the judgment history
> would pass on him He therefore made an effort to assemble
> the documents showing his actions that would ensure a fair
> verdict. He handed the papers to Biggini, who was ordered to
> save his own life so that he could write about those events and

shed some light over the facts. Biggini was a young man and nothing led him to believe that he would die so soon. Mussolini, however, wanted to be cautious and did not limit himself to his chosen historian; he also gave a copy of the documents to the Japanese ambassador, who at the time was residing in Venice. Hidaka was an extremely courteous and intelligent gentleman and somewhat of an archivist: during the Republic of Salò he was given other extremely important documents for safekeeping and strangely enough everyone seemed to forget that Italy was allied to Japan. We do not know where that diplomat is today; he may be growing roses in some far removed oriental garden. But if he is still alive today he could speak up. The publication of those documents will change many people's thinking. If Churchill cares, he should search for a copy of those documents in the ambassador's house in Venice, from the ambassador's friends, or from the ambassador himself. The fact that a copy of the documents had been given to Hidaka was something Biggini told me and he confirmed it insistently just a few days before his death.[1]

When Campini wrote these lines in 1952 no one knew what had happened to Shinrokuro Hidaka. This was because no investigation was made into the fate of the Japanese diplomat to see if he had managed to return to his own country, or whether he had been arrested and possibly subjected to the justice of American special courts because of his turbulent past involvement in the Japanese occupation of China, or if he had returned to diplomatic service. Actually, for an official of a defeated country his fate was to be better than most others: he returned to the diplomatic corps without being subjected to any kind of purge and was given the most sensitive kind of task as overseer of the diplomatic archives.[2]

Unfortunately, as we shall discover, Hidaka steadfastly refused to speak or reveal where he placed, or to whom he gave, the papers he most certainly carried with him when the RSI collapsed and he escaped to Switzerland—more precisely, to the Japanese legation in Bern.

Furthermore, Dino Campini is not the only source to attest to the unconditional trust Mussolini placed in the distinguished fifty-year-old Japanese diplomat known for his extreme courtesy, his gift for eloquence, and extensive cultural interests (he spoke fluent Italian and had memorized the great arias of the operas of Verdi, Mascagni, and Puccini). Campini's account is basically confirmed by Nino D'Aroma, director (under the Salò regime) of the Istituto Luce, the famous photo and film archive of the fascist period.[3] Nino D'Aroma relates that Mussolini summoned him around mid-February 1945, together with Minister of Popular Culture Fernando Mezzasoma (who would later be executed at Dongo). The Duce asked D'Aroma if he could quickly have some trusted photographers make three copies of a few hundred confidential documents. D'Aroma replied that he could not guarantee to Mussolini the discretion of the photographers. During another meeting Mussolini told D'Aroma that he had been able to make three typed copies of those papers, two of which had been given to Baron Hidaka and one to Minister Biggini. "At the right time," he confided, "after the period of struggle and persecution has ended, these documents must absolutely see the light of day."[4]

Another primary source regarding the handing of a copy of the secret correspondence to Biggini and Hidaka for safekeeping is *I 600 giorni di Mussolini* [Mussolini's 600 Days], by Ermanno Amicucci (editor in chief of the *Corriere della Sera* at the time of the Republic of Salò), who avoided the purges and discussed the issue throughout his book.[5]

Mussolini's full and unconditional trust in Baron Hidaka is further corroborated by other credible sources. Alberto Mellini Ponce de Leon, who was the head of the cabinet of undersecretary of foreign affairs of the RSI; Serafino Mazzolini; and, following Mazzolini's death due to illness on February 15, 1945, the main collaborator of the new undersecretary, Filippo Anfuso, witnessed several of Mussolini's protests to Hitler regarding the bold and bloody actions taken by German troops on Italian soil. Mussolini handed every copy of such written protests to Hidaka "with a request for a vigorous step towards the Führer by your colleague in

Berlin."[6] And again: "Mussolini was more and more annoyed and impatient by the endless interference on the part of German military authorities. He discussed the issue at length with Ambassador Hidaka on May 17, 1944, in whose sincere sympathy towards Italy and his high personal standards he placed the greatest trust."[7] Mellini kept a daily diary starting February 15, 1945. At the entry dated February 21 he writes: "Following the Duce's instructions I went to Ambassador Hidaka to inform him of the growing tension with the Germans. The Duce wants Hidaka to be informed of everything in detail so that he may, in turn, inform his government and use his personal authority to intervene even with the German ambassador to Italy, Rudolf Rahn, and, through his Japanese colleague, with the Führer."

During the daily confrontations with his difficult ally Adolf Hitler, Mussolini would seek and find support in the Japanese. One more confirmation comes from Filippo Anfuso, who during the weeks and days preceding July 25, 1943, often met with Japanese ambassador Oshima in Berlin. Through Oshima, Anfuso attempted to pressure von Ribbentrop, the German foreign minister, towards reaching a separate peace with the USSR in accordance with the Duce's requests (as we shall see in the next chapter).[8]

These points show how and why Mussolini increasingly felt that he could trust Shinrokuro Hidaka to the extent of making him, besides the extremely loyal Biggini, the second recipient of the secret papers that offered proof of his attempts to seek an honorable end to the war with the least possible damage to Italy; at first through a separate peace with the USSR; then, once that project failed, through a separate peace with the western Allies.

But was Mussolini's trust in Baron Hidaka well placed? During a conversation with Nino D'Aroma at the end of February 1945 Mussolini spoke of Baron Hidaka as "a gentleman, one of our friends and a friend of Italy." He added: "I have observed his attitude during the last few months and I am certain I have selected the right man. In due course, once the time of fighting and persecution has passed, these documents must absolutely see the light of day."

Unfortunately they never did. Almost certainly—though possibly not directly—because of Hidaka, but in any case (perhaps without his knowledge) through other Japanese public servants, they wound up in the hands of the British.

It is impossible to disagree with the lashing opinion of Fabio Andriola, who writes in his book *Mussolini-Churchill, carteggio segreto* [Mussolini-Churchill: Secret Correspondence]:

> Due to their professional attachment to confidentiality, dip-lomats often end up complicating the task of journalists and historians seeking to reconstruct the facts where those same diplomats were either observers or actual participants. After the war Hidaka proved to be extremely reserved: not only did he deny repeatedly to having any documents in his possession (but only "to having in my possession" at the time the question was being asked) given to him by Mussolini, but he also stated that he never went to Bern, the headquarters of the Japanese embassy in Switzerland, after 1943. After the war the Mussolini family dispatched a freight forwarder from Chiasso to the Japa-nese embassy in Bern, while Hidaka was a prisoner of the Al-lies, to take back whatever Hidaka had left there. The result was fruitless, since the Japanese stated that they had already destroyed everything in anticipation of Japan's imminent unconditional surrender. [...] Hidaka, on the other hand, was not a prisoner for very long and following his acquittal at a war crimes trial for crimes committed during the Japanese occupation of China, he was able to return to the Japanese diplomatic service, the only such case among Japanese diplomats involved in the war pe-riod. As an international inspector, Hidaka was the first Japa-nese diplomat to be allowed by the U.S. government to proceed with the inspection of several Japanese consulates in the United States. After that, Mussolini's chosen confidant resigned from politics to become president of a large central heating com-pany. [...] To anyone asking about the issue of Mussolini's pa-pers and diaries, Hidaka (back in Japan) was to deny any knowl-edge of those documents. Later on the Mussolini family at-

tempted a futile lawsuit against the ambassador, but Hidaka was obviously too well connected and averted that challenge as well.[9]

A vivid description of Baron Shinrokuro Hidaka is provided by Italian historian and journalist Piero Buscaroli, who published in the daily newspaper *Il Giornale* in October 1995 an account of his meeting with Hidaka on Wednesday, July 6, 1966, in Tokyo some thirty years before. In the course of that long interview (which lasted all day), the former ambassador told Buscaroli about the behind-the-scenes events of July 25, 1943, the day fascism was toppled. As Hidaka recalled, the Duce was hoping to secure, through him, Tokyo's mediation—since Japan was not at war with Moscow—towards an armistice with the Russians following the defeat at Stalingrad in the winter of 1942–43. However—according to the former ambassador—the conspiracies of the Fascist Grand Council and King Victor Emmanuel III put a stop to Mussolini's project as he was ready to place Hitler in front of an ultimatum.

Hidaka, as Buscaroli recalled, "spoke a very clear Italian." Buscaroli filled up two notebooks with annotations but decided to keep them locked in his desk because he was embittered by the attitude taken by the Italian press and historiographers. "For years I had witnessed how news stories, the truth or revelations published in *Il Borghese* or *Roma*,[10] were either ignored or kept silent, apart from a compact group of loyal readers. I decided to keep those two notebooks, where I had jotted down the conversations with Hidaka, to be used later on when the time was right."

Finally, some thirty years later, when Buscaroli decided to publish his notes he attracted the attention of the most serious scholars, who avidly read those impeccably written "reports." The dramatic mistake made by the conspirators of July 25, 1943, thus came to light, as well as the high regard that Mussolini had for the Japanese aristocrat ("He told me once," Hidaka said to Buscaroli, "that among all those around him, Italians and Germans, he considered me to be his only friend.") However, after speaking about his relationship to the Duce for many hours, "Hidaka rose," wrote Buscaroli, who no doubt was disappointed. "I tried to rekindle the conversation somehow and ask if it was true that Mussolini had given him for safekeeping his famous secret documents, or at least part of them. He smiled back in his sad and affected way: 'It is too early to discuss this . . . Perhaps after my death.'"

Along with the well-known story of the copies of the "Churchill" documents given to Hidaka, there still remains the even more mysterious and unclear story of the Duce's diaries, which—according to another popular account—were also handed to Baron Hidaka to be brought to safety in Switzerland.

First of all, there is no reason to doubt the existence of the Mussolini diaries. It is unimaginable that a prolific journalist such as Mussolini would not indulge in the pleasure of writing down every evening what had happened during the day. There are also too many eyewitnesses and "courtiers" who saw him on those evenings intently writing in those notebooks, or even simply on loose sheets of paper. However, there are serious doubts that the extracts that were published with great fanfare by the *Sunday Telegraph* starting Sunday, June 26, 1994, and reproduced by the world press, are in fact part of the Mussolini diaries. According to the British weekly the diaries covering the years 1935–1939 had been provided by a mysterious "Mr. X," who discovered them in a trunk in his father's attic. His father had been a partisan on Lake Como. The diaries were sold to the *Telegraph* by "Mr. X," showing an uncharacteristically pacifist Mussolini, who was decidedly hostile towards Nazism and illustrating the efforts of the most fanatic fascist extremists—they had been vetted by an American writer and researcher, Brian Sullivan, who reached an odd conclusion: "They are both real and false at the same time. They are real because Mussolini actually wrote them, but they are false because Mussolini wrote falsehoods in those notebooks in order to save his image. In other words, after having handed over to Japanese ambassador Hidaka the original diaries, Mussolini proceeded to write a new version at Salò."[11] This kind of fiction outdoes even Alfred Hitchcock. On that occasion the renowned British scholar of fascism, Denis Mack Smith, turned out to have a more "normal" reaction, stating that without a doubt it was the actual prose of Mussolini. Even though the Duce that emerged from those pages was a benevolent man, far removed from the bellicose ideas that instead characterized his actions, a kind of victim of Hitler ("Hitler wants war, he fears nothing and feels certain of victory . . . Unfortunately I will not succeed in proving him wrong"), a Duce who was a bit frustrated by power ("It's true that I am the Duce, and that people lose their heads when they see me . . . But it is also true that I cannot come and go as I please"), he was also a wise and very savvy politician who considered the ideas of the German dictator as expressed in the famous book *Mein Kampf* as "unreadable nonsense."

Fascinated by this discovery, Mack Smith did not hesitate even when faced with some gross mistakes, such as the wrong birth date ("This year I am 55 years old: August 29," while any encyclopedia will tell you that Mussolini was born on July 29, 1883).

The "scoop" by the *Telegraph* received with great skepticism by most of the competent Italian historians, starting with Renzo De Felice, did have a precedent. In 1967 another trio of British and Italians, including an engineer from Milan, Ettore Fumagalli, a retired English newsman, Clive Irving, and a man named Charles Dean, showed up at the editorial offices of the *Sunday Times*, offering four years of Mussolini diaries: 1940, 1941, 1942, and 1943 up to July 25. The *Times* was not counting its pennies and bought the "fake" sight unseen for one hundred thousand pounds in cash. The vetting began *after* the purchase. Two Italian historians, Silvio Bertoldi and Giorgio Pini (for many years chief editor at *Il Popolo d'Italia* and therefore the journalist who was closest to Mussolini), gave the Fleet Street daily the awful news that this was a colossal forgery. The *Sunday Times* took the bad news in stride, published the story of the forgery, and filed all the papers away. That bitter experience was not to prevent a second try, but with greater style, in 1983, when it acquired Hitler's fake diaries for 1.7 million pounds sterling.

The false diaries of 1967 came from a single "editing shop" belonging to a delightful lady from Vercelli, Amalia Panvini-Rosati, who had sold the four years of diaries to the trio while taking the precaution of warding off any legal issues by issuing a statement saying that this was an "author's forgery." This meant that she had written the diaries by giving a perfect imitation of the Duce's hand-writing. This was something like "black ink and old lace." Panvini-Rosati had already been at the center of a noisy affair that took place between 1957 and 1960 when it was extensively covered by the Italian newspapers. Together with her mother, Signora Rosa, the widow of a well-respected chief of police at the Questura of Vercelli from 1938 to 1947 (the year he retired) and who died in 1955, Amalia had sold to Oscar Ronza (who at the time was the secretary of the neo-fascist party MSI in Vercelli) a total of four-teen diaries in the Duce's handwriting. In exchange, the two ladies were paid five million Italian lire that they needed to purchase a spacious apartment. Mr. Ronza, however, had not bought the dia-ries as one might assume, to turn them into relics, but rather to resell them at five times the purchase price (25 million lire of that time) to the publisher Arnoldo Mondadori. Just like his British col-leagues, the Italian publisher was thoroughly taken in; but before issuing any worldwide press releases Mondadori sought the added expertise of two undisputed experts, the brothers Giulio and Duilio Susmel, along with Giorgio Pini, and even the Duce's son, Vittorio, who had been brought in from Argentina where he was living after his escape from Italy in 1945. The diaries had also been examined by Pino Romualdi, former deputy secretary of the Fascist Republi-can Party [PFR], and by Giuseppe Tassinari, former agriculture minister of the RSI. The reactions were not unanimous. The dia-ries were said, by the Susmel brothers and Pini, to be forgeries; while they were authentic for Romualdi and Tassinari; Vittorio Mussolini said he "couldn't tell." Assailed by doubts, the older Mondadori decided to cancel the deal and asked Mr. Ronza for his money back.

All those so-called "scoops" were quickly forgotten, which does not mean that the real Mussolini diaries did not exist. If (and every indication points in this direction) Shinrokuro Hidaka did have them for safekeeping and, probably following pressure from the Japa-nese government, handed them to the victors (meaning the Ameri-cans, since Allen Dulles' men were the first to enter the Japanese legation in Bern) then one may assume that they could have eventually wound up in London as a courtesy from Harry Truman to Winston Churchill, the most interested party—given his long acquaintance with Mussolini. This would have, therefore, logically meant their eventual destruction—unless one believes the Japanese historian Osamu Tezuka,[12] according to whom "Mussolini's diaries could be in Japan because one of the Duce's best friends was Shinrokuro Hidaka." However, all doors are bolt shut in Tokyo when this subject is discussed. Some years ago, Professor Romano Vulpitta, an historical researcher and university professor, went to the Tokyo State Archives in the course of research on behalf of Renzo De Felice. "So, here is one more person looking for the Mussolini-Churchill correspondence!" said the civil servant ironically, as he received the professor, hinting that the Americans had taken everything in 1946.

Many Japanese historians uselessly attempted to "hound" Hidaka. Japanese journalist and historian Hiroshi Kimura, who had lived in Italy for many years and translated several books about Mussolini into Japanese, published two books of his own: *Arrest Mussolini!* (on July 25, 1943) and *Kill Mussolini!* (on April 28, 1945). In 1982 this author also tried to ask the Japanese foreign ministry for information about the correspondence. The laconic and discouraging response was that "Baron Hidaka has given all his papers to the ministry and these are covered by secrecy."[13] This naturally does not mean that at some time or other the real Mussolini diaries could still appear (possibly coming from someone related to Churchill), who is tired of holding on to some ten notebooks covered with Mussolini's handwriting. They could possibly be sold to a publisher for many thousands of pounds sterling. If this were to happen, we feel we can safely predict that the Duce's diaries may indeed start during his youth, when he relished playing the role of the socialist anarchist, but they almost assuredly would end in 1944, the terrible year that could have spared so much of Europe from half a century of Bolshevik tyranny and that cost Mussolini and his companion their lives.

Chapter III

MUSSOLINI AND THE WAR

The Duce's desperate attempts to extract Italy from the war. From the missed meeting with Molotov during the meeting at Feltre on July 19, 1943, to the soundings with British agents at the end of 1944.

Mussolini decided to reach a separate peace with the Soviet Union early in 1943 to improve the chances of resisting an Anglo-American offensive that threatened Italy from the coasts of North Africa with a crescendo of terror bombings, causing thousands of victims among the civilian population. As we have shown in the preceding chapter, the Japanese ambassador in Rome, Shinrokuro Hidaka, was to play a key role. Since his arrival in Rome at the end of June 1943, Hidaka immediately asked Mussolini for his support in pressing upon Hitler an elaborate plan of the Japanese government. "General Tojo had informed the Führer on many occasions that it was completely senseless to keep on destroying his reserves with continuous advances and retreats in the expanses of Russia.

The Japanese ambassador to Berlin, General Hiroshi Oshima, had been working in this direction since July 1942."[1]

Hidaka found Mussolini receptive and ready to agree to that line of thinking. The Duce's attitude sharpened once the fortunes of war turned against the Axis powers (the German-Italian defeat in the USSR after the battle of Stalingrad during the winter of 1942–1943, the Italian surrender in Tunisia on May 12, 1943, and the Allied landings of July 9, 1943, in Sicily) to such an extent that during the Feltre conference between Mussolini and Hitler (July 19, 1943) there was to be the top-secret participation of Vyacheslav Molotov himself, Stalin's foreign minister.[2]

Delayed because of the Führer's hesitations, the secret summit with the man from Moscow would certainly have been put back on the agenda had Mussolini not been fired and arrested six days later, following the coup d'état by King Victor Emmanuel III on July 25, 1943. The famous university professor and philosopher from Turin, Norberto Bobbio, who was also a key anti-fascist, mentions a meeting he had with Biggini, who had just been appointed minister of national education while teaching at the University of Padua: "Fully aware that I was an anti-fascist he attempted to explain the reasons behind his loyalty towards Mussolini when he brought up his origins, coming from a socialist family from Sarzana. He also said that had Mussolini not been overthrown he would have taken Italy out of the war by attempting a separate peace with the Soviet Union."[3]

In a conversation with the author,[4] Giorgio Gervasi, nephew of Rachele Mussolini and first cousin to Vittorio Mussolini, the Duce's oldest son, summarized what his cousin had told him:

> Vittorio, and I also, felt that the key to his father's tragic demise lay in the events leading up to July 25, 1943. The year had started very badly for the Italo-German alliance, with the surrender of the troops in Africa, the landings in Sicily, and the beginning of the increasingly frequent and devastating bombings of the country. The bombing of Rome on July 19, which until then had been spared as the capital of the Catholic Church, was a tragic signal.

The Duce was not confident and he knew that the probability of defeat was increasing daily, so that it had become essential to unhook Italy from Hitler's chariot. From Hitler, not from Germany, since part of German public opinion, especially among the upper classes, was aware that Hitler was taking Germany into an apocalyptic bloodbath. Military operations in Russia were chewing up one division after another, along with resources that it had become impossible to replenish in a doomsday delirium that Hitler was totally wrapped up in. Mussolini, who as the watchful political animal that he was, had understood this state of affairs for some time and was working effectively to compel his ally to seek a separate peace with the USSR, so as to concentrate the powerful German military machine on a single front by giving up the endless vortex of the Eastern Front.

To reach this goal—as my cousin Vittorio told me on several occasions—the Duce had begun talking with Hitler himself, as well as with the other allies of the Axis and in particular Hungary and Romania, with whom he was setting the stage for a general conference of the Axis powers. Such a conference would have allowed the smaller nations taking part in the war—Romania, Hungary, Finland, and Slovakia—as well as neutral and non-belligerent countries such as Bulgaria, Spain, and Vichy France, to express their opinion about the general situation on the continent and try together—even against German—opposition to find a way out of the war that could no longer offer a strictly military solution. In planning such a conference the Duce had a specific ideological and political objective in the approval and launch of a Charter of the Rights of European Nations in opposition to the Atlantic Charter that had been for at least two years the main tool of Anglo-American propaganda.

The Führer naturally did not agree and felt that what had to take precedence was victory in the East, the destruction of Stalin's communism, and the total subjugation of the Soviet State with the corollary conquest of the land and riches contained in that "continent within the continent." It was the fulfillment of the unfinished grand design of Teutonic Knights, who saw in the expansion to the East and the rich fertile prairies of the Ukraine the key to German power. Hitler had always answered in the negative to the Duce's repeated observations, first by making demands that Stalin could never agree to (such as ceding the Ukraine), then later by declaring that he, Hitler, was convinced of victory thanks to the powerful new weapons that Germany was creating [a hope that was dashed with the U.S. bombing of the base at Peenemünde[5]].

Faced with these incessant denials the Duce tried to secure the help and support of Japan. At noon on that fateful Sunday, July 25, 1943, following the no-confidence vote of the Grand Council and just a few hours before his arrest on the King's orders to be replaced by Marshal Pietro Badoglio a loyalist of the monarchy, Mussolini summoned Japanese ambassador Hidaka. He asked the ambassador to transmit a message to President Tojo that on Wednesday, July 28, he, Mussolini, would take a strong and final initiative with the Führer so that after a careful review of the latest events he could be persuaded to stop the fighting on the eastern front to reach an accommodation with Russia.

This clear historical analysis by Giorgio Gervasi is confirmed by the diary of Undersecretary of Foreign Affairs Giuseppe Bastianini in his entry dated July 25, 1943:

The Duce had decided to take, in the course of the coming week, a strong step with the Führer to attract his most serious attention to the situation as it had evolved recently and encourage the Führer himself, as he had done on other occasions, to end the fighting on the eastern front and reaching a settlement with Russia. Once that had been achieved the Reich could then weigh in with all its war-making potential against the Anglo-Americans in the Mediterranean. The Duce had asked the Japanese ambassador to tell President Tojo that it was his strong desire to have the president support with all his strength such an initiative with the Führer.[6]

The success of such an "initiative" could have spelled disaster for the Anglo-Americans and had to be avoided at all costs. The easiest way was to block Mussolini and prevent him from taking any kind of action. This was how Ambassador Hidaka viewed the situation: "Without a doubt, by ordering Mussolini's arrest, the king, the Duke of Acquarone (his closest aide) and the military men prevented the Duce from concluding what he had started. (. . .) They could not have done any better if they had been British or American agents." He added, significantly:

> At Gargnano during the months of the RSI, Mussolini told me that despite his fall from power and that of the fascist regime, his arrest and the bitterness of the double betrayal by his own men and by the king he felt deeply relieved during the first few days because the action of the king and the generals had convinced him that they already had reached an understanding and an agreement with the Allies. Instead the truth was that they had nothing.[7]

Hidaka's statement denies therefore an extreme conspiratorial and unsubstantiated version of the coup d'état of July 25, 1943, purporting that the Great Masonic Lodge of London, through its connections with top fascist leaders and the king's entourage, was behind the entire affair. Hidaka confirms Mussolini's attempt to save as much as he could of Italy by trying to do away with the worse kind of bad luck that could happen to any nation at war, namely the need to fight on two fronts. They also announced what was to happen eighteen months later at the end of 1944 when the much hoped for but unfulfilled agreement with Stalin was replaced by the very concrete talks with Churchill, seeking the breakup of the alliance between the USSR and the Anglo-Americans and the loosening of the wrench that was crushing central Europe.

The Italians, who have mentioned contacts, meetings and the exchange of letters between Mussolini and British agents during the months of the RSI (and not just on the eve of Italy's coming into the war or the period immediately following it), make up a long list. Their accounts and memoirs have been assembled in books by researchers and historians of absolute integrity and good faith.[8] This author feels the book that best recounts in a complete and rigorous way the story of the secret relations between the Duce and the British prime minister is *Mussolini-Churchill carteggio segreto* [Mussolini-Churchill: Secret Correspondence] by Fabio Andriola.

Besides these books (which have become the classic texts on this subject), there are innumerable diaries, memoirs, interviews—always on the Italian side—where the secret Italo-British relationship is mentioned as taking place at the end of the war. Strangely enough, this large body of work is considered as trash by every British writer, to whom it is preposterous to even consider a possible relationship (other than war) between Winston Churchill and the man he often referred to as the "big devil" or the "bullfrog."

The snobbery of some British researchers is supported by a segment of Italian writing on the subject. We refer to the group of writers that places the correspondence during the months that immediately precede Italy's declaration of war on June 10, 1940, when Churchill tried by every means possible to avoid Italy's involvement in the conflict by promising a number of territorial rewards not only coming from Great Britain (Malta and Gibraltar), but even at the expense of France (Nice, Savoy, and Tunisia) and of other nations (Yugoslavia and Greece) in exchange for Mussolini's neutrality. According to other sources who claim to know the contents of the correspondence, during those months Churchill may have written to Mussolini but with the opposite in mind: to ask him to enter the war that appeared to be headed for a rapid conclusion with an unavoidable victory for Germany in order to mitigate Hitler's demands when the time came to discuss a peace settlement, for Mussolini to exercise some influence over the Nazi dictator who listened to his views. A good example—even though it came in an odd way—is the revelation in 1998 by a former leader of the partisan police in Como, who was by then 84 years old: Luigi Carissimi-Priori to the researcher and newsman Roberto Festorazzi. Carissimi-Priori, a former leader of the defunct Partito d'Azione and former head of the political office of the Como police after Liberation, emigrated abroad soon after those events. He became an engineer and having spent most of his life outside Italy he returned home to retire. Judging from his conversations with the author, Carissimi-Priori was rather disgusted, like many others, by the Italy that "was born from the resistance" and determined not to hand over to the archives what he claimed he had acquired, namely copies of the correspondence (or better, a part of the correspondence) between Mussolini and Churchill. One more person therefore who felt authorized to do as he pleased with papers belonging to Italy's history.

According to the elderly engineer's account, the Mussolini-Churchill correspondence stolen from the Duce at the time of his arrest and in the possession of the secretary of the Communist party of Como was "sold by him to the British with the Party's assent, while also ordering him to copy the material before handing it over to be placed in the Party's central archives." At that time, Carissimi-Priori, as a police officer, was in charge of investigating "the execution by firing squad of Mussolini and the disappearance of the Dongo treasure." It was during that investigation that he came across the copy of the documents. What did he do? He hid it in a safe place and now at age eighty-four he is promising that "it will be published in due course in a foreign country," adding that: "I shall back the delivery of this material to its rightful owners, namely the British." What about the Italians? Apparently they were to get nothing. The same kind of attitude can be found among the many partisans who took part in the events at Dongo and have written memoirs "to be published after my death." They all obviously have something to hide. However—and this is the most important question—what is the content of Churchill's letters to the Duce? According to Carissimi-Priori, "In his letters to the Duce in 1940 Churchill had very much exaggerated the offers he made to Italy as a reward for its continued neutrality. The British prime minister promised Mussolini significant territorial concessions, such as possession of Dalmatia and permanent confirmation of the Greek islands of the Dodecanese and of all of Italy's colonies (including Ethiopia), besides the acquisition of Tunisia and the 're-conquest' of Nice."

Still, according to the revelations of Carissimi-Priori—in one of the letters the English statesman was very clear to confirm that the British would have been favorable to the western borders of Italy ("to your western borderline" said the engineer). Carissimi-Priori emphatically denies that in any of the letters in the file Churchill asked that Italy go to war as an ally of Germany in an attempt to mitigate Hitler's demands. Churchill had actually done the opposite by trying in every way to draw fascist Italy to the side of the Allies. Carissimi-Priori also found no correspondence between the two leaders after Italy entered the war.

These are rather disappointing revelations and the enthusiastic Festorazzi must have also felt that way when he attempted at the end to elicit from the former policeman some details regarding the end of Mussolini and Claretta Petacci. What he achieved—and this appears to be, in our mind, the most intriguing part of the book—was that the former policeman agreed that the end did not correspond to the accepted official version that coincides with that of the Communist party, which is always ready to attack anyone casting doubt of any kind. Mussolini and Claretta Petacci were not lined up in front of the gates of the Villa Belmonte to face a firing squad, nor "done justice" in an appropriately solemn manner "in the name of the Italian people," but rather gunned down like animals.

In light of these remarks it is no wonder that a young British historian, Nicholas Farrell, was able to write an ironic and sarcastic piece entitled "The Conspiracy Factory."[9] The most significant parts are worth examining:

> Let us assume that Churchill and Mussolini really did have an exchange of letters. Why would Churchill then set up a whole operation to find and destroy the letters? What could be so terribly embarrassing in offering pieces of French territory and a handful of islands in the Mediterranean? Well, there could be some embarrassment but not enough to give Churchill insomnia. Yet Italian historians and journalists would like us to believe that he was so terrified by the prospect of everything coming to light to travel personally to Italy, first to Como then to

Lake Garda, and finally to Venice regularly for five years for the specific purpose of retrieving by any means necessary the letters and even to order the spies of his Britannic majesty the king to comb the peninsula to seize the correspondence regardless of the price. Actually, Churchill and Mussolini never wrote to each other except for that one exchange of letters in 1940, when the British statesman asked the Italian unsuccessfully to stay out of the war.

Smart, intelligent, well written and the inevitable conclusion of anyone who is intent on limiting the Mussolini-Churchill exchanges to 1940 with the highly likely and probable offer of territory to Italy in exchange for not going to war. Was it really worth being ashamed of it to the point of ordering the death of the Duce (and of his lover at the same time) so that they would not reveal that old and useless offer? And what damage could this do to Churchill's honor (perhaps a bit less for his political acumen) if odd letters from the British prime minister were to suddenly appear asking Mussolini something like: "Please enter the war. It will only cost you a few casualties, you can slow down the Führer's appetite for expansion, and I will know how to reward you."

Actually, the small embarrassment that the letters as described above could have caused for Churchill in 1940 was already overcome in December of that year when during a radio message Churchill told the Italian people that Mussolini was "the only one responsible for Italy's participation in the war." And it was also completely forgotten in the dramatic radio speech of November 29, 1942, following the Italian defeat at El Alamein: "One man, one man alone is responsible for the ruin of the Italian people. We tried our best to convince him to remain neutral. But he chose not to listen." Those words should end once and for all the issue of the "correspondence of 1940."

The documents, papers, and statements that could have been more compromising for Churchill had they been published were very different. Very appropriately, Fabio Andriola in his book points out how on May 10, 1945, Churchill wrote to Field Marshal Harold

Alexander requesting an investigation into Mussolini's death and in particular why his lover Claretta Petacci had also been executed. The prime minister in that letter even called the action "predatory and cowardly." The CLNAI (Comitato di Liberazione Nazionale Alta Italia) had just assumed responsibility for that execution. The CLNAI acted in the name and on behalf of the government of Ivanoe Bonomi and of the lieutenant general of the Kingdom, Umberto of Savoy. The shame for that "act of justice" or, depending on one's viewpoint, the double assassination, was to fall on a weak government and king in Rome. How could British fair play ever appear suspect to anyone?

Nine years later in the fall of 1954, one of Mussolini's nephews, Vanni Teodorani, became the first to write in the weekly magazine *Asso di bastoni*, which he edited, that the British may have been involved in the Duce's death. Churchill had no need to acknowledge that impoverished and desperate fascist publication. Instead, he reacted with a sharp denial to an article published in *Il Giornale d'Italia* in March 1947, denying that he had written any letters to Mussolini besides those published in his books. Once he again became prime minister he ordered the Foreign Office (on November 7, 1951) to issue a statement repeating the terms of his prior statement, following a series of articles that had been published in Italian newspapers.

Regarding the nature of the contacts (a more accurate definition than that of "correspondence") between Mussolini and Churchill starting in the fall of 1944 up to the collapse of the RSI we can only speculate. What may be debated is whether the initiative to reopen the dialog came from the Italian or the British side. According to Fabio Andriola, "in 1944 there were two elements that could induce Mussolini and Churchill to reopen the dialog: on the one hand the breakthrough of the Red Army in Europe and the need to oppose the new Soviet imperialism; on the other, Mussolini's extreme political and military weakness could have compelled him to pressure the British prime minister, who could be blackmailed for his offers of a few years before to obtain peace conditions that would not be humiliating." The initiative could therefore have originated with Mussolini.

However, it could also have come from the British in an attempt to slow the advance of the Red Army. What could Mussolini offer to Sir Winston Churchill? The surrender of the RSI for whatever it was worth and although it was impossible without the agreement of the German occupiers? Churchill could promise much more in case Mussolini succeeded in convincing the Führer to stop fighting in the west. It is a fact that the contacts did take place. We will demonstrate that there are too many corroborating accounts.

Chapter IV

THE EYEWITNESSES TELL THE STORY

*The contacts between Mussolini and Churchill that had been
interrupted by the war were renewed at the time of the Battle of
the Bulge, during the winter of 1944–1945.*

D ino Campini (Biggini's secretary when he was minister of education, in Padua) spent th second half of his life (after Liberation) trying to piece together the facts the minister had told him.
Campini wrote scores of articles on the subject as a contributor to
the weekly magazine *Tempo* and several other publications, and was
the author of two books about the role played by Churchill at the
end of the fascist republican regime. As we mentioned in the open-
ing chapter, Biggini repeatedly indicated that the Duce had taken
initiatives to shorten the war and spare the suffering of his men.
Those initiatives were aimed at the British and Mussolini kept
Biggini regularly informed because he trusted him implicitly. During the last days of his life, as he lay in agony in the clinic in Milan
where Campini went to visit him discreetly, Biggini, who was regis-
tered under a false name, kept complaining of having lost the copy

of the secret documents the Duce had given him. As Campini wrote, "It was clear from his words that these were not secrets regarding Hitler, but rather Churchill. From the context, from many statements and from very specific details, it became increasingly clear to me that the documents he was referring to were those regarding Italy's relations with England, between Mussolini and Churchill."

There are two other memoirs worth citing at some length: one by Sergio Nesi, an officer of the Decima Mas, and the other by Pietro Carradori, the Duce's orderly. This is what Nesi has to say:[1]

> The most important secret contact with the enemy took place in November 1944 and not just between individual emissaries coming from the south and Prince Valerio Borghese, but at a rather higher level. The author is not aware of any writer or journalist having ever mentioned it, since the event came to light only recently. The location of the meeting was on Lake Iseo, specifically on the base of the *Decima Flottiglia Mas*. It was on that lake near the seaplane landing of Montecolino that the Decima had an outpost and the CABI had set up a pontoon to test torpedoes. Commander Borghese's family lived on the island of San Paolo,[2] which was almost adjacent to the landing area. To anyone unfamiliar with the Navy it may appear odd that at the foot of the Alps there could be a seaplane base; however, up to September 8, 1943, there existed a Royal naval air reconnaissance school at that base with three "Cant Z 501" Airplanes. On the morning of September 9 the planes flew to Venice while all personnel followed over land. The base administrative commander was Royal Army Major Barsali, who also left that base to go to the base on the island of Sant'Erasmo in Venice, near the Sant'Andrea airbase (the former torpedo manufacturing plant). When he was ordered to go south and surrender to the Anglo-American forces just as Fecia di Cossato was to do later on, Barsali wrote a letter to his family ("I will not go to the enemy side") and shot himself.[3] [. . .] Getting back to the contacts in question, it is necessary to observe the movements

of Commander Borghese during those days in November. On November 7 he had a long private conversation with [Marshal] Graziani. On November 14, with an escort of a few sailors and Lieutenant Enzo Tartaglia,[4] he paid a visit to German ambassador Rudolph Rahn at a location on Lake Iseo; that evening he went to the outpost at Montorfano. The following day he was near Como, specifically near the base of the *Vega* battalion specialists. On November 16 a motorboat of the *Decima*, piloted by the sailor Caviglia from Sarnico, took Commander Borghese and Lady Daria Olsuviev[5] to the base at Montecolino. All the access roads to that location had been cut off a few days before by German units, as participants and historians of the local resistance recall today. The headquarters building was surrounded by a unit of fully armed Decima sailors with blue insignia, led by Lieutenant Enzo Tartaglia. Shortly after the other participants in that meeting arrived for an ultrasecret meeting chaired by Commander Borghese, who was presiding, and which included: Captain Fausto Sestini representing the Republican [Fascist] Ministry of the Navy; General Giuseppe Violante, the Commander of the *Etna* division of the GNR [Guardia Nazionale Repubblicana—Republican National Guard]; the MOVM and Francesco Maria Barracu for the RSI government; Ambassador Rudolf Rahn; Obergruppenführer SS Karl Wolff; senior British officers representing Prime Minister Winston Churchill and Marshal Bernard Montgomery; senior American officers, representing the U.S. government and General Dwight. D. Eisenhower; and other minor figures. Lady Daria was the only interpreter present.

The meeting had been called by Churchill himself and his plenipotentiaries had brought a top-secret plan by the British statesman, which, had it been followed, would have changed the course of the war and the face of the world.

The proposals were:

1. Official recognition of the RSI and at the same time an armistice with that State;

2. Switching of the front with U.S. Fifth Army and the British Eighth Army going on offensive on the eastern front against Russia;
3. Using German troops in Italy to help Allied forces;
4. Intervention of the four Italian divisions of the RSI *Littorio*, *Monterosa*, *Italia*, and *San Marco*, as well as the *Decima* in coordination with the other troops.

To Commander Borghese's question as to why the Allies did not also wish to involve the armed forces of the Kingdom of Italy in the South, the British answered that the government could not be trusted, given the presence of too many men in the cabinet with ideological ties to Communist Russia. That answer reflects rather faithfully the one given in the south to the covert volunteers who were to land at Trieste and in the Istrian Peninsula. This leads us to believe that the so-called "De Courten plan"[6] was nothing but a footnote of the broader plan hatched by Churchill and Montgomery: the 5,000 covert volunteers of Mastragostino and Cigala-Fulgosi[7] would probably have had to take part in an operation on the front of Venezia Giulia, Friuli, and Istria, together with the 10,000 men of the Decima already deployed on location.[8]

There must have been an animated discussion in that room at Montecolino; however, nothing besides the initial points that were made has survived, filtered through a door kept ajar if not the completely negative reaction of the American plenipotentiaries. Roosevelt and Eisenhower wanted no part of a break with their "friend Stalin," whom they fully respected as a friend and whose good faith they blindly believed in. The meeting therefore ended in complete failure. Yet something must have been written and perhaps Churchill went looking immediately after the war among the other documents for that account that was so embarrassing to him. This event was covered by impenetrable silence for almost half a century. Now we have shed some light on the matter.

Is this total fantasy? Fictional reality? A fabrication? But to what end?[9] Within the scope of Sergio Nesi's book of reminiscences the anecdote of the meeting at Lake Iseo is only of marginal importance. Nesi is not someone given to recasting history, he was a contemporary witness to the events, a volunteer of the Decima, simply writing "the history of the Italian navy's attack units in the south and north after the armistice," as his book announces on its cover.

But we should continue with other eyewitness accounts, such as that of Pietro Carradori, who was Mussolini's orderly.[10]

In the closing months of the RSI Mussolini negotiated with British representatives of Winston Churchill. I was a witness to at least two meetings, all of them ultrasecret and very confidential, that the Duce had with those mysterious characters. Both meetings took place at a villa located at via Roma, 5 (at least that was the name of the street that I noted) at Porto Ceresio in the province of Varese, just a few hundred meters from the Swiss border. The first meeting took place during the evening of September 21, 1944. We left Gargnano at 8:30 p.m., taking the rear door to escape Birzer's surveillance. He was the SS lieutenant whom Mussolini hated and whose orders were to never allow Mussolini out of his sight—even for a moment— and whom many a time I shoved aside unceremoniously to make him understand that his presence was totally unwelcome. Four of us got in the car. I was up front with the driver Cesarotti, the Duce sat in the rear with Nicola Bombacci, his Communist friend, the only one at Salò who addressed him in the familiar form. It was a silent trip for some two hours. Mussolini was carrying a yellow leather case with a zipper and no handle, the same one he was to hand me later on, saying that it was the most precious possession he had—this was when we left the Milan Prefecture on April 25, 1945.

Once we reached the villa Cesarotti I stayed in the car while Mussolini and Bombacci went inside. I never saw the British who had come—at least that's what the driver and I thought— with a rowboat or a motorboat from nearby Switzerland, reaching the villa from the rear. It was clear to me that they were British, given the few words the Duce exchanged with Bombacci during the return trip, which started shortly after midnight. Mussolini openly talked about them being English and commented to Bombacci how inflexible they were. He appeared clearly to be disappointed that things did not turn out as he expected.

I was to hear the same comments and identical conclusions laced with disappointment and bitterness (characteristic of someone who did not succeed at reaching an agreement he was anxiously expecting) from Mussolini on the night of January 21–22, 1945, returning from the same trip, also in the greatest secrecy, to Porto Ceresio. On that occasion the Duce was accompanied by Francesco Maria Barracu,[11] again carrying the dark yellow briefcase. A long time after these events I connected those two strange trips to other journeys that Mussolini had taken during the preceding months in the company of Maresciallo Apriliti to San Paolo island, owned by the Beretta family, on Lake Iseo. Beretta, the industrial entrepreneur, was the main Italian manufacturer of small arms and on friendly terms with Mussolini, but not just with him. Beretta also had as his guests in the luxurious villa on the little island Mrs. Daria Olsufiev, the wife of Commander Borghese, and her children. Beretta often visited Gargnano, sometimes twice a month. When he manufactured the famous "short machine gun" he brought over two samples, one for the Duce and the other for me. The Duce's gun had the trademark Mussolini M engraved in gold on the butt. Mine had the same M in silver. On that occasion I thanked Beretta. I could not imagine that he also generously provided pistols and machine guns to the partisans as well. In any case, weapons manufacturers must of necessity keep good relations with all belligerents. This obviously included the British, to the point of arranging meetings at his residence with the head of the fascist Republic.

One can make—and this has been done—the most wild assumptions regarding the content of the talks between

Mussolini and the British. I may offer my limited but accurate direct testimony that at Gargnano Mussolini was fearful of being captured by the British. He was negotiating with them but feared them and did not trust them. I can't say that I know the reason why but I can imagine that they wanted to shut him up so that he would not reveal the nature of those discussions that had taken place obviously without the knowledge of the Russians. All I know is that more than once, as if conversing with himself, I heard him talk about the risk of becoming a prisoner of the English.

Yet things had not always been like that. A short time before we entered the war I introduced into the Map Room [Mussolini's study] at the Palazzo Venezia a British delegation led by the British ambassador to Italy. At the end of the talks some members of the delegation asked Quinto Navarra[12] if they could take a few ashtrays that were in the anteroom as souvenirs, offering to pay for them. Navarra told them to help themselves to whatever they wished. One of them replied for all of them: "The Italian people are not aware that they have a leader who is so much bigger than they are. For us to take home a souvenir of Mr. Mussolini is an honor."

Once again: Were these inventions, fantasy, or fictional reality? And to what ends? Actually these accounts fit in perfectly with the political-strategic picture at that juncture of the Second World War that could only find Churchill and Mussolini in agreement to end the massacre in the west and stop the Communist advance. Hitler (due to his unreasonable fanaticism) and Stalin (the real victim of the operation) were both kept in the dark about those contacts for obvious reasons. The Americans were hesitating and were responsible in the end for the plan's failure. Nor was it surprising that the German commanders in Italy should know about the contacts, since they were as anxious as Churchill to end the war and save their own skin.[13]

Confirmation of these secret contacts and stabbing the Red Army in the back—there is no other possible explanation—are furthermore part of the effort to save Europe from communism. One of the more convincing accounts is in Filippo Anfuso's book *Roma-Berlino-Salò* (Milan, 1950). When Mussolini appointed Anfuso as undersecretary of foreign affairs he confided that he had attempted to act as mediator between Churchill and Hitler in a useless attempt to end the slaughter in the west but that he always encountered Hitler's opposition to the idea ("Whenever you mention England to Hitler he looks like he's been bitten by an asp!").

Ermanno Amicucci, the editor of the *Corriere della Sera*, who had Mussolini's trust, discussed the matter in his book *I 600 giorni di Mussolini* (Rome, 1948) in which he recalls several meetings between Mussolini—who was said to have gone to the meetings alone, driving a Fiat *Balilla*—with British emissaries in a villa near Brescia. Those meetings were to have started on June 14, 1944.

Undersecretary for Popular Culture Alfredo Cucco discussed the issue in his book, *Non volevamo perdere** (Bologna, 1950). He reported about more than one meeting on San Paolo Island between Mussolini (accompanied only by his aide de camp Colonel Vito Casalinuovo—later shot by firing squad at Dongo) and two British emissaries, who were staying at Maderno. Also according to Cucco the meetings would have taken place in June and July, to be interrupted by the attempt on Hitler's life on July 20, 1944, which threw the top German officials in Italy—from General Wolff to Ambassador Rahn—into an understandable state of high anxiety.

After the war the RSI's undersecretary of the air force, General Ruggero Bonomi, was to confirm those meetings to Dino Campini, Minister Biggini's former secretary who was continuously searching for any confirmation of the nature of the papers the Duce had given to his favorite minister for safekeeping. Furthermore, the fact that those papers included the complete history of the contacts and agreements that took place during the RSI between the Duce and the British prime minister was not a mystery to many eyewitnesses at that time, including Edmondo Cione, the philosopher whom Mussolini had placed in charge of creating a political party to

---

* We Did Not Want to Lose.

give a semblance of democracy to the RSI,[14] to Nino D'Aroma, the director of Luce Institute, as we have shown in chapter II.

All these witnesses remember the recipients of at least two copies of the papers: Minister Biggini and Japanese ambassador Shinrokuro Hidaka, whom the Duce considered a trustworthy friend. It is likely that the third copy Mussolini discussed with Nino D'Aroma was one he wished to keep himself once the originals were safely sent to Switzerland. To complete the picture of the accounts that had been ignored too easily by many official Italian historians, but placed in proper perspective by others, it is instructive to reproduce a passage from the book *Mussolini si confessa* [Mussolini Confesses] (Milan, 1948) by Mussolini's German doctor, Georg Zachariae, which Fabio Andriola aptly quotes. During one of many confidential conversations that took place between the doctor and his famous patient, who was sick with ulcers, towards the end of 1944, Mussolini said:

I know Churchill very well; I know him personally, intimately. He came to see me when he was not part of the government. He visited Rome as a private citizen and wished to be considered and treated as such. I must tell you in total candor at the outset that I always enjoyed my conversations with this man of the world, who is intelligent and very English despite our differences of opinion and points of view. I can say that during those days we genuinely became friends. […] Even during the war I made it known to the German government that I was certain to be able to reach a reasonable agreement with England. I think the initiative could have succeeded, since I intended to use my personal relationship with Churchill as the basis for the move. Ribbentrop could never have obtained anything of the sort. I know the prime minister and know how to appeal to him. […] Such a meeting could still be arranged anywhere in Spain or North Africa. Churchill is not narrow-minded. His intelligence and experience as a statesman are too great for him not to understand the advantages of an agreement in the interest of Great Britain and Europe. I can say this to you: I was ready to take such a step and promote a meeting with

Churchill. Hitler did not want it and still does not. He prefers to listen to the incompetent Ribbentrop.

But this is not all. For example, current historians have been too much in a hurry to file away the revelations made by Drew Pearson, the U.S. syndicated columnist who, in 1945, was active between Rome and Lake Como. On one occasion in particular, while Pearson was investigating the escape of General Mario Roatta, he stated that the general's disappearance had been engineered with the help of the British: "They feared that he would reveal the contents of the compromising Churchill-Mussolini papers and the scandalous double-cross game played by the British government with the pro-monarchist Yugoslav partisans of Mihailovic."[15] This author, along with Alessandro Zanella, the dedicated and honest historian from Mantua,* has been involved in that research, with interviews of eyewitnesses, consulting archives and written reports. In his seminal book *L'ora di Dongo,* Zanella[16] recounted the summons by Mussolini on April 23, 1945, to the Milan Prefecture of the notary Umberto Alberici to conclude the sale of the building of *Il Popolo d'Italia* to the businessman Gian-Riccardo Cella. This account includes a confidential revelation by the notary Alberici to Cella himself, a revelation that is not compromising in any way but essential for the unfolding of this book: "Among the most important files the Duce asked me to hold, there are his papers with Churchill, who begged Mussolini to intercede with Hitler to avoid signing a separate peace with Stalin. Mussolini was successful and had saved Great Britain by avoiding the terrible consequences of a war with the Führer on a single front in the west." It is possible that the notary Alberici—as Fabio Andriola has pointed out—glanced quickly at the papers in order to authenticate them, but certainly did not have them in his possession until the end. In any case Alberici quickly forgot the content, being the consummate professional.

No one could forget the ugly deaths of Captain Neri and the woman partisan fighter Gianna, as we shall see in the closing chapter of this book, or the firing squad at some remote rifle range. That

---

* He died prematurely on May 22, 2000.

was to be the fate of the Brescia chief of police, Manlio Candrilli, "executed" on September 1, 1945, by a firing squad at the rifle range of Mompiano, coldly witnessed by a British army officer.

This author met the son of the chief of police, Giancarlo Candrilli, in Rome in 1982 while engaged in research at the State Archive for the biography of Carlo Alberto Biggini. Candrilli, who along with his mother and since he was a young boy, had been fighting to prove his father's innocence and the cruelty of his execution. He was successful, thanks to a judgment overturning the sentence fourteen years after the fact by the Corte di Cassazione.* Candrilli was hoping that something would surface confirming "a British involvement" in his father's death, just as I had been searching for similar traces in the very mysterious death of Biggini.

However, no hard proof was to emerge and much suspicion lingered on. Candrilli was the only RSI chief of police to be executed following pressure by British agents on the CAS (Corte d'assise straordinaria)** in Brescia that had unjustly condemned him to death. Candrilli was the top Brescia police official in the province that was picked as the location of the most sensitive departments of the Italian Social Republic and also the area where the secret meetings took place between Mussolini and Churchill's men. Candrilli had been responsible for the Duce's safety and that of the other eminent persons involved. He knew who they were and what they looked like, as well as their names, and played a key role in a page that had to be erased from history.

The Brescia historian, Lodovico Galli, in his book *Una vile esecuzione* [A Cowardly Execution] (Brescia, 2001), has documented in great detail the false and invalid indictment of Candrilli and the completely unfair death sentence handed down to him. Candrilli was very well known to the population as a peaceful person, who was kindhearted and decidedly in favor of pacification. Following a series of false accusations written by some of his former collaborators who had changed sides he was arrested. Right after his arrest

---

* Italy's Supreme Court of Appeals.
** Special Court.

he was severely beaten. He requested, to no avail, that some well-known anti-fascists be allowed to testify in his favor, since had helped them during the civil war. All the lawyers appointed to defend him recused themselves for "health reasons"; the trial was a tragic farce. But what were the facts of the indictments? As Galli recalled, there were two: having ordered the execution of a partisan, who had actually been shot by machine gun fire in an escape attempt; and of having tortured a woman, who showed some of the scars on her body to the judges. Candrilli had never seen the woman before and her scars were actually caused by a smallpox infection. "My father's tragic death shows that anyone who knew too much had to die," was the comment of Candrilli's son.

Chapter V

THE PHONE TAPS AS EVIDENCE

Mussolini's phone calls to Claretta Petacci, Graziani, Pavolini, and other aides prove his attempts to convince the Führer to seek a separate peace with the Allies. The mystery of Tommaso David, head of Salò's secret intelligence: was a copy of the Churchill papers exchanged for a gold medal?

On March 28, 1973, General Karl Wolff, former commander of the SS and German police in Italy during the occupation and the civil war, handed to Italian newsman Ricciotti Lazzero, who had gone to interview him, the copies of a few letters and tapped telephone conversations of Benito Mussolini, which he kept in his private archives. General Wolff was not a man to give something for nothing. Freed from prison after twelve years and out of work, he survived by selling his memoirs and documents little by little to the journalists and historians who went to interview him. This author speaks from experience because just one year prior to Wolff's death in 1983 at age eighty-two, I went to interview him for a large circulation weekly (*Gente*, published in Milan). The meeting took place in the Bavarian town of Prien-am-Chiemsee, and I had to bring some four million Italian lire in German marks, or the equivalent of about five hundred U.S. dollars for each of four articles we then published. We may therefore conclude that Lazzero or his publisher had to pay much more money to obtain those documents. The added reason is that the documents are of a sensational nature and confirm without a doubt that the "elusive" Mussolini-Churchill papers were not a phantom at all; that the contacts between the two politicians (Mussolini and Churchill) continued up to the final days of the Duce's life—with Mussolini actually playing the role of Churchill's "envoy" to Hitler, and Churchill (through Mussolini) attempting up to the end to persuade Hitler to stop the fighting on the western front so that everyone (Italians, Germans, British, and in all likelihood the French) could stop the Communist wave coming from the east. Mussolini, thanks to the Churchill letters, was convinced he could save his own life and even, after the initial moment of confusion, return to politics in Italy! Had Stalin been able to use that file he could have immediately torn up the agreement reached at Yalta by accusing Great Britain of betrayal and then grabbing even more territory than just Poland, Hungary, Czechoslovakia, and half of Germany. Finally, in the contest between the Communists and the British to be the first to execute Mussolini and Claretta Petacci (who knew and shared in all of the dictator's secrets) it was the British who reached their target, thanks to one of their agents who had infiltrated the Communist ranks.

Ricciotti Lazzero, one of most authoritative and thorough historians of the RSI period has, for reasons unknown, kept those documents under wraps for some twenty-odd years. He finally published them in his very successful book, *Il Sacco d'Italia*, in 1994.[1] Before we examine those sensational documents we should offer a word of explanation to help the reader's understanding. These papers are absolutely authentic. The Germans had set up at Salò a telephone wiretap service that recorded all of the Duce's phone conversations. They also photographed all of his letters, a copy of which he regularly passed on to his mistress (more to keep her informed of every one of his steps than to seek her approval). Clearly, Mussolini knew about all this. He was also aware of the fact that Claretta would pass his letters along to SS Captain Franz Spögler, her bodyguard, so that he could make copies. The operation was set up in order to create more copies of the file. Mussolini was obsessed with the idea of distributing copies of the most important documents to provide to the most trustworthy persons in his entourage the true picture of the way he handled the war. These included Clara Petacci, Minister Carlo Alberto Biggini, Japanese ambassador Shinrokuro Hidaka, and Captain Spögler, who as the loyal SS officer he was made an extra copy for his commanding officer, General Karl Wolff. This was the chain that brought the documents into Ricciotti Lazzero's possession. Let us now examine the most important contents.

September 10, 1944. Letter from Mussolini to Marshal Rodolfo Graziani:

> . . . In order to protect us all in the future, I am assembling a maximum of written details and communications. From everyone in their own handwriting. I don't even exclude Hitler himself. Only this documentation, which is by now very thick, will speak up and break any attack against us. Just the knowledge of the existence of my papers frightens too many people: from Victor Emmanuel to Badoglio. But even Churchill and Hitler himself will be forced to remain truthful.

November 22, 1944. Phone conversation between Hitler and Mussolini:

> HITLER: But we can take action, Duce: repressive measures. I have been very clear in the letter I just sent you.
> MUSSOLINI: I also see no other way out. We are compelled to do it. These Anglo-Saxons are so crazy! They don't understand—especially the British—that this way they are digging their own grave. Or do they believe that with the victory they

are hoping for they can block Bolshevism at the English Channel? They are very nearsighted.

HITLER: Not nearsighted—the British are blind! Aren't they aware of the Russian colossus?

MUSSOLINI: Actually, Churchill had forecasted that danger many years ago. But...Führer, you are aware of this...

HITLER: Yes, I know. I know all the details. But Duce, believe me, that sword cuts on both sides of the blade. As long as that is the case we must not negotiate. You remember what I told you?

MUSSOLINI: I remember and I keep on expecting your understanding. We must not waste this opportunity. Give me your trust!

HITLER: You have my trust, there is no doubt about that. But if I . . .

The conversation stops here because the line was interrupted.[2]

January 9, 1945. Letter from Mussolini to Graziani:

I have a letter from Hitler dated January 2, 1945. He asks that in case it becomes necessary for us to fall back to the north, his advice is that I take all the papers I had discussed with him and proposed to make use of, now becomes clear. At this time I feel it is extremely important to put these papers in a safe place— first of all the exchange of letters and the agreements with Churchill. These will demonstrate the bad faith of the English. Those documents are worth more than victory at war.[3]

March 14, 1945. Letter from Mussolini to Claretta:

Claretta, my dear, you are right. The day is approaching when Hitler will become convinced of the need to seek direct negotiations with England. He knows what I can provide.[4] But he is fearful and I know the reason behind his fear. And I hate having this knowledge because it makes me feel that I am a coward, of not knowing when to act even though I sense that it is absolutely necessary, actually a duty, to finally take action. Yet to act with Hitler's approval means to risk endangering our situation and our possibility of saving whatever could be saved. To act on our own initiative? Alone? This is not what I would recommend. I do not wish to follow in the footsteps of the Savoy family and the other traitors! What a torment! And what a crisis of conscience![5]

March 25, 1945. Phone conversation between Mussolini and Minister of the Interior Paolo Zerbino:

ZERBINO: I followed your orders. Three photographic copies are ready. The material for that man from Milan[6] is ready to go.

MUSSOLINI: Send the material to Milan immediately. The other copies should be brought here along with the originals. The final destination for these has already been selected. The other two copies will have to be kept in different places. I will take only a few papers. One never knows what may happen and we must prevent the possibility that even a small part may fall into the hands of people with an interest in destroying or hiding it. I am referring to many Italians who have not hesitated to become the allies of Italy's enemies to enhance their own positions twenty years later.[7] You can bet that these people would not move a finger for our national prestige! Those losers have only betrayed: inside our country and abroad!"

March 25, 1945. Phone conversation between Mussolini and Alessandro Pavolini, minister secretary of the Fascist Republican party:

MUSSOLINI: At this time I feel that the most important and useful thing is to take our papers to a safe place, especially the correspondence and the files of the agreements with Churchill. Those papers will document the inevitable bad faith of the British. Those documents are worth more than victory at war!

April 2, 1945. Letter from Claretta Petacci to Mussolini.

My firm conviction is still only that we must not compromise! The Savoy, Badoglio, and company are leading us into a trap! To them you are a criminal, someone condemned to death. Listen to my advice: be on your guard! It is in everyone's interest to silence you forever! You say: the documents will do the talking. But they know that documents can be bought, stolen, or destroyed. One fact is clear: should you or the papers fall into their hands one day, your existence and that of the papers would come to an end! Ben, I beseech you, do not make any decision without consulting you know who.

Who was Claretta Petacci referring to as she showed a rather extraordinary lucidity and ability to forecast?

April 3, 1945. Letter from Mussolini to Graziani:

Your proposal is totally insane! To hand over to the Savoy family the documents to win the peace? Victor Emmanuel turned his back on me and will keep on betraying one after the other all of his companions by liquidating them once he has used them. The Savoy family will never be able to use our papers!

Among the phone calls made from Mussolini's telephone at the villa delle Orsoline that were intercepted and transcribed by the German soldiers reporting to Wolff and published in Ricciotti Lazzero's important book *Il Sacco d'Italia*, there is one dated November 22, 1944—as quoted above—that we will call "the double-edged sword." It is necessary to examine it rather carefully. Mussolini and Hitler are speaking on the telephone. The latter was busy preparing the Ardennes offensive that history shall record as the "Battle of the Bulge" and Hitler's final attempt. The Italian dictator was not informed of those preparations; he was bitter and depressed by the continuous Allied bombing, creating civilian victims and destroying the population's morale. Let us reexamine their words once again.

HITLER: But we can take action, Duce: repressive measures. I have been very clear in the letter I just sent to you.

MUSSOLINI: I also see no other way out. We are compelled to do it. These Anglo-Saxons are so crazy! They don't understand—especially the British—that this way they are digging their own grave. Or do they believe that with the victory they are hoping for they can block Bolshevism at the English Channel? They are very nearsighted.

HITLER: Not nearsighted—the British are blind! Aren't they aware of the Russian colossus?

MUSSOLINI: Actually, Churchill had forecasted that danger many years ago. But...Führer, you are aware of this...

HITLER: Yes, I know. I know all the details. But Duce, believe me, that sword cuts on both sides of the blade. And as long as that is the case we must not negotiate. You remember what I told you?

MUSSOLINI: I remember and I keep on expecting your understanding. We must not waste this opportunity. Give me your trust!

HITLER: You have my trust, there is no doubt about that. But if I...

Once the line was restored after some technical problem, the end of the conversation was not transcribed. However, there is enough available to understand what the ultimate goal was. The military situation, not only on the eastern front but in the west as well, was getting worse for Germany. Mussolini was continuing to try for some kind of exit through Churchill. At that juncture, Mussolini was the one making the request, but a few weeks later Churchill would again be the supplicant. Hitler was about to become a serious threat once again, thanks to the counteroffensive in the Ardennes.[8]

Following the liberation of Paris the Allied advance went on without pause. On August 21, 1944, Marseille fell: on August 30, Rouen; on September 3, British troops liberated Brussels; and on September 11 the Allies reached the German border. They were compelled to stop since they faced the fortifications of the Western wall and harsh German resistance, making any attempt to break through impossible. The only improvement came on October 21, 1944, with the fall of Aachen, but at the price of enormous casualties. The advance that appeared to be unstoppable had ground to a halt. Hitler was able to draw a deep breath and hope that all was not yet lost. "Operation Grief" was studied by the OKW strategic planners in the hope of repeating the success of 1940. The positions had reached that same starting point when the German army, by enacting the von Manstein plan, had broken through the enemy front, entering the Ardennes and closing up the British Expeditionary Corps and part of the French army in a pocket in Belgian territory. True, things had changed since then: enemy troop strength, with the addition of the Americans, had almost doubled and the German army, following the defeats and humiliations after D-Day, had lost its former optimism. However, the need to defend the threatened homeland could still work miracles.

The operation known as the "Battle of the Bulge" or "Hitler's final gamble," was prepared down to the last detail. German soldiers speaking fluent English were infiltrated behind enemy lines to create confusion among the Allies with fabricated news of attacks on their units, to blow up bridges and cause panic: these were the "Werewolves." The attack began on December 16 and for over one month a savage kind of war was fought amid the ice and snow, with the Allies retreating all along the front and a German advance of over one hundred kilometers.

Panic spread to the Allied commanders and their staff and it was felt that the offensive could well throw the invading forces back into the ocean. It was possibly during those weeks that Churchill secretly requested Mussolini's initiative to convince Hitler to call off the counter-offensive in the west and concentrate all of his forces against the fateful advance of the Red Army, which threatened to conquer all of Europe. The transcripts of the desperate phone calls from the Duce to the Führer that would turn out to be useless prove that this actually took place.

The Ardennes offensive could have ended in disaster for the Allies without the desperate resistance at Bastogne, which was surrounded by German armored troops. That battle was among the bloodiest of the entire Second World War and brought "Operation Grief" to an end. On January 20, 1945, General George Patton, in command of three armored divisions, began chasing the Germans from the positions they had conquered.

The chronology will help understand the role played by the two main protagonists of our story: Churchill and Mussolini. Each time one of the two felt himself weakening, he asked the other to do something; when one felt strong he became indifferent. Therefore, the meetings at Lake Iseo, which took place after June 6, 1944 (Normandy landings), and until July 20 (the attempt to kill Hitler), show Mussolini and the German leadership in Italy—by now estranged from the Führer—pushing hard for an agreement. With the failure of the first phase of the negotiations (due to the reasonable suspicion of British involvement in the attempt on Hitler's life by Count Klaus von Stauffenberg on July 20, 1944), Mussolini came charging back with the September 21 meeting, witnessed by Pietro Carradori. As the Ardennes offensive was about to begin, Hitler became more reticent than ever regarding an agreement directed against the Soviets—see the November 22 phone conversation ("the sword cuts on both sides"). Once the Battle of the Bulge failed with Patton's unstoppable offensive (beginning January 20, 1945), Mussolini, on January 21, was once again pressuring Churchill's agents—the second meeting reported by Carradori—but the Duce returned to Gargnano, disappointed by their tough terms.

As previously noted and as Nino D'Aroma wrote in his book, *Churchill and Mussolini*, the Duce ordered three photographic copies made of the papers regarding his relationship with the British. The original was taken from him at Dongo when he was captured. Of the three copies, we know for sure that two of them were destined for and handed to Minister Biggini and Ambassador Hidaka. But what happened to the third copy?* No one has yet investigated this in any detail. We may now be able to shed some light on the matter

---

* The latest documentary by Peter Tompkins states that the third copy may have been held by Mussolini's wife, Rachele.

thanks to the research of Riccardo Lazzeri, a tireless investigator of historical issues that we shall discuss once more in Chapter VIII regarding the Dongo treasure.[9] Lazzeri, in seeking to confirm the transcripts of the telephone calls as reported in the book by Ricciotti Lazzero that we mentioned at the beginning of this chapter, was able to obtain from Franz Spögler, former bodyguard to Claretta Petacci and SS officer in charge of recording the Duce's telephone conversations, the carbon copy of the originals he had given, at the time, to Karl Wolff and allowed the author to use them in the research for this book. Among the copies are a few previously unpublished conversations between Mussolini and the mysterious unidentified "man from Milan"—one in particular recorded right after the Yalta Conference and another on April 16, 1945, the day before the Duce left Gargnano to go to Milan.

During the first phone call Mussolini told the "Unbekannt in Mailand" that he was writing a report to Hitler to persuade him that "the Yalta conference shows that there is an abyss between the views of the United States and those of the USSR," to underscore how the proposed annexation of Poland and the Baltic states had shaken England ("England ist sehr erschüttert" in Spögler's notes) and finally to confirm that his relations with Churchill "are still good" ("sind heute noch die besten") and allowed starting negotiations for a separate peace. During the April 16 phone conversation to "an Unbekannt in Mailand," Mussolini confided candidly: "My dear old friend, don't be surprised by my sentimentalism, my fears and my assumptions, but right now I have very little left. Only our papers can provide our moral and material salvation. Should I perish, be murdered, executed or die in combat, use these documents judiciously: the national interest is at stake!"

In Ricciotti Lazzero's book, the man on the telephone is identified as Nicola Bombacci, but this does not correspond to the German original of the phone tap, which has on the cover "an Unbekannt in Mailand."[10]

Who was the "unknown" person who almost certainly received the third photocopy of the papers? A likely possibility is Tommaso

David, who was the head of intelligence at Salò, the "Silver Foxes" as they were called, a group of volunteer secret agents specializing in sabotage behind enemy lines.

Tommaso David was born in 1875 (eight years before Mussolini) at Esperia in the province of Frosinone (near Rome), and had begun his career at sea as a boy on oceangoing clipper ships. As head gunner first class he fought in the Italo-Turkish war of 1911 and was decorated with a bronze medal for military valor. At the end of the war he joined the navy as weapons master, teaching at the Livorno Naval Academy. In 1915, even though he was under no obligation because of his age to be in combat, he volunteered in the First World War and in December 1917 he was awarded a second bronze medal for military valor, as well as a promotion to lieutenant for war service. Once Italy went to war in Ethiopia in 1935 he went back into the service and was promoted to the rank of captain.

His son was sent to Croatia in 1942 to fight the Tito partisans who were constantly ambushing the Italian occupation units. This brought the older but always very brave Tommaso David to request (and be granted) an assignment to front line duty in command of a battalion of volunteers he had created, specializing in hunting down Communist Yugoslav partisans. With his men he took part in operations that caused havoc in enemy units, killing scores of Communists in their wake. But he was to face the greatest sorrow a father could ever experience when he was told of his son's death in combat. The awful blow greatly energized him as a fighter, up until the bloody clash at Zanton on December 8, 1942, where he was seriously injured and nominated for the silver medal for military valor.[11]

That silver medal was turned into a gold medal following his request by a decree of the Head of State dated June 28, 1956, something that had never happened before and that was truly extraordinary in a Republic dedicated to anti-fascism. Following the events in Croatia, David played a key role in the military organization of the Italian Social Republic as a dedicated fascist and faithful ally of the Germans. He should have been condemned to death but instead he was awarded a gold medal. How could this be possible? One of the best informed historians of the RSI, Teodoro Francesconi, asked the question in his book, *Le Bande BAC in Dalmazia 1942–43*[12] [The BAC Brigades in Dalmatia 1942–43], whether a copy of the Mussolini-Churchill papers had been given to the De Gasperi government by Tommaso David himself in exchange for the upgrading of the silver medal into gold. As Francesconi, who is a leader of RSI veterans, states: "Returning to northern Italy from Croatia in December 1943, because of his experience and ability and his rank of lieutenant colonel in the GNR (he had been a "Primo Seniore"* in the MVSN—the fascist militia—up to 1943), David was given command of a special autonomous army and GNR unit under the name of "Dottor De Santis," while the cover name of the unit was "Allevamento volpi argentate" [Silver foxes breeding farm]. David had a few dozen men and women under his command, with a number of young volunteers originally from Dalmatia with whom he was actively operating behind the front lines. He was in charge, first in Rome and later in Milan, of a network of informers and saboteurs behind enemy lines. Since his agents were extremely efficient he was frequently in contact with the head of state. At this stage, the information points to the briefcase that Mussolini was always carrying with him containing important State documents during the final days. There are indications pointing to the fact that it was very probable that part of or a "copy" of those documents had been given by Mussolini to David. There are traces of this in the testimony by Alcide De Gasperi at the trial for libel where the Italian prime minister sued the popular writer and journalist Giovanni Guareschi in 1953.[13] According to reasonably accurate information that was never officially confirmed, David had delivered the Mussolini papers to Alcide De Gasperi, when he was prime minister, as the legal representative of the Italian State, requesting in return an amnesty for those fascists who were in prison and the gold medal for himself for the events at

---

* A rank of officer in the Fascist militia.

Zaton on December 8, 1942. It may sound like a fairy tale but it would provide the only justification for the switching of the medal from silver to gold. Such an upgrading becomes even more diffi-cult to explain once we

learn that the ministry of defense of the Italian Republic blocked all proposals for decorations for military valor made *before* the armi-stice of September 8, 1943, in favor of military personnel who had in any way cooperated or served in the armed forces of the RSI. The facts speak for themselves.

Chapter VI

MUSSOLINI ON LAKE LUGANO AND CHURCHILL ON LAKE GARDA

*No one has ever explained why Mussolini spent so much time at
Menaggio—almost one and a half days. Winston Churchill's "vacations"
on Lakes Como and Garda were not related to his passion for painting.*

Mussolini's movements, once he left Milan during the evening
of April 25, 1945, have been witnessed and counted minute
by minute by the scores of people who followed him on the way to
Lake Como and managed to escape being executed by the partisans
and later to write their memoirs. What no one has been able to
explain, however, are the reasons why the Duce—if he truly intended, as he hinted to most of those following him, to go to the
"Valtellina redoubt" (also named R.A.R.) in order to wait for the
Allies to arrive and surrender to them—took a road going in a totally different direction. Actually, it was an absurd choice, because
the fastest and shortest way to reach Valtellina was the lake front
road on the eastern side of the lake starting at Lecco. On the con-

trary, the so-called "via Regina," the scenic coast road, winding and dangerous, was also controlled by the partisans of the 52nd Garibaldi Brigade, starting at Como, then through Cernobbio, Moltrasio, Argegno, Cadenabbia, Tremezzo, Menaggio, Musso, and Dongo—reaching Colico, the first town of the Valtellina, shortly after.

Many historians have speculated that Mussolini was really attempting to seek safety in Switzerland, leaving his followers in the lurch in a rather cowardly fashion—since they were obeying an order issued over the radio by the minister and secretary of the Fascist Party Alessandro Pavolini—and converging to Como from all parts of northern Italy. This was a mistaken and even childish assumption because had Mussolini really decided on that course of action he could have gone into Switzerland in a few minutes, since the border almost touches the town of Como. On the other hand, one fails to see why he should take the narrow and winding road that goes uphill from Menaggio to Grandola then comes down to Polezza and Lake Lugano. Also, one should bear in mind that the Duce was well aware that Swiss border guards had been reinforced on that occasion by army units with orders to not allow anyone into Swiss territory, per the request that the American and British ambassadors in Bern.

Yet at dawn on April 26, Mussolini, with only three of his most faithful followers (who would end up in front of the firing squad at Dongo—his secretary Luigi Gatti, Nicola Bombacci, and Paolo Porta, the fascist federal secretary of Como), got into his *Alfa* and drove to Menaggio where the local party secretary, alerted by phone, was on hand to welcome him. Just before leaving, he informed the other members of his party (including his son Vittorio, his government ministers, and the commanders of military units) that he expected them all later on at Menaggio "where they will be given orders at the Fascist headquarters."[1]

Obviously those who knew Mussolini's true intentions, and especially whom he had in mind, whom he was planning to meet and talk to, were those three faithful followers soon to be silenced forever by gunfire. All the other members of the convoy understood that the comings and goings, the waste of time, were only making things even more dangerous.[2] They felt that way because they didn't know Mussolini had a definite plan in mind to save himself along with his entire entourage. However, he could not discuss it because he still did not know whether it would succeed.

In the meantime, the fact that the stop at Menaggio was to continue until the next morning proves that Mussolini did have "an appointment on the lake," as Fabio Andriola entitled his book. But with whom? The logical answer is: with Churchill's envoys, to whom he would hand over the papers that were so compromising for the British prime minister and—as we shall see—to shed some valuables that he could not wait to dispose of.

Shortly after 9 a.m. on Thursday, April 26, most of the convoy of fascist officials and their families "invaded" Menaggio. At this point, Mussolini probably already understood that he had been misled since the person or persons he was to meet did not show up. "As those who had just arrived were speaking with Secretary Castelli, they saw Mussolini coming out of a house in military uniform with a machine gun at his side going to another villa nearby amid the curiosity of the townspeople who were going about their business."[3] In what must have been a pure coincidence, at a short distance from Menaggio at the center of Mezzegra (then part of the Tremezzina district) was the magnificent villa belonging to Sir James Henderson, president of the Cucirini Cantoni Coats Company, one of Italy's most important textile enterprises entirely owned by British investors. (Henderson was also a founder of the Rotary Club of Italy and a cousin of Sir Nevile Henderson, the British ambassador to Berlin in 1939). Sir James had left Italy at the beginning of the war to move to nearby Switzerland, leaving his property in safe hands. Actually, "even the war could not separate Henderson from his creation. The Scotsman returned to Switzerland, where he kept a small observation office and managed to keep in contact with Cucirini Cantoni and follow its operations, even at a distance."[4] Henderson was a very important person in Italy and had been president of the Banca d'America e d'Italia, founder of the Anglo-Italian Chamber of Commerce, representative of the Bank of England in Italy, and knight of the Order of Saint Gregory the Great.[5]

It was very possible that Sir James and Mussolini knew each other from past acquaintance. The Henderson villa and the offices of the Cucirini Cantoni were located a few dozen meters from the locations (the De Maria house and Villa Belmonte) where the tragedy of Mussolini and Claretta Petacci took place. However, this could also be a strange but complete coincidence.

While Mussolini, tense and irritated, was looking for those who had promised to meet with him but did not show up, the members of his entourage were requested by Prefect Gatti, the Duce's dedicated secretary, to go with their automobiles to Cadenabbia, where they would be given new orders. "There was some impatience and irritation for the prolonged stop on the part of the leaders, who complied nevertheless."[6] In the meantime the situation was becoming complicated and more enigmatic with every passing hour. One more aborted meeting due to another no-show by the mysterious contacts of the Duce must have led to the absurd order for everyone to drive up to Grandola, leaving Menaggio for almost half a day, to then return back to the banks of the lake. "The column returned to Menaggio in the evening under a steady rain. Everyone was annoyed because a whole day had been wasted."[7]

At that point Mussolini understood that the British had entrapped him. But he still did not envision the worse part. He did not know that a powerful German motorized unit, led by an officer whose name was to elude every historian (Fallmeyer or Schallmeyer?), would provide Mussolini with the illusion that he could still save himself. However, the German officer would proceed to hand Mussolini over to the partisans of the 52nd Garibaldi Brigade according to a plan carefully put together by the surrendering German commanders and the British secret services.[8] Edmondo Cione's complete surprise was amply justified: "All it took was a blocked road and thirty partisans here and there to stop a column of three hundred soldiers armed to the teeth."[9]

Some have actually hypothesized that Mussolini got into the military truck in a German overcoat knowing in advance that he was to be arrested thereafter by the partisans, to give them the satisfaction of having captured the Duce themselves and later deal and negotiate with the British. This kind of scenario could be confirmed—this author has no way of doing so—by events such as those described by Edmondo Cione and by the Duce's orderly, Pietro Carradori. As Cione wrote: "Mussolini, who believed in his good fortune, was found on a truck and taken to the municipal building, where he talked with the mayor and the partisans and, despite the 'weariness of life' that had descended upon him, managed to impress them by his eloquence. It seemed as if the situation was headed towards a normal conclusion, some time in jail or in internment, sentencing by a court, and later perhaps even a return home."[10]

The account given by Carradori is no less surprising, since he saw Mussolini again at the Dongo municipal building after he, Carradori, had been captured by the partisans following a firefight:

> Mussolini came up to me, worried and saddened because I looked awful. I summoned my remaining strength and saluted him with my right arm at attention as I had done every morning at the Palazzo Venezia. He put his hand on my shoulder and asked, "Where did they get you, Carradori?" I couldn't speak and was unable to explain to him that I had not abandoned him and that the Germans had prevented me from getting into the truck with him. He barely had time to tap me on the sleeve affectionately with his hand, lightly, to avoid hurting me. "Take heart, Carradori, take heart," he said. "The game is not over yet." I remember his words as though I had just heard them. What was he trying to tell me? How many times during the intervening years have I thought back to that sentence! The tone was that of a man who still had cards up his sleeve. But which ones? Today, after many years and having spoken to many other people, I have come up with a very clear picture. Mussolini was thinking specifically about his minister of national education, Carlo Alberto Biggini, to whom he had given a copy of the file regarding the agreements with Churchill. In my own mind I think that Biggini—to whom the partisans would certainly have never done any harm, if only because they owed him a debt of gratitude and respect—was also unable to

save himself because he knew about those political and diplomatic secrets that were never to be published under any circumstances.[11]

Obviously, Mussolini still counted on the original copies of the papers he had sent to Switzerland through Ambassador Hidaka, as well as those given to Biggini and those Claretta Petacci had given to her brother Marcello, who was to be executed because of this, even though he no longer had the papers that had been taken from him at the time of his capture.

These multiple copies (photocopies and typed copies) of the papers prompted Churchill, after the war, to spend time first at Lake Como, staying at the Villa Apraxin at Moltrasio (the location of British army headquarters); and later on Lake Garda, where he spent longer periods on the lakefront at Villa Gemma (the same villa where Biggini had left copies of the documents the Duce had entrusted him with); and finally on Lake Lugano, at Osteno, on the Italian side, which could easily be reached from the Swiss side across the way. No one believed the "official" reason given for the strange vacations of the victor of the Second World War—to pass the time painting landscapes. The independent press (the Swiss newspapers, for example) was the first to turn it into a joke in cartoons where Churchill was shown throwing papers into a fireplace.

The British secret services did not tread lightly in securing possession of all copies of the compromising papers. If payment was required they readily agreed (many Communist leaders chose to fatten their pocketbooks with British pound sterling rather that risk their own skin for their Russian masters). But if tough measures were called for, they did not hesitate. In a report to Prime Minister Alcide De Gasperi, the prefect of Como, Virginio Bertinelli, described how the British secret services went about finding the papers that Churchill was interested in. After describing how, in agreement with Chief of Police Grassi, he, Bertinelli, decided to hide a file of papers "that were very important and could be significant in explaining Mussolini's position, as well as to serve as a counterweight to some potential attitudes of the enemy-ally Great Britain," in the locked and unused tool shed of the Como Gymnastics Society. Bertinelli carefully used the stuffing of an exercise device left in a corner of the room. "No one but myself, Grassi, and Deputy Chief Cappuccio knew about it. One evening Cappuccio was asked to dinner by British officers, who gave him so much to drink that he loosened his tongue." The next day, May 22, 1945, a British officer of the Field Security Service came to the tool shed and went directly to the exercise device. His name was Captain Malcolm Smith (alias Johnson). With the help of another officer, Smith showed the custodian his orders to confiscate the device and then "proceeded to tear the stuffing apart, taking all the documents right in front of the custodian."[12]

Malcolm Smith is remembered by many "old timers" on Lake Como (where he went to live with his Italian wife after the war) as one of Churchill's most trusted men, almost his shadow. His name was back in the news regarding an important envelope full of documents the partisans took from Rachele Mussolini (the Duce's widow) and placed in a strongbox at the barracks of the Como Fire Department. "But here as well, the precious envelope did not remain very long. It was removed on August 31, 1945, by the same Captain Malcolm Smith, and handed directly to Churchill, who had come to the banks of the lake at the time to 'paint.'"[13]

Most of the time Churchill pretended to be painting. Here is an interesting anecdote by Andrea De Rossi, who at the time was living at Lake Garda, about a Churchill stay and one of his "sittings" to paint on the lake front near the villa that had been the residence of Minister Biggini during the RSI period:

> He set up his easel and two parasols to block the sunlight and heat and began his work. I saw all the preliminaries from the balcony of my house some 150 meters away and later I saw people try to come closer but being sent away by the guards. The statesman and painter was therefore totally isolated and could go about his task quietly. A few moments later I saw a

large motorboat arriving from Fasano. Aside from the pilot, the boat appeared to be completely empty. It was a trick: once the boat was a few meters from Churchill's chair suddenly from inside—where they had been hiding—several photographers quickly went about their work. The private guards reacted immediately by grabbing rocks from the shore and throwing them at the motorboat. But the photographers had enough time to take their pictures and the motorboat returned to where it came from. The pictures later published in the daily newspapers and magazines were precisely those taken from the strange motorboat. The painting was back in the news in 1992 when the Town of Gardone decided to organize an exhibit of the paintings of Lake Garda during the nineteenth and twentieth centuries. Amid the sixty-odd works requested from museums in France, England, Spain, Austria, Holland, and Switzerland (besides the Italian works), was also included—even though not of great importance from the artistic but rather the historical standpoint— the painting Churchill had worked on during that summer on the beach at Maderno. However, a year later when the exhibit was to take place, the painting by the British statesman was not present. The organizers had encountered insurmountable obstacles to get the painting on loan. Even during an exhibit of Churchill's main works at Sotheby's in London from January 5 to 17, 1998, the painting of the Gulf of Maderno was not among those shown.[14]

What was Churchill doing on that lakeside beach? Was he painting or waiting for someone to deliver him a sheaf of documents? The clearest confirmation, if it were necessary—that the Italian Communists, starting with their top leaders, preferred to accede to Churchill's requests rather than play the role of Stalin's spies—came recently from Massimo Caprara. Caprara was Palmiro Togliatti's[15] secretary for twenty years, and is today a respected writer and historian, having completely rejected his own Communist past. Caprara[16] has stated that there were secret contacts between Togliatti and Churchill during the months when the British statesman, in his

Fulton, Missouri, speech was promoting a permanent breach between Western Europe and the Soviet Union. As Caprara wrote:

> I am personally aware that Togliatti, faithful as he was to his
> habits at the Comintern where confidentiality was kept by not
> making copies, did not pass on the papers (which had eventu-
> ally reached his desk from Como—NDA) to anyone. He waited
> for the moment when he could best use them himself as bar-
> gaining chips—without Stalin's input—directly with the inter-
> ested party.

It happened in 1946. Churchill had been defeated in the July
1945 elections, the first to follow the end of the war. For obvious
reasons he was interested in retrieving that correspondence. Once
he became, following the Fulton speech at Westminster College in
1946, the leader of the world anti-Soviet bloc he took a trip to Italy,
purportedly for relaxation and sightseeing. As a member of Parliament he enjoyed greater freedom of movement than when he was
prime minister and he could follow much more easily not just the
itinerary of the compromising papers but also all the copies that
could possibly have been made. Churchill found out easily enough
that either a copy or the originals themselves had been in the possession of Gugliemo,[17] and from him had been sent to the head of
Communist party. The British politician found a way to meet with
Togliatti at the British embassy in Rome, near the Porta Pia, where
the Italian minister was invited. I found out about the invitation
and I was amazed that Togliatti went there completely aware of the
unusual motive for the meeting. The Churchill Archive in London
states that Churchill visited Lake Garda in 1946. The author of this
book received a fax from the British embassy in Rome dated February 10, 2000, detailing Churchill's travels. The document is signed
by Ann Ashford of the Press Information Section declaring that
the information came from London and the Churchill Archive and
the responsible person, a Mr. Gavin. The same fax reports on
Churchill's trips in July 1945, in 1949–1951, and 1955, as well as the
travels of Lady Clementine to Italy. We also know that Churchill

chaired the inauguration of the new embassy of the United Kingdom of Great Britain and Northern Ireland in the via XX Settembre
80/A in Rome, which offered the opportunity to repeat the contacts and assurances with the Italian Communist leader.

I was struck at the time [continues Massimo Caprara] by
something that often was recurring. Every time he came after
1946 Churchill was very insistent upon having his picture taken
next to Togliatti, the much-feared international enemy, as though
to confirm to those—in and outside the Conservative party
worried about the correspondence with Mussolini—that the
bomb had finally been localized and quickly defused. It had
reached one of the two destinations. The most dangerous potential user of the papers for negative purposes was clearly
"Ercoli"—Togliatti, who had been and still was the powerful
general secretary of the Comintern and of the PCI, as well as a
frequent visitor to the British embassy, to which he carefully
and deliberately accepted all of its invitations.

In brief, the Italian Communists betrayed Stalin (who knew
nothing about those papers aimed at him) to gain the friendship of
Churchill and of the British. This indicates a choice by the Italian
Communist leader in favor of the West long before the Atlantic
option of Enrico Berlinguer—the general secretary of the PCI in
the 1980s, who finally broke his allegiance to Moscow.

A dramatic coda to this chapter could be the still mysterious air
force bombing that took place after the end of the war, aimed at a
hotel on Lake Como where someone was attempting to "outsmart"
the British by refusing to hand over the documents they were actively seeking. This took place during the hours and days immediately following the executions at Dongo—of Mussolini and Claretta
Petacci, her brother Marcello Petacci, the ministers who were part
of the entourage of the head of the fascist government, and a few
others who were completely innocent. At precisely 10 p.m. on April
30 two bombs made a direct hit on the Bazzoni Hotel at Tremezzo,
a very short distance from the Villa Henderson and the location of

the execution of Mussolini and Claretta Petacci. The hotel was filled
with Italian Resistance leaders and among these most certainly someone who was well known to the British secret services. There were
many victims, dead and wounded, but the exact number was never
known since the entire matter was quickly buried among other war
news. The newspapers influenced by the CLN wrote that it was
German revenge because of Mussolini's execution. A German plane
from an unidentified airfield would have dropped its bombs as a
sign of contempt for the partisan fighters. It is incredible that such
a crazy explanation could be disseminated and believed practically
to this day. Just the day before, on April 29, the representatives of
the German military forces in Italy had signed their surrender to
the Anglo-American forces at the Royal Palace of Caserta (near
Naples). But this should come as no surprise since so many Italians
had become convinced of many other absurdities, including the
basic goodness of Bolshevik communism.

The truth became known, in part at least, only in 1990. The
person who revealed it was an exceptional witness, Urbano Lazzaro,
the partisan known as Bill, the man who arrested Mussolini on April
27 on the main square at Dongo. Bill had handled the Duce's two
valuable briefcases containing the papers, but not for very long.
After being handled by various other persons they wound up with
Luigi Canali (Captain Neri), the commander of the partisan unit,
who in turn passed them on to the local leaders of his party, the
PCI. Those big and small party stalwarts who were hanging around
the bar of the Bazzoni Hotel naively thought they could fool British intelligence.

As Bill states in his dramatic account:

At that time I was in the garden of the villa of Count Sebregondi
at Domaso, talking to an English major. We both heard the
airplane engines rumbling above. I said: "What's going on? What
are those German planes doing here?" The major answered,
"Those aren't German but British planes. There are two of
them." I looked at him puzzled, and asked: "How can you recognize them at night?" "I don't need to see them. To a veteran

pilot like me it's very easy to recognize a plane by the roar of its engine. You can believe me, those are two British planes." Suddenly we saw the lake being lit up by two extremely powerful flares. I then asked, "Is this to celebrate the liberation?" The major did not answer, appearing troubled.[18] A few minutes later, as the flares were still glowing, we heard two tremendous explosions. "Why did the British do this? Why?" I asked angrily, while the major looked more and more dejected. Then he said, "I don't know, I don't know. I must have been mistaken. They are not English. The war is over in Italy."[19]

Bruno Giovanni Lonati was back in the news and not only in Italy. Peter Tompkins (see Chapters VIII and IX) was OSS chief in Rome during the Second World War and has produced a two-part documentary on the air at the beginning of September 2004 by Italian State Television, RAI-3. The program was entitled *Mussolini: The Final Truth*, and it was based on Lonati's story as being truthful without however adding any new elements to the previous statements made by the former partisan commander and with a few small changes: the real name of Captain John was Robert Maccarrone, not Maccaroni, and he was said to have changed it to the more British—even Scottish—"McRoney."

Given a skeptical reception by the Italian press and moderate curiosity by the British,[20] the Tompkins documentary, which took years of research, interviews and fact checking, did contain some valid findings, such as a confirmation that the killing of Mussolini and Claretta Petacci had taken place in the morning rather than the afternoon of April 28, 1945. The recollections of the old partisan Roberto Remund, who was given the task with some others to lift Mussolini's body onto the truck waiting to take all those shot at Dongo to Milan for the public display at the Piazzale Loreto are very clear. Remund found that the body was already in rigor mortis, which would have been impossible had the shooting occurred just one hour before, as all the Communist leaders have repeatedly stated from the beginning. Remund also said that "there were no traces of blood" in front of the gates of the Villa Belmonte, the alleged location where the two lovers were executed, thus confirming the fact that they had been killed somewhere else.

Much less convincing in the Tompkins documentary is the repetition of an old story from some fifty years ago regarding the Enrico De Toma file. During the early months of 1954 De Toma, a former officer in the GNR sold documents to publisher Angelo Rizzoli, who published them in his weekly popular news magazine *OGGI*[21] as being the "Mussolini-Churchill correspondence." De Toma wrote that on April 23, 1944, as an eighteen-year-old second lieutenant in the GNR, he was summoned by his commanding officer Giuseppe Gelormini, who took him to see Mussolini. De Toma claimed that the Duce gave him a package of letters (many of them from Mussolini to Churchill and vice versa) to be taken to Switzerland for safekeeping.

Wearing civilian clothes and using false travel documents, De Toma claimed that he delivered the package to an Italian Jew in Geneva who had reason to be grateful to Commander Gelormini for saving his life. Nine years later De Toma claimed that he again visited the same person (whom he actually never identified by name), who returned the entire file to him. De Toma was then free to sell the papers to the highest bidder. From the very start the documents were considered bogus. Former Commander Gelormini denied everything and there wasn't a single expert who would vouch for the authenticity of those papers. The logical explanation was that the file contained some original documents that were already in the possession of RSI functionaries along with other papers that were absolute forgeries produced by a clever expert[22] (who was even identified by name). The matter ended when publication was halted and the material was seized by the courts, which then ordered that it be destroyed. Enrico De Toma was arrested for fraud and finally admitted that part of the documents had been forgeries. Shortly after he was freed from prison, De Toma emigrated to Brazil and never returned to Italy.[23]

The alleged correspondence between Churchill and Mussolini concerned the period preceding Italy's entry into the war (at that time the British prime minister was promising the Duce territorial gains at the expense of France if Italy decided to remain neutral) and the closing period of the war when Churchill requested the return of the old "compromising" letters in exchange for favorable treatment for the defeated Duce. However, as we have previously shown, the purported 1940 documents were not that compromising at all. Finally, the file itself contained such glaring forgeries (German letterheads with the swastikas drawn to the left instead of the right) and false letters clearly forged by RSI espionage units to discredit political enemies, such as Alcide De Gasperi, Pietro Badoglio, and others that somehow wound up in the hands of the very young De Toma and his friends. The "De Toma File" therefore lost any credibility for all the above reasons.

Mussolini during a speech in 1939. *(Charles Poletti Papers, Rare Book and Manuscript Library, Columbia University.)*

Claretta Petacci in 1939.

Winston Churchill as
First Lord of the Admiralty on
September 4, 1939.

Churchill with Queen Mary and King George VI in the summer of 1940,
shortly after becoming prime minister.

London, May 26, 1942. The signing of the twenty-year Anglo-Soviet Alliance Pact. *Seated from the left*: Soviet ambassador I. Maisky, V. Molotov, Anthony Eden, Churchill, Clement Attlee.

Churchill welcomes FDR aboard the *Prince of Wales* during the Atlantic Conference in 1941.

The Teheran Conference with Roosevelt, Churchill, and Stalin, November 29, 1943.

Algiers, May 29, 1943. Planning the invasion of Sicily. *Seated from the left*: Anthony Eden, Marshal Alan Brooke, Churchill, General George Marshall, General Dwight D. Eisenhower. *Standing from the left*: Marshal Tedder, Admiral Cunningham, Marshal Alexander, Field Marshal Montgomery.

Molotov at a reception in Berlin during his visit in 1940. Von Ribbentrop is on the left and Otto Meissner of the Foreign Ministry is in the center. Von Ribbentrop wanted to reach an accommodation with the USSR and later made several attempts to persuade Hitler to seek a separate peace.

Foreign Minister Matsuoka of Japan meeting with von Ribbentrop in Berlin in March 1941. The Japanese government did not want war with the USSR and considered the Western Allies as the main enemy.

At the Casablanca Conference in January 1943 Roosevelt announced the doctrine of "unconditional surrender," which Churchill fully supported. *From the left:* General H. Giraud, FDR, General de Gaulle, Winston Churchill.

General Eisenhower shakes hands with General Castellano on September 3, 1943, following the signing of the armistice with Italy.

General Walter Bedell Smith signs the armistice with Italy at Cassibile in Sicily on September 3, 1943. General Giuseppe Castellano *(in dark suit)* and his interpreter, Vice Consul Montanari *(far right)*, look on.

Otto Skorzeny, who liberated Mussolini
from his prison at Gran Sasso on
September 12, 1943.

Mussolini with his wife Rachele
and their grandchildren near
Munich in October 1943.

Carlo Alberto Biggini, in fascist uniform, was a full member of the Fascist Grand Council.

Biggini with his wife Maria Bianca in 1944.

At Salò in 1944. *From the left:* Serafino Mazzolini, Undersecretary of Foreign Affairs; Shinrokuro Hidaka, the Japanese ambassador and Mussolini's close confidant; C. A. Biggini, Minister of National Education; Rudolf Rahn, German ambassador to the RSI; Alessandro Pavolini, Secretary of the Fascist Republican Party.

Mussolini at Field Marshal Kesselring's headquarters near Parma in August 1944. *From the left*: SS Col. Eugen Dollmann, Mussolini, Col. Zolling, Col. Belitz, Kesselring.

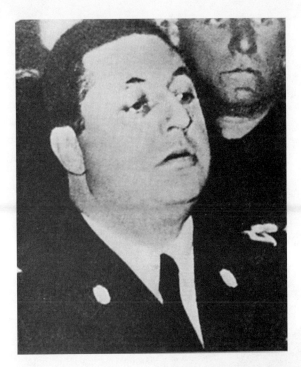

Guido Buffarini-Guidi, Minister of
the Interior of the RSI, 1943–1945.

Cardinal Ildefonso Schuster,
Archbishop of Milan,
in 1945.

Mussolini in July 1944 in Germany. At far right is Marshal Graziani. The photo was signed by Mussolini and dated April 16, 1945, twelve days before his execution. *(Charles Poletti Papers, Rare Book and Manuscript Library, Columbia University.)*

Mussolini with his German doctor, Georg Zachariae, on Lake Garda in 1944.

The main offices of the Head of State of the RSI (Italian Social Republic), where Mussolini worked with his staff at Gargnano on Lake Garda.

The last photograph of Mussolini alive, taken during the late afternoon of April 25, 1945, as he returned to the Milan Prefecture from a meeting at the Archbishop's residence with Cardinal Schuster. An angry Mussolini is shown with SS Lt. Birzer *(left)*. The man behind Mussolini is Mario Bassi, the fascist head of the Milan province.

Tommaso David, one of the heads of RSI espionage and possibly the mysterious "man from Milan" referred to by Mussolini in his phone calls to Claretta Petacci.

Chapter VII

THE BIG LIE: DONGO

*How I was able to prove that Communist partisans had not killed
Mussolini and Claretta Petacci.*

K ing Louis XVI of France was tried and condemned to death in
a solemn court procedure in Parliament in the presence of
dozens of writers and journalists. He had lawyers to defend him—
among the best of the Paris bar of the time—and they were free to
proceed with their summations. Every deputy was called by name to
cast his vote and the sentence of death by guillotine took place on
January 21, 1793, *coram populo*—in front of all the people of Paris.

Thomas Moore, the English prime minister of Henry VIII, was
tried for high treason by the High Court of Justice and a majority
voted for his death because he had refused to convert to the new
Anglican Church and to recognize the king as its leader. He was
publicly decapitated in London on July 6, 1535.

Benito Mussolini, prime minister of the king of Italy for twenty-
one years, then head of RSI for eighteen months, the ephemeral

state in northern Italy under German military occupation. Was he tried and condemned to death? By whom and when? Which crimes was he accused of having committed? Who witnessed his execution and how did it take place? Was an official report of the execution submitted and who was its author? Is the report filed in the State Archives?

There is no single answer to any one of these questions, which is reason enough to attempt to reconstruct as completely as possible the history of the sentencing to death of the leader of fascism. It must be made clear that none of the top world historians who have written and continue to do research on Mussolini have ever spent much time investigating his death.

Four major British historians have dedicated their efforts to Mussolini's death sentence: Denis Mack Smith, F. W. Deakin, Martin Gilbert, and Richard Collier. All four are or were prestigious university professors. The best known and probably most knowledgeable was F. W. Deakin, since his book, *The Brutal Friendship*,[1] has served as a beacon for entire legions of Italian historians. Deakin is laconic but does not seek any justification; to him, Mussolini's death sentence was not legal. As he writes:

> The manner of his sentence, and the responsibility of individuals, are of little import, as are the details of his death. The controversy in Resistance circles about the formal legality of his execution and on whose orders is of little historical relevance. Mussolini died by a revolutionary act.
>
> On the afternoon of April 28, 1945, together with Clara Petacci, he was taken from the custody of local partisans by a killer squad acting on orders from Milan and shot down without warning at the gates of a villa on the outskirts of the hamlet of Mezzagra.[2]

After some 800 tight pages chronicling the most minute details of Mussolini's moves, words, and thoughts, the end is limited to the words quoted above.

As for Denis Mack Smith:

...the partisan commanders had ordered that he be executed at once if captured (...) Members of this committee, [the CLNAI] as it seems he heard later on 25 April, confirmed a final order for his summary execution. [...]

Many different stories have been told by presumed eyewitnesses of what happened next. The one certain fact is that on 28 April, the sixty-one-year-old Mussolini was executed by Communist irregulars before he could be reached by the Americans, who were only a few hours away.[3]

Martin Gilbert, famous historian, author of *The Second World War: A Complete History*, points to how Mussolini's death should be recorded for history: "In Italy, April 28 witnessed the ignominious end of the fascist regime installed twenty-three years before: on that day near the village of Dongo on Lake Como, Mussolini was executed by Italian partisans in a reprisal for the killing of fifteen of their comrades that took place in Milan nine months before; they also shot fifteen people who had been captured with him. Among them were Alessandro Pavolini, the secretary of the fascist party, four cabinet ministers, and some of Mussolini's friends. His lover, Claretta Petacci, was also killed. Her body and Mussolini's were taken to Milan and hanged by the feet on the morning of April 29."

That is the extent of the description. We looked in the index for other names and we found neither Sandro Pertini, Leo Valiani,[4] Luigi Longo, nor Palmiro Togliatti.[5] The lieutenant general of the Kingdom of Italy, Prince Umberto of Savoy, who was the head of State at the time Mussolini and his followers had been killed, was not mentioned. There is only the mention of Ferruccio Parri as "a leader of the Resistance, freed in Switzerland by General Karl Wolff." The fall of fascism receives no other space in a world-embracing history.

The account written by Richard Collier is far more exciting and even, in a sense, cinematic.

Simultaneously, from San Leocco, south of Naples, Allied forces headquarters had instructed twenty-five OSS teams poised for action in the woods and the mountains: "It is the desire of the Allies to take Mussolini alive. These HQ will be notified if he is taken and he will be held in security pending the arrival of Allied troops." [...] To ensure that the Communists maintained their hold on the people the implications were plain. The armed insurrection must go ahead, heedless of the Allied warning. Already Luigi Longo's orders had gone out: "No passes, no golden bridges for those retreating—only a war of extermination." And as patriots, the other left-wingers, too, saw the need to prove that they no longer depended on the Allies but were their equals and collaborators. Argued Sandro Pertini: "We're not their servants. To kill Mussolini would be to assert our independence." [...] Every man who had marched on Rome would face a popular tribunal—which in the case of the Duce and his bigwigs, would hand down only the death penalty. Such was the Communist decision, and the others had little choice but to follow.[6]

What about the victorious Allies? As Collier further writes: "As long ago as 26 July 1943 Franklin Delano Roosevelt had set the search in motion, with a memo to Winston Churchill suggesting that in the event of a separate peace with Italy 'the head Devil should be surrendered.' Churchill had agreed [...] 'Personally, I am fairly indifferent...provided that no solid military advantages are sacrificed for the sake of immediate vengeance.'"[7]

Finally, there is the vivid account of the meeting between Walter Audisio, accompanied by Aldo Lampredi and General Raffaele Cadorna,[8] confirming that the latter agreed with the Communists:

A few minutes later Palombo heard Daddario ask, "What is the latest information on Mussolini?" And Cadorna's voice was rock-steady as he replied, "To date we have no information whatsoever."

How long, Palombo wondered, could each side sustain this elaborate double-bluff? If Daddario knew the partisans held Mussolini, he was giving nothing away. He had not even once announced that the Duce's person was among his primary objectives. But tonight Cadorna and the duty staff held all the aces. From his frequent trips into Switzerland, one man on the premises knew both Daddario and Allen Dulles intimately—fifty-four-year-old Ferruccio Parri, the professorial white-haired Chief of the Action Party.

[. . .]

Around Palazzo Cusani, the secret was closely guarded. Minutes after Mussolini's departure, Cadorna was conferring with his Town Major, General Emilio Faldella, when the door opened and Audisio swaggered in. The Communist, Faldella recalled later, was carrying a rifle at the trail, a tricolor scarf at his throat, and shrugging into a brown leather raincoat. "Well," he announced, "I'm off." "All right," Cadorna replied, "let's do things properly."

"What's all that?" Faldella asked. "Where's he going?" Cadorna was calm. "They've caught Mussolini and he's going to collect him." He wasn't more specific.

It never occurred to Faldella that Mussolini would not be taken alive. On his own initiative, back in his office, he uncradled the phone and called the governor of San Vittore Prison: twenty cells were to be put aside to receive the Duce and his bigwigs.[9]

Mussolini's death is viewed as nothing more than a marginal episode in the broad landscape of the Second World War in other classic texts, such as in Sir Basil Liddell Hart, who describes it this way: "The Americans moving still faster took Verona a day earlier. The day before, April 25, a general uprising of the partisans took place and Germans everywhere came under attack from them. All the Alpine passes were blocked by April 28—the day on which Mussolini and his mistress, Claretta Petacci, were caught and shot by a band of partisans near Lake Como."

The French historian I. M. Chassin, author of a *Histoire de la Seconde Guerre Mondiale*,[10] does not even mention the death of the founder of fascism. There is not a single line to be found in the chapter regarding the end of the war on the Italian front.

Winston Churchill, in his monumental six-volume work, *The Second World War*,[11] chooses to summarize the tragedy he had no wish to take part in, in less than half a page:

> In the evening followed by a convoy of thirty vehicles containing most of the surviving leaders of Italian Fascism, he drove to the prefecture at Como. He had no coherent plan, and as discussion became useless it was each man for himself. Accompanied by a handful of supporters he attached himself to a small German convoy heading towards the Swiss frontier.[12] The commander of the column was not anxious for trouble with Italian Partisans. The Duce was persuaded to put on a German greatcoat and helmet. But the little party[13] was stopped by Partisan patrols: Mussolini was recognized and taken into custody. Other members, including his mistress Signorina Petacci, were also arrested. On Communist instructions[14] the Duce and his mistress were taken out in a car next day and shot. Their bodies, together with others, were sent to Milan and strung up head downward on meat hooks in a petrol station on the Piazzale Loreto, where a group of Italian Partisans had lately been shot in public. Such was the fate of the Italian dictator. A photograph of the final scene was sent to me, and I was profoundly shocked. But at least the world was spared an Italian Nuremberg."

Let us turn to the Italian historians. There are two "official" historians whose works are always cited in textbooks and by historians and journalists who cannot be called "revisionists." These are Roberto Battaglia and Franco Catalano. The book by Battaglia, *Storia della Resistenza Italiana* (Turin: Einaudi, 1964), is by now considered the "standard" work on the subject. On page 643 one may read:

During the morning of April 25, 1945, the CLNAI issued the three basic decrees that mark its legislative contribution. [...] The second decree involves the administration of justice. Article 1 states: "The members of the fascist government and

those fascist leaders who are guilty of having suppressed constitutional guarantees, destroyed the people's freedoms, created
the fascist regime, compromised and betrayed the country, bringing it to the current catastrophe are to be punished with the
death penalty and in lesser cases with life imprisonment."

As Battaglia commented: "The fact that Mussolini was condemned to death was implicit since it was so obvious."

Reading the second official text on the Resistance by Franco
Catalano, *Storia del CLNAI* (Milan: Bompiani, 1956), we learn that
the Article in question was not 1 but rather Article 5 of paragraph
2. Subtleties perhaps, but what was the exact historical truth?
Catalano reproduces the legal decree in its entirety. It is a very detailed document taking up twelve pages of fine print describing the
famous CAS (corte d'assise straordinarie) [Special Criminal Court],
the CAP (corte d'assise del popolo) [People's Criminal Court], the
Commissioni di giustizia [Justice Commission], the Tribunali di
guerra [War Courts], and so on; none of these entities were part of
the Statuto [the Constitution of the Kingdom of Italy], nor the
product of the laws issued by the Bonomi government.

The Decree then describes how to identify a fascist, who was
and was not a fascist, how to gather information about such a person in order to capture him if he was in hiding by pressuring the
next of kin and his friends, and how the condemned person was to
be shot on sight with no opportunity to enter an appeal. We must
also mention among the official histories the much-quoted *Una guerra
civile* [A Civil War] by Claudio Pavone (Turin: Bollati-Boringhieri,
1991), which discusses Mussolini's death in the chapter entitled "La
violenza internazionale." Pavone writes: "The time was coming
where in order to escape the nightmare of death and for it to really
be permanent demanded still more death. The order issued by the
Military Command of the Piedmont Region was a wise one: only
quick and exemplary justice can avoid excessive killing on the one
hand and undeserved impunity on the other."

The Command mentioned above had decided the death penalty for all those—except for the military draftees—wearing an RSI

uniform. All of them, without exception. Not only the GNR (Guardia Nazionale Repubblicana) and the *Brigate Nere* [Black Brigades], or the *Decima Mas*, the *Legione Muti*, but even the members of the *Polizia portuaria* [Maritime Police] the Polizia ferroviaria and stradale [the Railroad and Highway patrols]. A death sentence for 350,000 people that was not carried out only because it was cancelled by a "higher authority," meaning the CLNAI, which stepped in to mitigate the order: execute only those refusing to lay down their arms.

As for Mussolini's death sentence, Pavone writes:

Mussolini's execution was the episode that symbolically represented the violence of those days. […] It draws its legality from the complex institutional system characterizing the final phase of the Resistance and later on the insurrection. Without going back too far, on April 12, 1945, the CLNAI had denounced Mussolini and the members of the fascist leadership as "traitors to the homeland and war criminals." The CLNAI fully approved of the execution once it had taken place. Contrary to France and England, Italy did not have any regicide in its history as the dividing line between different periods of history. As the last country to appear even in that field, Italy had the execution of the Duce in the middle of the twentieth century.

Interestingly, on the issue of the legitimacy of the sentence and the way it was carried out, the comment in *L'Unità*, the daily newspaper of the PCI, is quoted by Pavone on page 514 of his book: "The Communist Daily," he wrote, "supported the fact that the main war criminals were executed in Jacobin style through an act of popular justice, which is the inevitable corollary of an insurrection." The newspaper handled the display of the bodies rather contemptuously: "The corpse of the Duce, surrounded by a number of his acolytes, lay in the Piazzale Loreto for all to hate." Since these words represent a Communist point of view and interpretation, the language seems absolutely normal and true to the Party's traditional rhetoric.

While it was not necessary to mention the scores of secondary writers or journalist-historians in the Communist and Resistance tradition, who invariably repeat a similar version of the facts, it is worthwhile to cite the meticulous description by the journalist Gian Franco Vené. Vené, who died prematurely,[15] relates that at 8 a.m. on April 25, 1945, in Milan at the Salesian College in the via Copernico, "five men under the rain quickly crossed the threshold of the cloister and entered the cold and darkened library. Priests dressed in cassocks were watching the entrance. The five were Arpesani, Marazza, Pertini, Sereni, and Valiani."[16] Thus began the most significant meeting of the CLNAI. Inside the Salesian library the three left-wing representatives (Pertini, Valiani, and Sereni) had little to object to concerning the first decree, entitled: "All power to the CLNAI." The second decree that was proposed and discussed addressed the administration of justice. It stated: "The members of the fascist government and fascist leaders who are responsible for the suppression of constitutional guarantees, of having destroyed popular freedoms, created the fascist regime, compromised and betrayed the country and having brought it to the current catastrophe are to be punished with the death penalty and lesser cases with life imprisonment." Valiani, Sereni, and Pertini were puzzled. No one had mentioned Mussolini's name but it was obvious to all that Mussolini would be the first to be executed. It was not yet 9 a.m. on April 25 and Mussolini was free but his death sentence had already been issued.

Vené does not say who voted for and against. He simply states: "The Decree was approved by a majority." But he adds later on: "Marazza and the liberal Arpesani also signed the insurrectional proclamation that Longo in the name of the PCI had issued twenty-four hours earlier."

One may conclude that in the historian's opinion Marazza and Arpesani had not signed and the same two always refused to give any details as to how they voted that morning, true to the decision to not create any break within the CLNAI. In any case, they were to sign the communiqué of 29 April, whereby after the executions were consummated the CLNAI took full responsibility not only for Mussolini's execution but also for that of the top fascists and the murder of Claretta Petacci.

Vené's dramatic and vivid account of Sandro Pertini's role in the so-called negotiations that took place on the afternoon of April 25 at the Archbishop's residence in the presence of Cardinal Ildefonso Schuster between Mussolini and a few representatives of the CLNAI is worth quoting:

> Sandro Pertini could not control his anger. He harbored the suspicion that the moderates Marazza and Arpesani had been taken in by Mussolini and had agreed that he could save his own life. He quickly ended a rally with the workers at the Borletti factory, jumped into his car and, using his horn like a madman, drove at top speed to the Archbishop's residence. On the steps he ran into a group of men who were coming down and gesticulating. He paid no attention to them. However, Mussolini was part of that group. "You let him get away!" he yelled and, hitting his own forehead, said, "Like an idiot I did not recognize him!"—"Why what would you have done?" "I would have shot him on the spot on the steps with my gun!"

Valiani and Sereni reached the Archbishop's residence right after Pertini. They appeared calm on the surface and now felt it had been a mistake to allow the moderates Marazza and Aspesani to organize the meeting. Had Mussolini followed the agreed-upon schedule and returned at 8 p.m., the Christian Democrats and Liberals could have made the decisions. Marazza, standing in the middle of the room, was facing Pertini: "If Mussolini surrenders we must be true to our word and hand him over to the Americans! We are not murderers!" And Pertini shouted back: "We have only one thing to say: summary justice." Tiengo came into the smoke-filled waiting room and went up to Marazza but no one paid attention to him. Pertini was rabid: "Should Mussolini return there is only one thing to do: shoot him! This very evening!" The prefect Tiengo tried to speak at one point but did not. He left discreetly and ran to the prefecture, where he said: "They want to shoot the Duce…this evening!"

The firm desire of the left-wing leaders to shoot Mussolini in any case is also confirmed by the famous episode of the American cables. In Vené's words: "On the evening of the 27th several radio messages arrived from Allied headquarters in Siena to CVL headquarters in via del Carmine. Each message was passed on from one table to the next: "To the CLNAI command—stop—let us know exact situation of Mussolini—stop—will send aircraft to retrieve him—stop—Allied Headquarters." "To CVL and CLNAI—stop—aircraft to pick up Mussolini will land 1800 hours tomorrow Bresso airport—stop—prepare landing signals—stop—Allied Headquarters." And again: "To CLNAI—stop—Allied Headquarters requests immediate information Mussolini—repeat Mussolini presumed location—stop—If already captured we order he be immediately turned over to Allied Command—stop—Request you deliver these orders with absolute priority to partisan units that may have effected the capture." And finally: "To CLNAI repeat CLNAI—stop—XV Army Group wishes to take Mussolini and Graziani—repeat—Mussolini and Graziani to Allied Headquarters—stop—." At 11 p.m. Pertini, Sereni, and Longo arrived in via del Carmine. While the cables from Allied High Command were on the tables all they had to do was decide "who" would go and pick up Mussolini. Perini proposed Italo Pietra, the commander of the partisan brigade. Pietra answered that it was the job of the police. Luchino Dal Verme—another partisan leader—gave the same answer. Then Pertini pointed to Walter Audisio (Valerio): "You are military police!" Valerio simply answered "yes." A little later, even before Valerio left for Dongo, a cable was sent from CVL general headquarters answering Allied headquarters: CVL TO AGH SORRY COULD NOT DELIVER MUSSOLINI WHO JUDGED BY POPULAR TRIBUNAL WAS EXECUTED SAME PLACE WHERE FIFTEEN PATRIOTS PREVIOUSLY EXECUTED BY NAZI-FASCISTS. 3 A.M. APRIL 28, 1945. This constitutes the overwhelming proof that Mussolini was to be taken to the Piazzale Loreto and be executed there. Something went wrong but the Communists have never wanted to say what it was.

Many Italian historians and journalists should be commended for disbelieving the incredible mistakes and actual lies contained in the official version. Among these two who certainly stand out are Franco Bandini and Giorgio Pisanò.[17] Bandini deserves credit by proving through sheer logic that the official time of death of Mussolini and Claretta Petacci was false. It was not Walter Audisio who did the shooting in the afternoon of April 28 but rather Luigi Longo that same morning; while what took place in front of the gates of the Villa Belmonte at 4:30 p.m. was the grisly shooting of two dead bodies. As for Giorgio Pisanò, an RSI veteran, newspaper reporter, historian, and politician (senator of the MSI neofascist party), he discovered Dorina Mazzola, and persuaded her to speak after decades of silence—due to fear—as the only eyewitness to the execution of Mussolini and Claretta Petacci. Dorina Mazzola was 19 years old when she witnessed the murder on the morning of April 28 at the entrance of the house of the farmers De Maria: she was well hidden behind the shutters of her house, directly across the way.

Many years before, Paolo Monelli, one of the grand masters of Italian historical journalism, dedicated several pages to the mystery of Mussolini's death sentence in his biography, *Mussolini piccolo borghese* [Mussolini: The Petty Bourgeois] (Milan: Garzanti, 1950), a book that was much too quickly forgotten. The reason may be found in some of his pointed comments, such as the one on page 368: "One should not believe what Colonel Valerio has written in his many reports and other writings—all of them different and contradictory." Monelli spends some eight pages in a critique of the "accepted version" of Mussolini's death. He lends so little credence to the circumstances of a presumed "death sentence" of the fascist dictator that there is no mention of that famous detail in his book (it appeared in any case in the works of Battaglia and Catalano, both published many years later). Monelli was writing some forty years before the so-called "revisionist" history published by Renzo De Felice.

It is worth noting some of Monelli's most significant comments:

Colonel Valerio (the accountant Walter Audisio), who always repeated that he was the executioner, has written at least three different versions, occasionally contradicting each other, relating to his and other individual's actions. Was Colonel Valerio the only executioner? This is what can be found in the Communist party's documents and the officially accepted version. But I must say that the partisan fighter Sandrino (Gugliemo Cantoni (Sandrino)) has given a completely different account of that event. According to what Sandrino said, there was no reading of a death sentence or any such thing. It was a quick and hurried execution that took place long before Mussolini and Claretta Petacci reached the wall where no traces of any bullets could be found. I feel we may safely conclude the following. The accounts of the event by the very few eyewitnesses contradict each other and there are no elements that allow us to believe one more than another. The detail of reading the death sentence was to give the killing some appearance of legality; the verbose description of Mussolini's fearful attitude is consistent with the Communist effort to make the tyrant's demise appear obscene and grotesque. Once the Communist party leaders understood that it was impossible to keep the details of the killing secret, they decided to turn Audisio into the big hero of the whole incident. Audisio was placed on the ballot by the Communist party and elected as a deputy to Parliament for no other reason.[18]

These words, half a century after they were first written, are an awful indictment, and actually amounts to a massive accusation of the Communist party for deliberately making false statements. It is clear that Paolo Monelli did not believe a death sentence against Mussolini existed, or that there was a trial or a decree of any kind. It was quite simply a homicide that took place in very obscure circumstances. Monelli was never sued for having written those words in a book that sold over 250,000 copies at the time. No one even threatened legal action or even accused him of libel in 1950, which leads us to further observations.

Leo Valiani gave this author his last interview, regarding Mussolini's death sentence, in February 1994. I published it in the

Milan daily *La Notte*, at the end of a long investigation where, for the first time, I hinted at the "British hand" at work in the execution of the Duce and Claretta Petacci. The idea was restated by Renzo De Felice a year later.* In that piece I said that Luigi Canali (Captain Neri), chief of staff of the 52nd Garibaldi Brigade, was the one who led the British-inspired executioners to the De Maria house where he had hid Mussolini and his mistress. How did Leo Valiani respond?

> I have no knowledge of Neri's moves. I never met him, I never was at Dongo. I never asked any of those who witnessed those events how things actually took place. Longo never wrote a report to the CLNAI. [...]
>
> The death sentence that the CLNAI, given the authority it had in occupied Italy from the Italian government and issued on April 25, 1945, was aimed at "the members of the fascist government and fascist leaders guilty of suppressing constitutional guarantees, destroying popular freedoms, creating the fascist regime, compromising and betraying the country and having led it to the present catastrophe." For them that decree implied the death sentence and, in lesser cases, life in prison. Collaboration with the German occupying forces was to be punished "according to the military laws of war in force as of September 8, 1943." Those laws also called for the firing squad. I do not know whether all those killed at Dongo and at Giulino di Mezzegra had collaborated or not with the Germans. If yes, their execution was mandated by the CLNAI decree. If the answer is no, then it was arbitrary. The sentence in any case should have been issued by a military court to be formed in accordance with the CLNAI's decree.

On that same occasion and following the disputes in the press after my theories were published, Valiani reiterated to the news agen-

---

* Renzo De Felice, *Rosso e Nero*, interviews with Pasquale Chessa (Milan: Baldini & Castoldi, 1995).

that the Partisan High Command did not issue orders to shoot Claretta Petacci. "I can confirm this without any hesitation," said the senator as he recalled that "the CLNAI decree provided to limit the death sentence to the members of the fascist government and fascist leaders."

"The shooting of Claretta Petacci had never been ordered," added Valiani, responding to the AND-Kronos news agency. "We did not even know that she was with Mussolini at the time." Regarding the circumstances of the shooting of the Duce and his mistress (who the executioner was, at what time, and how it happened), Valiani concluded: "Unfortunately I know nothing. I don't even know whether Luigi Longo did actually go to Dongo. The CLNAI never received a written report from Longo as to how those events took place." Even Claretta Petacci's sister, Myriam, a theater and film actress, was unable to understand the motive behind her sister's execution. A few years before her death Myriam Petacci published a book that commented on her sister's fate:

> Everyone heard Valerio cry out at Dongo: "Clara Petacci: to death!" But in his memoirs he wrote that as he was about to shoot at my sister he said: "Get out of there if you don't want to die as well!" What does this mean? Had Claretta been condemned to death or not? Sandro Pertini clearly declared in 1983: "Claretta Petacci should not have been killed. Her only sin was to have loved a man. I was certainly not the one who wanted Claretta Petacci to be shot. I must say that Pertini, who was a member of the "troika," in command in Milan in those days, is telling the truth. I also know that Leo Valiani did not want my sister to die. The third member of the "troika," Luigi Longo, the Communist party's future secretary, was in no way responsible for that crime.[19]

What was my 1994 statement based upon when I said that British agents had "worked faster" than the Soviet agents, namely the Communist partisans, in order to silence two uncomfortable voices—those of the Duce and his mistress—and seize the compromising Mussolini-Churchill papers? First of all, to refute the official and unofficial versions that had been disseminated until then. Second, by examining the movements of an enigmatic character, the key player in the whole story, Luigi Canali—Captain Neri of the Como Resistance. Canali was the man who had Mussolini under his complete control (from the afternoon of Friday, April 27, 1945) and was himself to be murdered on May 7 of the same year by his own Communist party comrades, with the excuse that they were carrying out an old death sentence by a partisan court for Canali's allegedly having been a traitor.

Before picking up the "British thread" we must revisit the most significant claims and clues that have been repeated for over half a century, beginning with the official version that Italian children still learn in their textbooks. It is the best known and the one that is the most patently false; namely, the one shown in films where Mussolini and Claretta Petacci are shot in front of the gates of the Villa Belmonte at Giulino di Mezzegra by Walter Audisio (Colonel Valerio) at 4:30 p.m. on Saturday, April 28, 1945.

Audisio, a minor party "apparatchik," was for many years a PCI deputy in parliament and faithfully played his role to the end—he died in 1973—as the "executioner," which the Communist leaders had ordered him to act out since the dramatic year of 1945. The newspaper *L'Unità*, the official mouthpiece of the Party, published, between November 18 and December 17, a total of twenty-four installments entitled "How I Executed Mussolini." Those articles were full of grammatical errors, contradictions and mostly vulgar images (for example, Claretta Petacci was worried about putting on her panties while her executioner shouted at her: "Forget about the panties! Come on, let's go!" The name of Walter Audisio was never mentioned in those pieces. The identity of the "executioner" was revealed two years later in 1947, at a public rally in Rome.

Just two years after Audisio's death in 1975, the Communist party publishing company, Teti, posthumously published the so-called "memoirs" of Colonel Valerio, entitled *In nome del popolo italiano* [In the Name of the Italian People]. The book was obviously written by some Party journalist who was just as imprecise and confused as the one who had written the 1945 newspaper "memoir." For example, the last name of the driver—G. B. Geninazza—was repeatedly misspelled as the man who drove the "executioner" to the location, even though he had been interviewed by scores of newsmen. The book is faithful to the initial version only by its vulgar tone. Even though Petacci's panties were no longer mentioned, the attempt to demonize Mussolini after his death is clear on every page. To begin with, Mussolini's purported stupidity—when he takes seriously a person (Valerio) who states that he has come to liberate him and addresses him in the familiar form, treating him like some poor idiot; no fascist military man would have dared speak to the Duce in such a way—up to the description of a cowardly and frightened man slobbering when faced with the machine gun of the "executioner," to whom he appeals in a trembling voice, "But Colonel . . . But Colonel . . . "

This particular detail (and we find this to be the most unacceptable part), having been fed to four generations of Italian students, was flatly denied in 1996 by the posthumous revelations of Marino Moretti. Moretti (*aka* the partisan Pietro, whose memoirs were published by the Como researcher Giorgio Cavalleri[20]) said: "While Valerio, having raised his machine gun, recited the death sentence, Mussolini did not look surprised. And when the weapon was aimed at him he loudly cried out "Long live Italy!" ("The suffered admission," said Cavalleri, "was made during the afternoon of Thursday, October 25, 1990.")

It would be too simple (and too long) to analyze the contradictions and falsehoods written by the ghostwriter of the book signed by Walter Audisio. Other excellent writers, such as Franco Bandini, have already done so. We think it more important to dwell upon the content of the "official version." Who gave Colonel Valerio the order to go to Dongo and execute the purported fascist "leaders"? Who, and more importantly how many persons, had he been ordered to shoot? Which sentence was he applying? And why, regarding those capital executions, was no official report ever written to the legitimate Italian government having as president of the council of ministers Ivanoe Bonomi and the lieutenant general, Prince

Umberto of Savoy, as head of state? And, what was even more amazing, why was no report provided to the CLNAI, the Committee of National Liberation of Northern Italy, which in effect represented the Rome government in the north?

The answer to all these questions can be found in the number of persons shot at Dongo. Neither Audisio in his book nor the PCI would ever admit that what took place at Dongo, rather than being a capital execution "in the name of the Italian people," was actually a reprisal that directly imitated the savagery of the methods used by the SS to avenge the fifteen martyrs executed at the Piazzale Loreto (the fifteen partisans had been shot at Milan during the preceding August following an attack by GAP[21] units against a German truck in the viale Abruzzi in Milan). Colonel Valerio left Milan with his well-armed team and a precise order given to him not by the CLNAI but rather by the Party: bring fifteen of them back to Milan, one for each one of those who had been executed at the Piazzale Loreto, and shoot them there along with Mussolini, their leader, in full view of the people of Milan in an historical act of vengeance.

When Colonel Valerio, whoever he may be, reached Dongo, where Captain Neri had taken control of the situation—Neri had miraculously reappeared after disappearing for some two months—and was immediately warmly welcomed back by his men. Valerio was handed a list of fifty-one Italians who had been captured in the escaping German convoy "with, in addition, a Spanish diplomat with his wife and children." This "Spanish diplomat" was actually Marcello Petacci, Claretta's brother, his wife, Zita Ritossa, and the two boys, Benvenuto and Ferdinando. Valerio knew every word of Article 5 of the CLNAI decree of April 25 by heart: "The members of the fascist government and the fascist leaders guilty of having contributed to the suppression of constitutional guarantees, having destroyed the popular freedoms, created fascism, compromised and betrayed the country, leading it to the present catastrophe are to be punished with the death penalty." Valerio understood that the description that fit the requirements of Article 5 could apply at the most to nine of the prisoners: Alessandro Pavolini;

Francesco Barracu; Fernando Mezzasoma; Augusto Liverani; and Ruggero Romano—all of them ministers of the Salò government—as well as (stretching things some more) the former prefect of Milan, Luigi Gatti; the Fascist Party federal secretary in Como, Paolo Porta; and the Black Brigade commander, Idreno Utimpergher. But he "had to" find fifteen of them, and he therefore made the tragic check mark next to six more names of those who could hardly be described as "creators of fascism," such as the former founder of the Communist party, Nicola Bombacci, or as "suppressors of constitutional guarantees," like air force Captain Pietro Calistri. It didn't matter. The names of Bombacci and Calistri; together with those of Goffredo Coppola, dean of the University of Bologna; of Ernesto Daquanno, a newspaperman; of Mario Nudi, an employee of the Duce's secretariat; of Vito Casalinuovo, Mussolini's military aide were added to the list. All were shot on the lakefront. To these was added—we shall attempt to understand why in Chapter X—the unfortunate Marcello Petacci, who tried unsuccessfully to save his own life by diving into the lake. The full count was then sixteen. After this the "executioner" went to Bonzanigo to shoot the two dead bodies of Mussolini and Claretta Petacci. He found the two bodies on his way to Dongo in the late morning, was informed as to their location, hesitated, and then decided that he could no longer follow his orders to bring those "condemned" to the Piazzale Loreto alive. He therefore decided to shoot the fifteen others on the spot. He certainly must have consulted with his "bosses" in Milan over the telephone since—contrary to the "official" version—the telephone was operating perfectly.

It is therefore the identity of the mysterious executioners of that morning, the real killers of Mussolini and Claretta Petacci, that has been the continued focus of the attention of those historians who chose to go beyond the "official" version for the last half century in an Italy that to this day quietly feels it is perfectly normal for a massacre to take place without trial, any kind of sentencing, or official report to the Head of State or the government.

We must therefore examine the main hypotheses known up to now as to the identity of the "executioner" at Bonzanigo and his companions. The best-known scenario identifies him as Luigi Longo, the number two man in the PCI leadership, said to have left Milan as soon as the exact location where the Duce was held became known, in order to personally handle the execution. The most detailed description of the death of Mussolini and Claretta Petacci by Longo can be found in the book by Urbano Lazzaro, *Dongo, Mezzo Secolo di Menzogne* [Dongo: Half a Century of Lies]. Lazzaro, *aka* the partisan Bill, or the man who captured the Duce in the German convoy, did not physically witness the killing of Mussolini and his mistress but claims he can reconstruct the event in detail through the accounts provided to him by his former "comrades." It should also be said—as we already mentioned—that credit must go to historian Franco Bandini for identifying Longo as the "executioner" in 1978, the year his book *Vita e morte segreta di Mussolini* was published.* This author published an article announcing Bandini's conclusions in a large circulation weekly magazine at the time by addressing a loaded question to Luigi Longo, who had recently handed over the leadership of the PCI to Enrico Berlinguer: "Answer us: is it true or false?" Longo kept silent forever. Will it be sufficient to state that the account given by Bill—and earlier by Bandini—is a true reflection of what actually happened? It is not easy to provide an answer to that question.

Another hypothesis that is perhaps more suggestive, but no less fitting as to the identity of the "executioner," was offered by Alessandro Zanella in his book *L'ora di Dongo* [The Hour of Dongo], which is key for the moment-to-moment reconstruction of the movements of Mussolini and his entourage from their escape from Milan on April 25, 1945. In Zanella, the killer of Mussolini and Claretta Petacci was the same Captain Neri, the man who had placed them in hiding in the house of the farmers De Maria. The motive for the killings was to enable Captain Neri to regain his status within the PCI, which considered him a traitor. The assumption is perfectly logical and is based upon converging and unambiguous clues

* Franco Bandini, *Vita e morte segreta di Mussolini* [Mussolini's Life and Secret Death], (Milan: Mondadori, 1978).

(we must not forget that Zanella, besides being a scrupulous historian, was also a successful criminal lawyer). There may be reason to cast doubt on the fact that Neri's rashness would be considered serious enough by the PCI for Neri and his mistress, the partisan fighter Gianna, to deserve the death penalty. Or was Neri and Gianna's misdeed something of a very different nature? We shall see towards the end of this book.

We then reach the final and most sensational version, the one offered by Bruno Giovanni Lonati, a former partisan fighter (he was actually a political commissar in the Garibaldi Brigades). Lonati was residing in Brescia and states in his book, *Mussolini e Claretta: la verità*,[22] that he was the Duce's "executioner," following the orders of a British secret agent, identified as the mysterious Captain John, who personally shot Claretta Petacci. Where did the order come from? According to Lonati it came directly from Prime Minister Churchill. The purpose was both to retrieve the famous documents and silence the couple, who if interviewed by newsmen would most certainly reveal all the agreements—those agreements could not be aired at the time—between the fascist leader and the British prime minister to attempt to turn Hitler against Stalin's Russia.

In all fairness it must be said—in closing this mystery—that Bruno Lonati was unable to provide any proof to back up what he was writing. He did not even reveal Captain John's last name. However, unknown to Lonati, there exists one potentially serious clue that could corroborate the truthfulness of his account that this author was able to find, as we show in Chapter XI.

Chapter VIII

PLUNDERING
THE GOLD STOLEN FROM THE JEWS

Many surviving Republican fascists stated that the "Dongo treasure"
was made up mostly of the valuables stolen from Jewish families when
they were deported to the concentration camps. Most historians, however,
have omitted this testimony. Why? We reopen the files to see what they
said in order to understand what really happened between
Como and Dongo.

"What I would like to understand," asked the elderly but vigorous Peter Tompkins, the former OSS agent in Rome during the Second World War and one of the growing crowd of historians who have decided to follow the "British thread" in the deaths of Mussolini and Claretta Petacci, "is why the Communist party, for some fifty years, has espoused a convenient version of the facts and prevented any kind of debate."[1] We shall attempt to explain why.

In the book by Urbano Lazzaro, *aka* Bill, there is a first-hand, eyewitness account about the way the executions were to be handled in the early afternoon of April 28, 1945, in the main lobby of the Dongo City Hall. We are authorized to reproduce the central and most dramatic part of that account.

> Pedro turned to Valerio and said [...] that not a single soldier of the 52nd Garibaldi Brigade would participate in the execution. Valerio was listening to Pedro very carefully and his face took on an angry and tense expression as Pedro kept on talking. "All right!" he answered in an irate voice. "Now let's look at the prisoner list!" He read out loud: "Benito Mussolini!" and quickly added: "to death!" He marked a cross next to Mussolini's name. Pedro and Giulio kept silent. There was an oppressive feeling in the air as if it were impossible to breathe. Valerio went on: "Clara Petacci: to death!" But the list of 31 prisoners given to me the evening before by Pietro, which I returned to Pedro when he went back to Dongo alone on the morning of April 28, did not include the name of Petacci. Mussolini was the 30th name on the list. If we can accept the fact that Colonel Valerio decided to read Mussolini's name first, marking it with a cross, he could not do so for Claretta Petacci because she was not on that list.

We must stop right here, because this eyewitness account—which strangely eluded historians up to now—by one of the main protagonists, should be enough to prove that Colonel Valerio already knew everything, namely that Claretta was dead and that he would have to bear the responsibility for her death by lying for the rest of his life. But we must read on to appreciate the flavor of that tragic farce.

> At that point Pedro felt he had to step in and did so quickly and decidedly. "Valerio!" he cried, "I don't find it right that you condemn a woman to death just because she was the Duce's mistress!" Valerio gave him an angry and contemptuous look. "I am the only one," he said, "to decide who must or must not

be shot! Barracu: to death!" He drew another cross next to that name. "But Barracu is a soldier, a gold medal of 1915. You can't shoot him. And then there's no record of him doing anything wrong!" Pedro said quickly. "He was the Undersecretary of the Council of Ministers of the Republic and that is enough to erase even the purest and most worthy career!" answered Valerio.

"Liverani: to death! Coppola: death! Utimpergher: death! Daquanno: death! Captain Calistri: death! Mario Nudi . . ." "Just a minute," said Pedro, I'd like you to know that Captain Calistri was not captured by us in the convoy or on the armored car but came to us freely asking that his position be taken into account very carefully. This indicates that his conscience is clear. And then he was not part of the Salò government!" "He was part of the convoy and that is enough," replied Valerio impatiently. At those words Pedro stood up, looking angry: "Then why don't you just shoot the drivers, the women, the children, the wives of the ministers just because they were in that convoy. This is all inconceivable!" Pedro had never lost his self-control but faced with Valerio's absurdities he was unable to hold back. Valerio, hearing Pedro's words, also rose to his feet, his face turning white with anger and pounding his fist on the table. He screamed: "I repeat that I'm the only one making the decisions here! Just stop these interruptions and comments! I don't want to hear another word! Do you understand?" Pedro looked at him pitifully as he wondered how the high command could give such an important and extremely delicate responsibility to such a person. [...] "Mario Nudi: death!" Valerio went on. "Pavolini: death! Mezzasoma: death! Romano: death! Zerbino: death! Bombacci: death! Paolo Porta: death!" Next to each name he made a check mark in the shape of a cross in black pencil. Valerio had an aggressive and slightly satisfied tone to his voice; he seemed to be filled by a need to impart justice. Pedro felt as if he were living the days of the terror in the French Revolution. He could not stand it, but he also understood that there was nothing he could do. Suddenly Valerio said: "These are all to be shot: assemble them all and get ready to hand them over to me immediately! [...] Get a move on as soon as you can. Then we'll go and get Mussolini and the Petacci woman."

This vivid and unforgettable account proves that at 3 p.m. on April 28 Valerio already knew that the execution of Mussolini and Claretta Petacci had already been carried out by a commando under orders coming from the British and had already decided (or it had been "suggested" to him) to proceed with the second "execution" of the two dead bodies. He had also been informed about the amount and origin of the valuables found in the cars used by the fleeing group: the famous "Dongo treasure."

The available testimony

On January 17, 1949, *Life* magazine published an investigative piece by newsman John Kobler under the title "The Great Dongo Robbery." For the first time the treasure of the RSI taken by the Italian Communist party following the capture of Mussolini and the convoy of fascist leaders fleeing Milan could be quantified. According to Kobler—who was well versed in these matters since he had been with the OSS during the Italian campaign—the treasure in Italian lire, foreign currency, coins and gold ingots, and precious stones came to about 66.2 million U.S. dollars of 1945, equal to some 5 billion U.S. dollars of 2000. Of these, about 61 million dollars (in Italian lire, gold coins and ingots, jewelry and valuable currency) represented the "secret funds" of the RSI; 4 million dollars (in lire and Reichmarks) were the German funds; and finally 1.2 million dollars (in lire and Swiss francs) was Mussolini's personal fortune, coming almost in its entirety from the sale to the industrialist Gian-Riccardo Cella of the building of *Il Popolo d'Italia* and the SAME printing plant in Milan's Piazza Cavour.

This total, less about some twenty percent that wound up in the pockets of many—real or fake—partisans who "handled" the prisoners at Musso and Dongo with their respective baggage, did not reach the vaults of the Bank of Italy as it should have, but instead found its way into the coffers of the PCI. According to *Life* magazine this money was used to finance two electoral campaigns in 1946 and 1948 (14 million dollars), to purchase the building at the Via Botteghe Oscure in Rome (1.3 million dollars, including the expenses for refurbishing), and the balance to finance covert paramilitary forces and set up the imposing network of provincial federations, sections, and cells all over Italy. It must be pointed out that all the accounts that followed, including the one that is best informed by Urbano Lazzaro (the partisan Bill), do not follow the old but extremely detailed account published in *Life*.

The Italian State would remain totally passive in the face of Communist boldness. Five reports were sent to Premier Alcide De Gasperi at the end of 1945 by the Como chief of police, attorney Luigi Davide Grassi, and by the prefect, Virgilio Bertinelli. All remained unanswered and were not acted upon. A report sent to "His Excellency Mario Scelba"[2] by the ex-agent of RSI secret services, Rosario Boccadifuoco, one of the survivors of the Mussolini convoy who declared "he was prepared to recognize those who mishandled the Dongo treasure." The Christian Democrats at the time were busy avoiding any confrontations with the PCI—a precursor of the "historic compromise" of the 1970s and 1980s.

In 1949, during the preliminary inquest of the Padua trial, best known historically as the "trial of the Dongo gold"—a trial that was to be interrupted, as we shall see later on, due to the mysterious suicide of a juror and never reopened as sometimes happens in the confusion of the Italian judicial system—the PCI produced an inventory indicating that it had actually received from the 52nd Partisan Garibaldi Brigade that had captured the Mussolini convoy: "128 million lire* that were used as severance for the Garibaldi units." However, the commander of the 52nd Brigade, Pier delle Stelle, *aka* Pedro, stated with bravery at the Padua trial on June 5, 1957: "That inventory included only a very tiny portion of the mountain of valuables that were stacked on the tables of the Dongo city hall." And he then added: "An inventory of that kind could certainly not fit in a room and a half full of valuables. Everything that

---

* Over 7 million in 2004 U.S. dollars.

is not listed must have gone to someone. I don't know whether it went to the PCI or someone else but that is what happened."[3] The presiding judge commented bitterly: "We understand. The only ones who knew were Neri and Gianna."

Captain Neri had been murdered by the Communists—something the PCI officially admitted—a few days after he supervised the gathering of the Dongo treasure in May 1945. His mistress Gianna (her real name was Giuseppina Tuissi) was to encounter the same fate a few weeks later. It was to be the start of a series of homicides that were never fully explained until now.

Further disputes over the facts

For decades there was more talk about the "secret funds of the RSI," with respect to the "Dongo treasure." The bank notes, gold coins and ingots, even the jewelry (watches, rings, necklaces, bracelets, and pins) were robbed from the State for the benefit of Mussolini and the fleeing fascist leadership. In fact, there was not a single ounce of "gold belonging to the State," as shown in the very detailed study by Riccardo Lazzeri (*Economia e Finanza nella RSI*): "there was not a single gram. The gold reserves were located at Fortezza at the headquarters of the Bank of Italy where they were retrieved untouched." Another very credible confirmation regarding the fact that not a single lira of State treasure had been taken from the "Mussolini convoy" fleeing from Milan was made by one of Italy's foremost experts of numismatics, Guido Crapanzano, in collaboration with Ermelindo Giulianini. Investigating the Bank of Italy archives and consulting the reports written after the war by Roberto Mori (director of the Bank of Italy in the south under Allied control), Crapanzano and Giulianini made the following annotation: "We are surprised to note that inflation is practically nonexistent in the north and prices are very low because of price controls and other measures, while inflation is very strong in the south, fueled by the Allied occupation expenses and the government's refusal to take any kind of initiative."[4] But that was not all:

On May 1, 1945, the Allied Military Government—AMGOT—issued General Order n. 44 controlling the printing of banknotes during the RSI period and the existing supplies. Inspector Ernesto Ambrosio was in charge of the investigating team and certified that the plants in charge of monetary production for the RSI had not been the object of removals or damage by retreating Germans or Fascists. Furthermore, based on Ambrosio's reports, it appears that the companies producing the banknotes still have large quantities on hand at various stages of production or ready for shipment. At the end of May Ambrosio returned to Rome with enough information to provide a very favorable picture of the situation in the north. Regarding the attitude of those responsible RSI functionaries the initial investigation by the Bank of Italy concluded that the management had acted properly and the quantities shown in the Decrees appeared to have been strictly adhered to. Further checks that took place until 1950 were to prove that not only had there been no administrative irregularity on the part of the Bank of Italy officials operating in the north, but that the RSI officials had also behaved correctly when, at the time of the catastrophe and in fleeing rather than taking advantage of the confusion, they gave strict orders to save the national treasure.[5]

It was too simple for over half a century to accuse the fascists who were busy fleeing Milan. No one could possibly have sued since they were all dead. At the same time the legend of the gold wedding rings offered to the homeland by Italian women in 1935 at the start of the war in Ethiopia purportedly hidden in a few secret trunks by Mussolini and his "predators" only to resurface in the Dongo convoy, has been totally debunked. The wedding rings were immediately melted down into gold ingots to pay for the war. There were many wedding rings in the "Dongo treasure" but they were not those of 1935.

Urbano Lazzaro, in his book, *L'oro di Dongo*, writes: "When, in the late evening of April 27, Captain Neri, and Gianna reached Dongo, Pietro[6] immediately informed them of what he had seen at

Musso and nearby.[7] At that point the energetic trio from the 52nd Garibaldi Brigade was able because of the authority it had been granted, to retrieve most of the valuables. [...] Everything that Pietro, Captain Neri, and Gianna were able to find was brought to Dongo and placed in a room on the first floor of the municipal building."[8] Did Neri and Gianna understand right away that those valuables were not the "RSI's secret funds"? Did the temporary custodians of the treasure, Prefect Luigi Gatti and his secretary Mario Nudi, tell them the origin of the contents? Whatever actually took place was written so that the truth about the "Dongo treasure" would never surface. Only after several decades did the most incredible assumptions about the treasure emerge.

In 1983 Mussolini's valet, Quinto Navarra, revealed:

On the morning of the 23rd Prefect Gatti left Gargnano, taking a few suitcases and many boxes of confidential documents. Those suitcases contained the so-called "treasure" of Mussolini, which included 65 kilos of gold and many hundreds of thousands in foreign banknotes (sterling, Swiss francs, pesetas, and reichmarks). The gold had been taken in the Abruzzi from the Jews who sought refuge over there. It included rings, necklaces, medals, and bracelets, and it was not all of good quality. The gold was at the disposal of Minister of the Interior Buffarini-Guidi first and then of Paolo Zerbino until Mussolini decided to hold it himself.[9]

How did Navarra know all this? He was old and ill but he was present at Gargnano and came regularly to the Villa delle Orsoline. As Alessandro Zanella explains: "Quinto Navarra was the oldest of the Duce's valets, had been in service up to July 25, 1943, and was at Lake Garda. He closely followed what was happening at the Private Secretariat, which he knew well from experience and because his son Lamberto was working there, holding the eighth place out of about sixty civil servants, in front of Werther Samaritani and his father."[10] Historians, including those who until now have chosen not to mention that fact since it is such a sensitive issue, now have first glimpse of the truth about that "treasure" and how it reached the secret rooms at Gargnano; who took it just before the end, and why it was part of the Mussolini convoy, as Zanella narrates:

Secretary Gatti left Milan at about 7:30 p.m. (on April 23, 1945). He reached Gargnano about two hours later, accompanied by Mario Nudi, Pietro Carradori, and the prizefighter Antonio Brocchi, his very loyal bodyguard. He had the time to meet with Donna Rachele. The others had dinner at the cafeteria of the secretariat. [...] They took the six leather suitcases, size 50 by 60 [centimeters], used to convey the valuables. Those suitcases came from Rome when the Administration was moved to Lake Garda. In Rome they were held by Colonel Modesto Mileti, the head archivist at the Palazzo Venezia, who did not go to Gargnano. The valuables were made up of a series of packages shipped to the ministry of the interior by the Provincial Leaders—starting with the provinces of Latina and Frosinone and up the peninsula to Bologna, which was excluded at the time of evacuation because of the enemy's advance. The packages were marked with what was inside (gold, Swiss francs, pound sterling, etc.) and the province of origin. As long as Buffarini[11] was in charge, these valuables were held at the ministry, the Foresteria at Maderno. When Zerbino took over the treasure, Doctor Samaritani brought it to the headquarters at the Villa delle Orsoline where it was assembled and stored. At headquarters, the treasure was kept in good order, package by package according to the provinces of origin (Frosinone, Rome, Terni, Viterbo, Grosseto, Siena, Florence, Pistoia, La Spezia), in an office next to the archives, always guarded by two soldiers.

All the Communist historians, for example, have speculated that the treasure was made up of the wedding rings donated to the homeland in 1935, but Carradori categorically denied it. The Duce's orderly said that the chief of police, Tullio Tamburini, was responsible for assembling the valuables. The wedding rings donated to the homeland years before had been sent to the Mint in Rome. There were no valuables from the

Mint at Gargnano. The fact that Mussolini tried to concentrate the valuables at his headquarters in order to best prevent Wolff and Rahn from taking them confirms the hypothesis of Quinto Navarra and Carradori. The remaining question is: Why did Mussolini want the treasure brought to Milan? It is possible that the timely inventory of the valuables that Gatti made on April 23 was due to an order by Mussolini, who was preparing to return the valuables to their owners. [...] By returning the valuables belonging to the Jews, Mussolini could show the Allies that the RSI was acting independently from German interests. In any case, we may exclude any idea on Mussolini's part to take the valuables. Had he decided to steal them he could have made them disappear at Gargnano or Milan.

There is also another confirmation in *L'oro di Dongo* by Urbano Lazzaro:

The RSI's chief of police, Dr. Tullio Tamburini, ordered the transfer of the valuables, and particularly the jewels, in the greatest secrecy. These had been accumulated by the fascist police through the systematic depredations inflicted on the many Italian Jews who had been arrested, detained, or even worse, handed over to the awful German SS units. [...] A further confirmation that these were the possessions belonging to the Jews is provided by the account given to the district attorney of Como during one of the many useless trials regarding the robbery of the Dongo treasure by an RSI functionary at the ministry of the interior, the accountant Raffaele La Greca, the head cashier of the RSI police.

According to the testimony at the Padua trial by Dr. Werther Samaritani, who was not asked whether he knew what the origins of the valuables were, the suitcases taken by Gatti contained 66 kilos of gold that came from various jewelers in the Marche and Abruzzi regions (they had obviously proceeded to melt down the rings, bracelets and chains under orders from the prefectures), 2,150 pound sterling in gold, 147 thousand Swiss francs, 16 million French francs, 10,000 Spanish pesetas, besides an unspecified quantity (or that he could not be more specific about) in British pounds, American dollars, and Portuguese escudos.

Apparently all those in the Mussolini convoy, from the prefects down to the last driver, knew that the valuables belonged to the Jews. It would be very logical that those in the convoy would have immediately informed the man who was proceeding with such determination and authority to confiscate the valuables, namely, Captain Neri. Furthermore, the way the packages were put together (heavy wrapping paper with the metal stamps of the prefectures of origin—then called "provinces"—and the markings of their contents but not necessarily the quantity) must have led any person sharp enough (and Neri was certainly among these) to ask himself and others a whole list of questions. What were those valuables? Where did they come from? Where were they supposed to go? Why, actually, would the prefectures of places such as Teramo, Ancona, Frosinone, Arezzo, and so on, in dozens upon dozens of packages large and small, possess banknotes and gold wedding rings, gold bullion and Swiss gold coins, necklaces and bracelets? Everyone in Italy knew—even the newspapers had published the news—that RSI legislation called for the arrest of the Jews, their internment in special concentration camps, and the seizure of their belongings.[12] Furthermore, a few weeks later, the seizure was changed to confiscation. These measures were enforced by the police and therefore the "questure," or police stations, and finally the prefectures, whose stamps were affixed on each one of the packages now stored in huge stacks in a room at Dongo.

Pietro Carradori again confirmed what he knew to the author. In his own words:

> On the morning of April 23, 1945, I received an order to accompany the Duce's secretary, Prefect Luigi Gatti, to Gargnano. Traveling with us were Captain Mario Nudi, who would be executed at Dongo, and the prizefighter Antonio

Brocchi, a Spanish-Italian, who was a friend of Gatti's. Our mission was to transport to the Milan Prefecture building what was to be later known as the "Dongo treasure." The treasure contained an unknown amount of gold and banknotes in dozens of packages wrapped in heavy yellow paper, each one bearing the stamp of the province of origin. These were the possessions of Jews that had been confiscated on orders by the various province heads up to the time when the chief of police, Tullio Tamburini, refused to do that kind of "work" and issued orders to local police chiefs to stop providing lists of names and addresses of Jews to the Germans. That decision was to trigger Tamburini's arrest by the SS and his imprisonment in a concentration camp in Germany.

The packages had been stored at Maderno at the headquarters of the ministry of the interior as long as Buffarini-Guidi was minister. Once Paolo Zerbino came in February 1945 the packages were taken to the Villa delle Orsoline, and kept in perfect order in an office constantly guarded by two armed soldiers. The Duce was planning to use those valuables in his negotiations: they were to be handed over to Allied authorities at the time of surrender to be returned to the Jews, as opposed to those stolen by the Germans and permanently lost. Mussolini had no intention of keeping them for himself. Had he wished to do so he could have made them disappear long before, possibly to Switzerland.

There was no time to open the packages and verify their contents, so we limited ourselves to dividing them up by content, gold or banknotes, and weighing each one. I can remember vividly the weight of those valuables: gold bullion—about 52 kilos, gold pounds sterling—25 kilos, banknotes of 100 Swiss francs each, and about 16 kilos in denominations, I can't remember, of dollars, Swiss francs, pesetas, marks and French francs. We packed everything into five leather suitcases, 50 by 60 centimeters, that came from the Palazzo Venezia inventory and we returned to Milan.

When we left for Como the five suitcases were loaded on to the gray platinum Alfa Romeo cabriolet belonging to Prefect Gatti, with Mario Nudi also abroad. The suitcases were taken by the partisans who captured and then shot Gatti and Nudi.

Finally, another corroborating statement that should be taken into account—but that has been ignored like the others to this day—came from newsman Franco De Agazio, who had started a series of investigative articles in a news weekly he edited in Milan (*Il Meridiano d'Italia*) on the fate of the "Dongo treasure." In the issue dated October 6, 1946, he wrote:

> It is difficult to say today whether its possession [of the "treasure"] was legitimate or whether it was the result of the innumerable thefts, acts of blackmail, extortion committed high and low by the top brass of the self-styled republic at the expense of the Jews [...] From all the information and confidential conversations, given past events and those still taking place, from private conversations with a few Communist party leaders, and their silences, surprises, and contradictions we may conclude that the issue of the "Duce's gold" cannot be isolated, but is connected to a much wider, politically important and very confidential situation due to the continued presence within the government in the most sensitive positions of leaders of the Party. Should the truth come to the surface, not only regarding the "Duce's gold" but about all of the underground activity connected to it, [the Party] would be permanently damaged, with consequences that are rather difficult to forecast right now.

Therefore, Franco De Agazio—who would, a few short months later, pay with his life for his candor and journalistic honesty—knew that those valuables came from the Jews. Did the Communists who arrived at Dongo immediately following Mussolini's capture know that what would be later called "the treasure of the RSI" was made up of valuables stolen from the Jews? Was that the real reason for the dispute between Captain Neri, Gianna, and their Party comrades? The disagreement turned into a deadly power play between those who knew and wanted to talk and those who wished to silence everyone and hold on to their stolen goods.[13]

Such questions cannot be answered with any kind of certainty and we must make clear that we do not intend in this book any calumny or to defame any freedom fighters who were members of the PCI at the time or any others who were Party members or part of other groups within the Resistance. We can only proceed by conjecture, unsupported by any proof. We may assume that no one in the fascist convoy volunteered to tell Captain Neri where the treasure originated. We may also assume that having found out the truth, Neri told his British contacts about that detail, asking them to step in so that the valuables could be returned to their rightful owners. This was presumably what Mussolini intended. Then Neri was given an answer he did not at all expect: "We have decided to effect an 'exchange': they give us Mussolini's papers and take responsibility for Petacci's death and we let them keep the gold belonging to the Jews."

During the same investigation on the disappearance of the "Dongo gold," *Il Meridiano d'Italia*, in its October 20, 1946, issue wrote:

The British police,[14] as we know, did step in. Since it had no interest in "monetary" valuables but rather in those of historical importance, such as Mussolini's documents, it concentrated only on the documents once they were in hand and dropped everything else. The British followed Mussolini's treasure up to the Como *Casa del Popolo* [People's House] where Pedro, Neri, Francesco, Gatti, Gianna,[15] and company took it by car. After that they divided the precious stones and the boxes looking for the larger cases full of documents that prompted Churchill to come personally, as we know, staying at Lake Como for a few weeks to select the papers he was interested in. Those papers would have also been of the greatest importance to us, and to Italy."

Massimo Caprara, historian and journalist, who was at that time Palmiro Togliatti's secretary, has verified in his articles and books how the "Dongo treasure" always was a taboo subject for the Communist party.[16] Caprara mentioned how in an interview in *L'Unità*—introduced at the useless Padua trial—Togliatti stated: "It was false that the Mussolini convoy was loaded with Italian and foreign currency." He revealed that the valuables stolen on the road between Musso and Dongo that were taken to the Dongo city hall by Captain Neri and scrupulously inventoried by Gianna all wound up in the Party coffers. From there an expert attorney was able to recycle everything to Switzerland.

This was how Caprara remembers the attorney: "Every two weeks he would travel to Rome and chat with me while he waited for Togliatti to be free to see him. At every visit he went through an odd triangular set of stops that I found curious. After visiting with us on the second floor he would go to the third floor where the administrative office was and then to the fourth to see Pietro Secchia. One day at lunch that same lawyer told me what was going on: his job was to recycle the Dongo booty, turning it into bank deposits and stocks in a few Swiss banks so that it could be reused in Italy."

The question still open is: Why did Neri and Gianna, assuming they knew the real origins of the "Dongo gold," not discuss it with the people who were close to them, such as their families? One possible answer—but this is also speculation—could be the desire to avoid exposing their kin to the kinds of risks they were facing. But in examining the accounts and the documents it becomes clear that Neri and Gianna did reveal something. Maddalena Canali, Neri's mother, in recalling her last meeting with her son, which took place on May 1, 1945 (one of the last days of his life following his experience at Dongo), stated, according to the trial transcript: "He came home that day. He was extremely sad and we did not discuss certain things. That evening we went to sleep and I could see that he was unhappy. When he used to come home we would always have a little party. But that day he was worried. 'What's wrong?' I asked him. He answered, 'How can I be happy? I found such dishonest people . . .'"

At that point the judge—who unfortunately did not think of asking what "those things we did not discuss" actually were—asked: "Did he tell you what that dishonesty consisted of?"

MADDALENA CANALI: That famous gold appeared and there was an excited conversation with Gorreri . . .

JUDGE: Did your son tell you anything regarding the valuables at Dongo?

MADDALENA CANALI: He told me, "Listen mother, these useless dishonest types are ruining the entire movement. I have seen such things . . . There was so much stuff, of enormous value, jewels, money from many countries, billions mother . . . I didn't think I was among such people . . . But now I must do a transaction at a bank, an important operation and I want to do this myself and alone."

JUDGE: And did he go through with that transaction?

MADDALENA CANALI: He left and I never saw him again. And when he didn't come back, when he did not return . . .

Maddalena Canali's voice broke as she was sobbing.

As for Gianna, she also hinted at something. When she was told to stay as far away from Como as possible she wrote a letter to Bill and asked her brother Cesare to deliver it. However, the letter wound up with Pietro Terzi, *aka* Francesco, and was never given to Bill. What kind of message did it contain? Bill, in his book *L'oro di Dongo*, writes that he is convinced she wrote about the treasure that wound up in the coffers of the PCI. He remembered the testimony at the same trial at Padua by Vincenzina Coan, one of Gianna's friends and her confidante:

> One day Gianna told me that Fabio had issued an order to her to stop showing any interest in Neri or else she would end up like him. As far as Fabio was concerned—she added—they were all spies but she said she had something she had held back and that if they did not tell her what had happened to Neri she would tell everything.

Finally, a strange detail: at the Padua trial the fascists cited as witnesses, Samaritani, Tamburini, La Greca, and their other former comrades were careful to avoid stating that those riches belonged to the Jews. Why? Were they ashamed of the past or fearful of the future?

All the evidence ends up in Switzerland

THE DUCE'S TREASURE IS IN SWITZERLAND was the banner headline of the *Corriere della Sera* in October 1996, adding: "Mussolini's secret bank accounts that were opened following the race laws are surfacing." But that was not the end of it. Even Galeazzo Ciano, the former foreign minister and the dictator's son-in-law, executed by firing squad at Verona along with the "traitors" of July 25, 1943, was said to have hidden sums of money and immense treasures in both Swiss and Argentinian banks when the times were good.

The source of this "news" was in three "secret reports" sent to Herbert Cummings, an official of the U.S. Department of State by the American embassies at Bern and Buenos Aires: two in the final months of the war (December 1944 and March 1945) and the third from Buenos Aires in February 1946.

These were anonymous reports, or rather "information notes," drafted by OSS informants, who for a few dollars did their best to produce as much information as they could. A simple letterhead (that of the U.S. embassy) a date, a mysterious numeric code, and then it was open season. Had it not been so and those "notes" had been the result of real discoveries, rather than the invention of some improvised spook or the result of a confidential conversation gleaned without too much propriety, they would certainly not have been kept gathering dust for over half a century in Washington's National Archives where they ended up after a stop at the desk of Mr. Cummings, who at the time had given them the importance they deserved. It is not so with the PRO (Public Record Office)— the British archives. The head of the British SOE (Special Operations Executive) at Bern was John McCaffey, a former bank manager who had worked for Hambro's Bank and who would not have missed the juicy news of a Mussolini account in Switzerland.

The three reports were released by the National Archives, to be delivered with other documents of various origins to Elan Steinberg of the World Jewish Congress. He had announced their existence to the press and to Paul Volker, former head of the Federal Reserve of the United States, appointed by the courts to investigate the issue of the "Nazi gold." This is the background of the case we are discussing.

The power play that has been going on for some years between major Swiss banks and the World Jewish Congress is about the gold stolen from the Jews that ended up in German accounts in Switzerland. It also involved the many accounts opened in Switzerland by German Jews at the start of the racial persecution and never claimed, due to the death of their owners in the extermination camps.

According to the World Jewish Congress the Swiss banks should return some 20 billion dollars to Jews. The bankers in Zurich and Geneva, on the other hand, answered that nothing was due, given a fifty-year-old agreement signed by the Swiss federal government and the Allies. At the time Switzerland agreed to pay 250 million Swiss francs as "war reparations," an amount that was the equivalent of 50 million dollars, or about 2 billion dollars in 2003: ten percent of the gold value—according to accounting of the World Jewish Congress—would have actually been recycled by the Nazis due to the connivance of the Swiss bankers.

Following a number of lawsuits in U.S. courts brought by the Jewish survivors of the camps, an international commission chaired by Dr. Volker was formed to investigate. It was as a consequence of that decision that every recess of the archives in Washington and London was combed in search of the unlikely "scoops" that actually never materialized. In any case, had Mussolini or Ciano hid treasure in Switzerland and elsewhere, their families would have certainly not lived in such modest circumstances. "Donna" Rachele, Mussolini's widow, earned a living as a cook in the small restaurant she opened in the Romagna region and by selling her memoirs to weekly magazines. Her son, Romano, the father of Alessandra

Mussolini, a member of Parliament, earned a living playing piano in a jazz band. And so on.

It certainly would be a "coup" to find out that Mussolini—out of whose pockets, according to dictum often repeated by the neo-fascists, "not a single penny dropped out" as he was hanging by his feet at the Piazzale Loreto—stole jewelry and money from the Jews and hid it all in Switzerland. Ciano, Mussolini's foreign minister since 1936, was to have done the same, having Buenos Aires as his final destination. Actually Ciano did have a real "treasure"—his diaries, which were smuggled to safety in Switzerland by his wife Edda two days before he was executed on January 11, 1944, in the Scalzi prison in Verona. However, she gave them to an American publisher for publication only after the end of the war, exactly according to her husband's wishes, since he was not seeking to make money but only posthumous justice: "Because I believe that to honestly tell the truth," he wrote on a piece of paper in the Verona prison just before being sentenced to die, and smuggled to Edda by the German agent Felicitas Beetz, "is still useful in this troubled world to help the innocent and punish those who are responsible." In fact, the Ciano *Diaries* do represent the final moral condemnation of fascism.

If Edda and her children then benefited from owning the copyright (the book was sold in very large numbers) and survived the tragedy of the war and the private tragedy of their lives, it has nothing to do with the OSS reports and even less with the "Dongo treasure."

Chapter IX

HOW THE BRITISH BEAT THE AMERICANS

While Churchill's men secretly activated their network on Lake Como,
American OSS agents were setting up fruitless meetings between the fleeing
fascist leaders and the representatives of the Italian government in Rome to
guarantee the safety of Mussolini ("whom the Americans hold in the highest
esteem and regard"—as they said themselves), should he decide to surren-
der to them rather than become a prisoner of the partisans.

I n order to understand how a small but very aggressive group of
British SOE (Special Operations Executive) agents were able to
beat the extremely tough American OSS (Office of Strategic Services) and reach their number one target, Benito Mussolini, it is
necessary to place the events in historical context. Ever since Italy
declared war on the United States on December 11, 1941, following the treacherous Japanese attack on Pearl Harbor of December
7, 1941, the Roosevelt administration was uneasy about the large
Italian-American community that had thrown its full support to
FDR's reelection. A majority of Italian-Americans had pro-fascist
leanings, or at least showed a sincere admiration for Mussolini. He

was viewed as the man who had known how to uplift Italy—their country of origin and the homeland of their fathers—from being a backwater secondary European country to a major world power. Besides the six million Italian-American voters, many anti-fascist émigrés had found refuge in the United States, some of them with very prestigious names, such as the conductor Arturo Toscanini, nuclear scientist Enrico Fermi, historian Gaetano Salvemini, the founder of the Catholic Partito Popolare Don Luigi Sturzo, the former foreign minister Carlo Sforza, and the former commander of the International Brigades in Spain, Randolfo Pacciardi. For some time the émigrés were grouped together in the *Mazzini Society*, backing the project of its president Max Ascoli to create an Italian Legion to fight alongside the U.S. Army. Randolfo Pacciardi was the top contender to be its leader, given his undeniable military ability. However, the idea was dropped rather quickly, in part due to pressure from the State Department. Max Ascoli was persuaded to accept some of the more moderate members of the Italian-American community who had no intention of fighting against other Italian soldiers.

An OSS document from the Foreign Nationalities branch, dated August 3, 1943,[1] slices up the Italian-American community into left-, center- and right-wing groups. The majority was clearly on the right with the American Committee for Italian Democracy, chaired by Judge Ferdinand Pecora along with Boston Judge Felix Forte, the head of Sons of Italy, with half a million members; the famous editor and journalist Generoso Pope, owner of the daily *Il Progresso Italo-Americano*—who never hid his admiration for fascism; Dr. Charles Fama, head of the AMA's New York chapter; and so on. The main spokesman for the Committee was syndicated columnist Drew Pearson of the Hearst newspaper chain. The Committee also attracted other prestigious members, such as Bank of America founder Amedeo P. Giannini; Colonel Charles Poletti, the former lieutenant governor and governor of New York, who was to be the military governor of Palermo, Rome, and Milan; and Congressman Thomas D'Alessandro. "The cream of the former fascist group that was to be engaged in a furious campaign against the Popular front in the 1948 Italian elections."[2]

A few émigrés who were disappointed by State Department procrastination and its fear of losing the electoral support of the vast Italian-American majority decided to ally themselves and work with the British. Such was the case of Alberto Tarchiani who, as one may read in a secret intelligence report to the Department of State signed by Earl Brennan in March 1945, "is surrounded and dominated by a handful of individuals who are paid by the British or subjected to their influence—such as Dino Gentili, Max Salvadori, Emilio Lussu, Alberto Cianca—most of whom are in the active leadership of the Partito d'Azione and at least two of them (Gentili and Salvadori) are known to be operatives of the British intelligence service."[3]

Max Salvadori was much more than simply a "member of British Secret Intelligence." Forced to leave Italy due to the threats of violence to him and his family Salvadori emigrated to the United States first and later to Great Britain where he acquired British citizenship. When the war began he joined the British army and was quickly promoted to the rank of major when he participated in the landings in Sicily and Anzio where he was wounded. Due to his flawless knowledge of Italian and the impeccable reputation he enjoyed within anti-fascist groups (he had been a friend to some top anti-fascist leaders such as Ferruccio Parri and the Rosselli brothers) but also because of his daring and personal courage and military leadership he was appointed Allied representative to the CLNAI in Milan. The CLNAI was headed by the liberal Alfredo Pizzoni, known as Longhi, with whom Salvadori had an excellent relationship. Before going to Milan in February 1945 Salvadori was parachuted into the region of Piedmont, known as the Langhe, where he spent two months with the local partisans fighting the Germans.

There have been some attempts to connect Max Salvadori's name to secret SOE operations and to Special Force 1 in Italy. True, he did have a key assignment and played an important official role to the point that, with nothing to hide, he quickly published a very detailed memoir about his war experiences in Italy, *Resistenza e*

Azione—Ricordi di un liberale (Bari: Laterza, 1951) [Resistance and Action—Memoirs of a Liberal]. In the book Salvadori is very explicit about his ideas and the people he came into contact with during those months preceding liberation. As he wrote: "On the morning of April 22 Mussolini was convinced that everything would proceed smoothly as far as his personal fate was concerned. It is sure that the British were out to get him. However, the Americans were really in charge and he felt that he could make a deal with them. They would need him to reestablish order in Italy."

Salvadori never attempted to interfere with the decisions of the top leaders of the CLNAI and was always careful to defer to the legitimate government of Italy. "I did not take part in the discussions (during the meetings of the CLNAI). I was there as an observer and kept quiet. I could see taking shape the vision that had drawn us forward during the difficult years of conspiracies and exile, a vision of citizens revolting against dictatorship." As a loyal soldier—during the last few months he had been promoted to lieutenant colonel because of his merits as a soldier—he was worried about the extremism displayed by the Communists. "There were excesses," he wrote. "It was necessary to repress those who aspired at becoming as many Marats or Robespierres. That was why I tried to accelerate the arrival of the Allies (…) at the same time I reminded the CLNAI leaders that with the arrival of the Anglo-American armies all government authority would automatically pass on to the Allies and with it the control of all prisoners, whatever category they belonged to." This was not the thinking of a "007 with a license to kill."

Salvadori's attitude toward the bloodthirsty inclinations of a part of the Resistance is clearly expressed in one of his more polemical writings published many years later in the February 1981 issue of the journal *Storia Contemporanea* when commenting on the book, *La campagna d'Italia e i servizi segreti* (Milan, 1980) [The Secret Service and the Italian Campaign] by Raimondo Craveri. Salvadori was critical mostly of Vincent Scamporino and Max Corvo, who had financed and supported the ORI (Organizzazione Resistenza Italiana) that Craveri had created. (It should be noted that Craveri was the son in law of the philosopher Benedetto Croce.) Scamporino and Corvo were aware of the fact that the ORI promoted a violent and bloody kind of partisan warfare based on sabotage and terror attacks behind German and Fascist lines. The ORI's "progressive" line was opposed by SOE that felt—as Max Salvadori stated—that it was "irresponsible." It is difficult to envision that such an open and direct man could be involved in the murky affairs at Dongo.

Furthermore, it was obvious that with respect to the future of the Italian peninsula American and British interests did not coincide. In an OSS report dated August 14, 1944, reproduced in the book *Gli Americani in Italia,* one may read: "Great Britain aims at the elimination of any minimal Italian threat along the British Empire's lines of communication connecting the Mediterranean to the Red Sea and the Indian Ocean and Italy's complete economic and political dependence upon Great Britain. Great Britain therefore wishes to have a conservative regime in Italy that will guarantee the implementation of an armistice treaty, will block the Communist threat, and follow a line that is favorable to British interests."

One of the clauses of the armistice treaty was the turning over of Mussolini alive to the XVth Army Group Command under General Mark Clark, who at the end of April 1945 had his headquarters in Siena. The British secret services, however, did not agree. They moved with great speed and efficiency as soon as they received the news that Mussolini had become a prisoner, in the early afternoon of April 27, of the partisans of the 52nd Garibaldi Brigade on the main square at Dongo.

It actually may not be out of the question that Mussolini's capture had been planned in advance down to the smallest detail, thanks to an agreement between SS General Karl Wolff and the British secret service. This is what Erich Kuby writes in his book *Il tradimento Tedesco*[4] and is confirmed by a very convincing scenario offered by Italian researcher Luigi Imperatore,[5] who states that the arrival of forty trucks of German anti-aircraft units under the command of Lieutenant (or Colonel) Fallmeyer (or Schallmeyer?) coming from Lombardy on their way to the Valtellina via the western lakeside road of Lake Como had been ordered by General Wolff to allow a group of partisans under the British (i.e., the leaders of the 52nd Garibaldi Brigade) to proceed with Mussolini's capture. It should be noted that between the long and mysterious stop by the Duce at Menaggio—that began during the night of April 25–26—and the time of the interception of the Italo-German convoy on the morning of April 27 at Musso, between Menaggio and Dongo, the two German platoons that were to provide for the Duce's security— but also to control his movements—the one under the command of SD Lieutenant Otto Kisnatt, who was part of RSHA, and the other an SS unit led by Lieutenant Fritz Birzer, practically disappeared, leaving the very mysterious Fallmeyer in complete control.[6]

It is possible that Fallmeyer, following Wolff's orders and in accordance with the surrender talks secretly begun in Switzerland (without the Führer's knowledge) by the supreme SS leader Heinrich Himmler himself, was to deliver Mussolini to the Allies and precisely to the British, not directly but through a group of partisans under British control and whose commander, Count Pier Bellini delle Stelle, even had an English mother.

An unimpeachable confirmation of such speculation is provided by an excellent source, General Dwight D. Eisenhower, who in his book, *Crusade in Europe* writes:

> One early hint of German defection was a feeler that came through the British embassy in Stockholm. Its stated purpose was to arrange a truce in the west; this was an obvious attempt to call off the war with the Western Allies so that the German could throw his full strength against Russia. Our governments rejected the proposal. Another came out of Switzerland, under mysterious circumstances, from a man named Wolff. There was apparently afoot a plot to surrender the German forces in Italy to Alexander . . . In the Wolff incident the Western Allies, although proceeding in good faith to determine the authenticity of the message and the authority of the man who initiated it, incurred the suspicion of the Soviets . . . Until the very last the Germans never abandoned the attempt to make a distinction between a surrender on the western front and one on the eastern . . . [7]

We are aware of the requests by cable from Allied Headquarters in Siena to the CLNAI in Milan in the late afternoon of April 27 as soon as news of the Duce's capture was broadcast on the radio, clearly requesting that Mussolini be handed over to those responsible, who were to land at Bresso airfield. We also know the response—written by the Communist members of the CLNAI—that fatefully stated it was impossible to hand over Mussolini because he had "already been shot in the same place where fifteen patriots had been previously shot by the Nazi fascists."

The first American OSS officer to be taken in was certainly Captain Emilio Q. Daddario. Based in Lugano, he rushed to Milan as soon as he was informed of Mussolini's capture and demanded that Mussolini be turned over to him. He was accompanied by Lieutenant Aldo Icardi,[8] who was part of the "Chrysler" mission. The heads of the insurrectional committee (Longo, Pertini, Valiani, and even General Raffaele Cadorna, commander of the CVL) requested that the two American officers provide a safe-conduct document to Colonel Valerio. To this day the precise identity of Valerio is not known with absolute certainty; however, Daddario, without going into any great detail, accepted the false name he was provided: Giovanni Battista Magnoli di Cesare.

With the safe-conduct document in hand, written in English and signed by an OSS officer, Colonel Valerio left on his mission to bring back Mussolini and, in addition, the fifteen others, so that they may be "solemnly" executed by firing squad at Milan's Piazzale Loreto. However, Daddario did not know all this; he was told, and believed, the exact opposite. The CLNAI leaders gave him a cable sent at 6:30 p.m. to read that had been sent to Remo Scappini, an officer of the Guardia di Finanza, who was in command of the Dongo barracks: "Guard the prisoner properly with every courtesy. Do not harm him. Rather than using violence in case he attempts to flee, let him go."[9] Only later, once he learned the truth, and having personally witnessed the shameful display at the Piazzale Loreto, did Daddario forcefully take charge from the Communist executioners in the Resistance, preventing by his decisions and firm attitude—as reported by Max Corvo in his book[10]—their seizure of Marshal Rodolfo Graziani, the head of the RSI armed forces, whom he had arrested at the Villa Locatelli in Como and taken to the Grand Hotel Milan in the via Manzoni (in the center of Milan). Then, even the most bloodthirsty partisans who would have preferred to shoot the marshal right then and there, were compelled by Daddario's tough attitude to stand down. Graziani was taken to the safety of the headquarters of the American Fourth Army at Bergamo.

Daddario was not the only American to be roundly deceived concerning Mussolini's death. As Zanella wrote: "In the meantime John McDonough, the American special agent of the CIC (Counter Intelligence Corps), attached to the First Armored Division as it was nearing Como, was advised by radio in the late afternoon of April 27. A handwritten message from McDonough was sent by a partisan dispatch rider to Lieutenant Colonel Giovanni Sardagna of the CVL, who was at the prefecture. The message read: "Mussolini and Graziani are to be brought to Brivio for the disposition of the American police. John McDonough, special agent CIC, First Armored Division." It was as a result of that direct order from the Americans that Mussolini was transferred from the Dongo city hall building to the closer and more secure barracks of the *Guardia di Finanza* at Germasino, where he was treated with every consideration. As for McDonough, it is important to point out that he was in contact with the American deputy consul at Lugano and OSS officer Donald Pryce-Jones, alias Scotti, who, having been informed of Mussolini's capture, immediately ordered two of his men—Salvatore Guastoni and Italian navy captain Giovanni Dessi—to take Mussolini out of the Communists' control and deliver him to the American military police."[11]

Actually, Salvatore Guastoni had been on the scene for some time and was attempting to convince Mussolini, who was still free, to surrender himself to the Americans. As the vivid description of a meeting—by Ermanno Amicucci, former editor of the *Corriere della Sera*—that took place in the offices of the Como prefecture on the afternoon of April 26, attests:[12]

At the Prefecture the head of the province, Renato Celio, was with CLN leaders, Resistance leaders, and Allied agents who had also crossed in from the nearby Swiss border. There was an ongoing discussion and a "modus vivendi" being considered with a peaceful conclusion projected for this intricate situation, while at the Federation the fascist leaders were reorganizing their units and issuing orders to their troops.[13] In the afternoon—in the meantime Pavolini had traveled to Menaggio to meet with the Duce—province head Celio, in agreement with the other top officials, called a meeting at the prefecture of fascist and CLN leaders to work out the conditions for the fascists to leave and for the CLN to take over peacefully. There were many fascists but they were disorganized and rather demoralized. [...] Vito Mussolini and Vanni Teodorani[14] wanted to go with the Duce's convoy and asked that if all fascist forces could not be allowed to go to the Valtellina that they allow at least to freely transit to Menaggio. Hearing this statement, a man by the name of Guastoni and calling himself an agent of an Allied secret service made the following offer to Vito and Teodorani. In a friendly way and calling himself "an old fascist," he said he was convinced of the ultimate victory of the Allies and had not approved of Italy's going to war. He had, therefore, gone over to the enemy camp, commuting between Lombardy and Switzerland on secret missions. He told the two men that he fully approved of their intentions, but asked that they prevail upon the Duce to convince him to return and give himself up to the Allies. He then sang the praises of the loyalty, humanity, and wisdom of the Anglo-Americans, and attempted to convince Mussolini's two nephews that the Duce—for whom, he was able to state with certainty, the Americans had the highest esteem and regard—had everything to gain by giving himself up to the Allies, who would treat him chivalrously rather than run the risk of falling into the hands of the Communists, from whom one could not expect anything good. Guastoni also confided that the Anglo-Americans would soon, and radically, eliminate the Communist organizations.

This "man by the name of Guastoni" was very concerned with Mussolini's safety and well-being and was speaking on behalf of the U.S. government. On April 21 he had already met separately with Vittorio Mussolini, the Duce's oldest son, in Milan to try to reach a bloodless surrender.[15] However, Mussolini had a different (and secret) project in mind that he had not even discussed with his son, which was the reason the Guastoni operation was unsuccessful. Yet Guastoni's credentials were impeccable. The letter he had shown Celio, the prefect of Como, as soon as he arrived from Switzerland read: "Bern, April 26, 1945. The Foreign Service of the United States of America—American General Consulate—Bern. Dr. Salvatore Guastoni, in our service and part of the Italian navy, is hereby authorized to negotiate the transfer of power in the best possible manner and avoiding any victims." David Pryce-Jones, who was Allen Dulles' man in Lugano, signed the document.[16] He was just the first and probably the most important of the many men working for Dulles, who was to be overtaken by Churchill's operatives.

The chronicle written by Amicucci was confirmed by the memoirs of Vanni Teodorani, published nine years later in October 1954 in the weekly *Asso di Bastoni* under the title "Perche fu ucciso Mussolini?"[17] "Guastoni assured me that Mussolini would be well treated as a prisoner of war of the United States Armed Forces without being separated from his escort or his entourage. Those who wanted could remain with him and serve him as a prisoner. There would be no threat to his physical well being and certainly not to his dignity then or in the future." It should also be noted that no British agents took part in the meetings at the Como Prefecture. All those who were present worked for the Americans or reported to the Rome government. All the fascist leaders present who were later able to save their own lives (Pino Romualdi, Vito Mussolini, Vanni Teodorani), as well as the anti-fascists (Navy Commander Giovanni Dessì, Major Cosimo Maria De Angelis, and the prefect Renato Celio) agree in their recollections regarding this odd incident.

Even after Mussolini's capture American agents were confident they could succeed. Pino Romualdi, who at that time was deputy secretary of the Fascist Republican party—and a post-war founder of the neo-fascist MSI party—remembered: "At about 9 p.m. [on April 27] navy commander Giovanni Dessì again returned and told me that Mussolini and all the others had been stopped at Musso and that during the night they would be taken across the lake in boats to Bellagio. He told me: 'They will take them to Bellagio. Do you want to be handed over here at the Como police station, which is under partisan control, or do you want to go with the group?' I answered: 'I don't want to be given to the partisans. Put me in with the group.'"[18]

British agents were already operating on location and Mussolini, together with Claretta Petacci, was about to be taken from the small barracks of the Guardia di Finanza at Germasino and transferred to a place known only to Captain Neri. It was a small, modest house in the hills near Bonzanigo, a hamlet of the village of Tremezzina, some thirty kilometers to the south, about half a kilometer from the villa owned by Sir William Henderson.

Churchill's decision to control Italy politically was confirmed by one of the best known American agents in Italy during the Second World War, Peter Tompkins, who writes unambiguously in a recent book: "It was very easy for the British to prevent the Americans from taking the Duce. The Italian partisans arranged everything, but a British secret service agent of Italian ancestry actually encouraged them to quickly close the Mussolini chapter. [...] The death of Claretta becomes meaningless if it is not factored into the Mussolini-Churchill correspondence. She knew about it and had to be eliminated."[19]

Tompkins further speculates:

> Why must an agreement between Churchill and Mussolini, which had been reached during the meetings at Porto Ceressio and on Lake Iseo, be so radically erased as to require the killing of Mussolini and Claretta Petacci? Churchill's reputation would have been seriously damaged had it become known that he was plotting with the Duce of fascism and a few Nazi generals in Italy in order to have Italian and German forces join the Western Allies to fight the USSR together. This especially from some-

one who knew that the 20 million Soviet dead in the Second World War had saved Europe from the rule of Hitler and the Nazis. It was much too early for the world to accept the ideas that the former British prime minister would announce at his speech in Fulton, Missouri.[20]

The military espionage career of Peter Tompkins is of great interest. Born in Athens, Georgia, in 1919, Tompkins spent much of his childhood on the estate his parents owned in Forte dei Marmi, the well-known resort area in Tuscany. Since childhood he spoke flawless Italian. When the war began Tompkins was already a Rome correspondent for the *New York Herald Tribune*. In 1941 he was recruited by Colonel William Donovan, then "Coordinator of Information" for President Roosevelt, and participated in secret operations in Greece. After the American landings in Sicily in July 1943 he was sent to Rome where he had many friends in high places, among them Crown Prince Umberto of Savoy—who was to become King Umberto II; Duke Aimone of Savoy Aosta, who was King of Croatia; and Camillo Caetani, who had been his classmate at Harvard. But it is interesting to note the circumstances as Tompkins describes them: "I was unaware of the fact that the British, who wanted exclusive control of espionage in Italy, had refused to provide an aircraft for me to parachute to the outskirts of Rome. [...] Only at the beginning of September 1943 was the local OSS-Italy chief, Vincent Scamporino, an Italian-American who had been a labor leader in Connecticut, able to organize my parachute drop with the 82nd Airborne just to the north of Rome on the morning of September 9."[21]

The 82nd Airborne's drop was cancelled at the last moment and Tompkins had to reach Rome from Palermo via a PT boat, which stopped in Salerno. His mission took him to Rome, where by the spring of 1944 he became the head of the OSS in the city. Tompkins was active in military operations along the Gothic Line during the winter of 1944–1945. At the time of the liberation of northern Italy, rather than being sent to Milan, he was transferred by Allen Dulles to Weisbaden, "to work against the USSR" as he writes in his memoirs. In those days American intelligence did not hesitate to recruit former Nazis and fascists, who were thought to be very important, to fight the cold war against the Soviet Union. Tompkins did not agree and his commanding officers preferred to move him far away from Rome, where James Angleton took over his duties.

In the end some of these ideological disagreements within American intelligence may very well explain why the keys to the bloody conclusion of fascism were held by the British.

Chapter X

CLARETTA PETACCI
AND THE MYSTERY OF HER DIARIES

The mystery of Claretta and her brother Marcello, whom no one had ever condemned to death. They both knew too many secrets. Over sixty years have passed since their executions and the Italian State remains silent about the papers and notebooks Claretta had left to her sister Myriam and that the authorities had illegally seized. In the meantime, many of those papers have disappeared.

I n August 1999 in the popular column by veteran journalist Indro Montanelli, entitled "La Stanza" in *Corriere della Sera*, an ongoing discussion began regarding the diaries of Claretta Petacci, which had either disappeared or perhaps had been classified as state secrets. The issue of the diaries was revived by a dispute that started some years before, involving this writer and his friend and colleague, the historian and researcher Alessandro Zanella, and a number of ministerial offices.

A reader of the *Corriere* asked why former Minister of the Interior Giorgio Napolitano had prevented Luciano Garibaldi and Alessandro Zanella from being authorized to view the diaries of the Duce's mistress. Indro Montanelli answered that he "very much doubted that a diary of Claretta Petacci in fact existed," and added: "I think in any case that its author would be unable to go beyond simple gossip. Therefore, I do not understand why Napolitano would have prevented the historians from seeing it."

To Montanelli's reply came a response from Giorgio Napolitano, repeating in great detail the various requests made by Luciano Garibaldi and Alessandro Zanella and explaining why his secretary, Mr. Abate, in his response to the two scholars had denied them any access to the Petacci papers. In his answer Montanelli wrote that he agreed with Napolitano.

This author, who, up to that point, remained discreetly at bay from the debate, then decided to step in by writing the following letter to Montanelli that was published in its entirety:

> With reference to the letter to the editor by Francesco Satta ("Stanza" of August 21) and the reply by the Hon. Giorgio Napolitano ("Stanza" of August 23) regarding the diaries kept by Claretta Petacci. What the Hon. Napolitano states as former minister of the interior is unexceptionable. Actually it is since 1995 (the ending of the fifty-year "secrecy" period of documents containing state secrets) that with my colleague Alessandro Zanella, author of the book *L'ora di Dongo*, I have been expecting some kind of response. Precisely—as written in the request to the ministry of the interior, the latest one—"the confirmation within the diaries of Claretta Petacci of information that we already have secured regarding State relations during the four final months of the RSI between Benito Mussolini and British Prime Minister Winston Churchill." Once again we repeat our original request: "What the writers are requesting is a consultation limited to the specific event as described in the preceding paragraph having nothing to do with what was established in the 2nd part of the quoted DPR

1409/63 ("secrecy" for seventy years of papers regarding purely private circumstances of individuals), but that historical researchers cannot be further prevented since the fifty-year provision of the law covering confidential State documents has passed. In conclusion, these writers are requesting partial access under the supervision of the archivists, barring which we must conclude that unjustified obstacles to the work of free historical researchers are being created by the representatives of the State." Undersecretary Abate answered no, in the name and for Minister Napolitano [literally: "for the Minister"]. And, my dear Montanelli, do you know why? Because—and this is his exact response—"in the course of the required expert research no information has been found relating to the scholar's field of research." Therefore, dear Montanelli, as our master you must be correct, since you have written that poor Claretta's diaries could only contain gossip.

Montanelli's comments to our letter finally closed the dispute with these words: "I do not intend to turn this page into an arena of tensions about the historical value of Claretta's diaries that, as far as I am aware, did not excite the appetite of a document collector such as De Felice."

This was true. Probably De Felice did not have the time to get interested because he had died prematurely, to everyone's regret. However, before his death De Felice had time to state his belief in the "British connection" to the death of Mussolini and Claretta Petacci. He did so on three occasions: in a book of interviews[1] and in the course of two interviews—in *L'Espresso* of September 11 and in the *Corriere della Sera* of November 19, 1995. In the interview in *L'Espresso* one can read the following statement: "The British had decided that Mussolini must not be alive to stand trial because what he was liable to say could create gigantic problems." Not only because of what *he* could say but what could be gleaned with definite and precise references to times and dates and written documents from Claretta Petacci (from the pages of her own diary). This was the reason why Claretta died and her diaries disappeared. De Felice was even more explicit in his interview in the *Corriere della Sera.*

> The documents in my possession lead me to draw one conclusion: Benito Mussolini was killed by a group of partisans from Milan upon the request of the British secret services. There was interest in preventing the fascist leader from ever going to trial. The British suggestion was "Get rid of him," even though the clauses of the armistice called for his being turned over. For the British it was much better that Mussolini be dead. Their national interest was at stake, tied to the explosive compromises in the correspondence that the British prime minister was thought to have exchanged with Mussolini before and during the war.

As for the always intelligent and deep comments of the final book of interviews, De Felice made one in particular that this author sees contradicting the rest of his historical account when he states that the Duce's death was not "the most important thing in his life." Yet the fact that all of the Italian press gave space—among all the non-conformist and courageous positions he set forth in *Rosso e Nero*—almost exclusively to the short chapter dedicated to Mussolini's death showed that the opposite was true. It showed that the truth about Benito Mussolini's death was and will continue to be one of the keys to the history—not only of Italy—but of the twentieth century.

As far as scientific research per se is concerned, Mussolini being killed by the partisans following a decision of the Communists is one matter and his death at the hands of the British or, at least—as De Felice was speculating—of Italian partisans inspired by one or more British agents, is something else.

This is obviously a conundrum of contemporary history that needs to be unraveled to avoid having mythology and legend (the "vulgate," as De Felice rightly described it) replace historical truth. While Mussolini appears to have been acting with patriotic and long-term perspectives in mind when he created the RSI (as De Felice states it, in order to avoid having Hitler "transform Italy into a new Poland"), he also showed a keen and far-reaching vision in his approach to the great powers that beginning with 1943 appeared to be winning the dreadful world war. With Roosevelt and Stalin, who both loathed and hated him, Churchill was the only remaining leader with whom Mussolini could hope to seek the least bloody ending for fascism. And Churchill was an early admirer. After meeting the Duce in Rome in January 1927 as Chancellor of the Exchequer in the government of Stanley Baldwin, Churchill held a press conference at which he expressed excessive praise for Mussolini and fascism: "If I were an Italian," he said, "I would have been completely with you fascists from the beginning to the end of your victorious struggle against the bestial appetites and the passions of Leninism: your movement has rendered a service to the entire world."[2]

Many people at this time are "discovering" the supposedly bizarre "truths" regarding the Mussolini-Churchill correspondence by copying (poorly, in many cases) the work of historians, journalists, and researchers, such as Arrigo Petacco, Franco Bandini, Silvio Bertoldi, Gaspare Di Sclafani, Alessandro Zanella, Fabio Andriola, and others. There should be a renewed sense of the "official Italy," to guard the archives, the documents and the sources of its history. Some sixty years after the events it is still not known officially how many Italians were executed after April 25, 1945, while daily newspapers and weekly magazines regularly publish extremely detailed accountings of the "desaparcidos" in Argentina. Can it still be possible that the Italian State will remain officially silent about the exact numbers of members of the armed forces of the RSI who were executed *after* the war had ended, when they were being held as POWs and as such were entitled to the protection of the Geneva Conventions? This was clearly stated in the text of the surrender document signed on April 29, 1945, at the Royal Palace of Caserta by the German plenipotentiaries empowered to act in the name and for the account of the commander in chief of the fascist forces, Marshal Rodolfo Graziani. Why is it so threatening to inform Italians, and especially the new generations—who never even imagined such horrors—that the dictum "Italians are nice people" can be rather hollow? Who is keeping the archives closed? Why are the letters and diaries of Claretta Petacci not returned to her nephew and legitimate heir Ferdinando? Do the authorities fear somehow revealing the true role that this woman played, not just in the life of one man, Benito Mussolini, but in the history of Italy? And, above all, to reveal that she played a positive and not a negative role—otherwise wouldn't the diaries have been published a long time ago? Actually the Petacci papers must first be examined by a group of historians representing every faction and not only the faction favored by current political correctness. What is of historical interest must be made public without anyone benefiting financially from it. This applies to both the Left, which had been in power until the mid-1990s, and the Right, which has been in power since then, but that displays the same indifference to history and to the rights of individuals.[3]

In 1983 this writer had a long interview with General Karl Wolff—the former head of the SS and of the German police in Italy during the RSI period. General Wolff stated that, among other information, the Germans were reading all the correspondence and recording all the phone calls between Villa Feltrinelli (Mussolini's residence) and Villa Mirabella (where Claretta was living). The content of the exchange of letters and telephone calls, especially during the final months of the RSI, was certainly not devoted to amorous messages—that period had long passed—but rather dealt with dramatic political, military, and diplomatic issues. These also included Mussolini's contacts with Winston Churchill through intermediaries. Wolff had similar contacts of his own and even traveled to Bern in Switzerland as he negotiated with the Allies (and Allen Dulles in particular) for the surrender of all German armies in the south. Why did the Italian government at the time (in the 1990s) refuse to let those papers be read by those who had legitimately requested to have access to them?

The political context: the requests for access began after April 25, 1995, when the post-Communists and their allies controlled the Italian government. The historical context: Luciano Garibaldi and Alessandro Zanella could not make the requests before that date since the answer could only be negative because of the fifty-year limit the State must enforce to cover such secrets. Since the documents contain "State secrets," classified as such by the Supreme Court of Italy in April 1956, the lifting of the secrecy was supposed to be effective as of April 25, 1995. The travesty used by the State Archives, the ministry of cultural affairs, and finally the ministry of the interior, was that since the diaries include the "purely private situations of individuals" they were to remain secret for seventy years. This was an absurd allegation, made even more serious by the fact that those making this decision had been—at least officially, according to the documents—a few bureaucrats inside the ministry who had established that the diaries "do not include information pertinent to the field of research of the two scholars." Meaning that Claretta's diaries did not mention either the British or Winston Churchill.

How can those conclusions be trusted? Unless the most important pages had been torn from the diaries, which would be more than plausible and consistent with this author's long activity as a historian and his experience with the diaries of Carlo Alberto Biggini the RSI's minister of national education. The most important pages from those notebooks that I obtained in 1982 were missing, the ones relating specifically to the copies of the correspondence with the British that the Duce had personally handed over to the minister.

There exists a very eloquent precedent to the legal action taken by the parents of Claretta Petacci, namely Doctor Francesco Saverio Petacci, medical doctor at the Vatican, and Giuseppina Persichetti, as well as her sister Myriam, against the State for the return of the letters and diaries of their loved one seized by the Italian State in 1950. At first the court in Rome ruled in favor of the Petaccis; however, the sentence was overturned by the prosecution and the case went to the court of appeals. A harsh battle took place between the State attorneys and those of the Petacci family, Domenico D'Amico and Ugo De Pilato. The State attorneys requested that the first ruling be reversed "because Clara Petacci was Mussolini's political adviser and his inspiration and had such influence on him in determining fundamental decisions affecting the nation's fate.

All the writings of Clara Petacci therefore acquired a political significance and historical value requiring their preservation in the State archives." The attorneys for the defense unsuccessfully argued historical precedents involving Virginia Oldoini, the "Countess of Castiglione,"[4] and Margherita Sarfatti.[5] The former had sold (at a very high price) in 1889 at an auction in Paris the love letters addressed to her by Napoleon III, while Margherita Sarfatti had sold the love letters she had received from Mussolini to an American publisher. No legal authority had attempted to prevent those sales. The Rome court of appeals ruled that "the texts are so important that their publication could harm good diplomatic relations with other countries.[6] The ruling was later confirmed by the Supreme Court in April 1956 regarding the ultimate fate of the material in the State Archives "because the documents provided by the ministry of the interior indicate that Claretta Petacci was in the habit of taking initiatives or at least of interfering in government matters, particularly regarding the appointment of individuals to important state positions."[7]

How did Claretta's papers end up with the Italian State rather than her legitimate heirs according to her will, namely with her sister Myriam? The events leading to that outcome are as follows.

April 19, 1945, was a rainy cold day over Lake Garda and all of Lombardy. The Stefani Agency (the official Italian wire service) on its teletypes was spreading the news of the piercing of the Gothic Line by the Allies. Mussolini, the 61-year-old leader of the RSI, left the Villa Feltrinelli at Gargnano to go to the Milan prefecture to decide what course to take (either surrender or fight to the last man). Mussolini told his 32-year-old mistress Claretta Petacci, who was spending endless days in solitude at the Villa Mirabella at Gardone Riviera inside D'Annunzio's Vittoriale Park, to remain safely at the villa under the guard of German troops. The Duce said he would tell her when and how to leave with her family for the safety of Spain.

But Claretta could not stand by and wait. She put on a blue suit, an embroidered silk blouse, and raccoon fur coat. Then she asked her orderly, SS Captain Franz Spögler, to drive her to Milan at top speed in the Volkswagen military van he used. Spögler obeyed and took her to the Piazza San Babila in Milan at the corner of the Via Matteotti (then known as Corso Littorio), where Claretta's parents and sister Myriam were living in a rented apartment as they were getting ready to flee to Spain. They were hoping Claretta had decided to join them but she quickly disappointed them: "I came to Milan to be near him." She told only her sister Myriam that before leaving she gave to Carlo and Caterina Cervis, the caretakers of the Villa Mirabella, her most precious world possession, for safekeeping: two large boxes containing six hundred love letters the Duce had sent to her in the course of twelve years, as well as a diary started in 1933 (the year when, at age twenty-one, she first met Mussolini) and ending on the day of his departure to Milan, April 18, 1945.

In October* the Cervis couple became her best friends and confidants. Villa Mirabella was the property of Countess Maria Gallese di Montenevoso, the widow of Gabriele D'Annunzio. Caterina Cervis was the Countess' lady-in-waiting. Therefore, the Cervis couple and Claretta were living under the same roof. Claretta spent her interminable days waiting for rapid and increasingly rare visits by Mussolini, while at a table in the enormous sitting room she wrote page after page in her diary. Claretta wrote everything the Duce confided to her in letters and over the phone in those pages: not gossip (there was no time for that), but political, military, and diplomatic information. He also mentioned his final hopes to save his life. Those pages are therefore an extraordinary historical document.

A few days later her parents and Myriam left for the military airfield at Ghedi, near Brescia, where a plane was to fly them to Barcelona. When she went to say goodbye Claretta slipped an envelope into her sister's handbag, telling her: "Please open it only when you reach Spain." Myriam fought back her tears. The letter was Claretta's last will and testament; this is the complete text:

---

* October of 1944, when she was transferred from the Villa Fiordalisio, which had been the scene of a violent argument with Donna Rachele, to the Villa Mirabella.

Don't be sad about us. I am following my destiny that is the same as his. I will never leave his side whatever may happen. I will not destroy by a cowardly choice the great beauty of my offering and I will not stop trying to help him and be with him as long as I can. You know where all my papers are. Guard and respect them. You should be the one to have them: you should hold them and then in due course you will give them to your child, if God gives you one or to Benghino.[8] You will understand which one can best understand them. You, who have witnessed my entire love life, since you were a small child; you, who have been the little "peacemaker," the "go-between," our "little idiot" of the happier days, you know everything. No one better than you can be the keeper of my writings. You will find his letters. They are a part of me, a sacred remembrance, and an indivisible possession. Whatever may happen, I beseech you, make sure that the truth is finally told. Do not cry over what I am telling you. It is not pessimism nor sadness; it is a desire to feel secure about what is closest to me. Only you can understand me.

April 19, 1950. Following a few years of what was an understandable terror (the Petacci family had every reason to fear ending up like Claretta and her brother Marcello), young Myriam returned to Italy and failed to retrieve those papers. This is how she explains the events in her book:

The matter began in February 1950 when Ferruccio Lanfranchi, a reporter at the *Corriere della Sera*, received an unsigned letter giving the exact spot in the garden of the Cervis couple at Gardone where the crates belonging to my sister were to be found. Lanfranchi, to avoid any responsibility, contacted the police and our family. After digging two crates were found containing sixty-eight packages, a few envelopes, and a small trunk. The representative of the ministry of the interior took everything to Rome. From the brief official information we found out that they contained my sister's diaries from February

1933 to April 18, 1945, or fifteen volumes in all; the diary of
the thirty-six days she spent at the Novara prison; six hundred
letters from the Duce; notes, newspapers, books, recorded
speeches by Mussolini; photos and other things.[9]

This valuable material was the reason for the lawsuit between
the family of Claretta Petacci and the Italian State, which ended as
we have mentioned earlier in defeat for the Petaccis.

From that time until her death in 1991, Myriam Petacci never
ceased for one instant to demand possession of those papers as
her property. However, her efforts, her legal battles, her petitions
to the various ministries, were all in vain. The attempts made by
Ferdinando Petacci, Claretta's only living heir and nephew (the
son of Marcello, who had been savagely murdered at Dongo) to
recover his aunt's diaries have failed. Ferdinando now lives in dig-
nified poverty in the United States[10] and the Italian State, shamelessly, after abetting the murder of his father and only brother
Benvenuto, nicknamed "Benghi" (he lost his mind after witness-
ing his father's murder from the balcony of the hotel in Dongo
and then died at a very young age), continues to deny an inherit-
ance that is guaranteed to him by law.

What is the official reply? A decision by the Italian Supreme
Court dated April 12, 1956, gives the papers to the Italian State
"since they contain references to Italy's foreign and internal policy."
However, the Italian State, having reached the fifty-year limit for
"state secrets," still refuses to release any of them.

We cannot close the chapter about Claretta Petacci without
denying another legend that sounds like some cheap romantic novel
or soap opera. This concerns the traditionally held belief that
Mussolini told his jailers that Claretta was part of the convoy so
that he could see her and speak to her. Nothing could be further
from the truth. Claretta was traveling under a false name with false
Spanish documents in her brother Marcello's Alfa Romeo, along
with Marcello's companion, Zita Ritossa, and their two boys
Benvenuto and Ferdinando, who were also using documents pro-

vided by the Spanish consul in Milan. Marcello had been for some time—under the Duce's instructions—in contact with British agents, a fact that was well known within Mussolini's entourage—to the point that the fascist leaders, as they were lined up along the lake front at Dongo about to be shot, refused to have him with them, calling Marcello a traitor. Today we may say for sure that, along with his sister Claretta, Marcello Petacci "had to be" executed because he knew too many embarrassing secrets. This was confirmed in a phone conversation that took place in March 2003 between Ferdinando Petacci and former partisan leader Bill. This is how Ferdinando Petacci recounted the phone call with Bill to this writer:

> Before starting the executions at the lake front Colonel Valerio gave Bill the order to take my father from the Dongo hotel because—said Valerio—he was Vittorio Mussolini, the Duce's son, and that he too had to be shot. Bill quickly discovered my father's real identity. He revealed that he was really a British agent using the cover name of Fosco and produced proof to back this up. Bill told this to Pedro, who quickly went to tell Colonel Valerio. But Valerio did not change his mind and repeated his order to get him so that he could be shot with the others.
>
> Why do you think he did this? I asked Ferdinando Petacci. "Because he already had a deal with the British to get rid of my father, along with Claretta. Since my father was not on the list of the fifteen to be shot, he still needed an excuse to have him executed. And the excuse—either created on the spot or perhaps also suggested by British agents—was that he really was Vittorio Mussolini.[11]
>
> The final confirmation comes from Myriam Petacci: "When Bill brought Marcello to the square, Valerio, who had taken my brother's gold possessions, said: "If we don't shoot him for being Vittorio Mussolini we'll shoot him as Petacci." But no one had ordered the killing of Vittorio Mussolini. And no one had ordered my brother's execution. What then?[12]

Chapter XI

AN EXECUTIONER WITHOUT PROOF

*In 1994 a former Italian partisan commander, Bruno Giovanni Lonati,
revealed that he had killed Mussolini, following the orders of a British
agent who, in turn, murdered Claretta Petacci. No one believed Lonati
because he could not produce convincing proof to back up his story.
Many unimpeachable confirmations surfaced later on. They are
mentioned here for the first time. But perhaps the commander
did not tell the whole truth.*

Lonati's book is published

In the fall of 1994, without any kind of public relations effort,
Mursia Publishers in Milan printed and distributed a book entitled *Quel 28 aprile. Mussolini e Claretta: la verità* [That April 28.
Mussolini and Claretta: The Truth]. The author, Bruno Giovanni
Lonati, wrote that he had shot Benito Mussolini and had done so at
the request of a British secret service agent called John, who in
turn shot Claretta Petacci to death. It was a startling revelation, of
worldwide interest. But as the conventional wisdom goes, if other

more important publishers had turned down the manuscript, and if Mursia had been the one to finally decide to publish it almost silently, it could mean that the story itself had little credibility.

This seemed to be the case, and it did appear to lack credibility. The story could have been invented from the first line to the last. There was no corroborating evidence, no proof, no confirmation. It looked like a fake and nothing less. That was how it looked, as far as I was concerned when I first read the manuscript some six months before it was published.

My articles had just been serialized in the Milan evening newspaper *La Notte*,[1] regarding the events of the tragedy at Dongo and Mezzegra, where for the first time I offered the theory of the "British thread" in the executions of Mussolini and Claretta Petacci. I received an excited phone call from the editor-in-chief, Massimo Donelli.

> "You hit the bull's-eye! I have a gentleman sitting in front of me who has read your articles and claims to be the one who killed the Duce under orders from the British. He left me a copy of the book he's just finished writing and would like you to read it before it gets published.
>
> "Who is he? What's his name?" I asked
>
> "Lonati, Dr. Bruno Lonati. He's a retired manager at Fiat."
>
> "Lonati...Lonati. I know who that is. When will his book be published?"
>
> "Well, in the fall, from what he told me."
>
> "By whom?"
>
> "By Mursia."

I said that I would pick up the manuscript and then meet with the author face to face. Did he have the phone number? Yes, he lives in Brescia. Fine.

I read the text in one sitting. First of all, who was this man Lonati? His name was well known in the tight-knit circle of those who specialized in the Dongo events (they are called the "Dongologists") and who never could believe that the Italian

Communist party as an emanation of Soviet Russia could tell the truth about anything and certainly not about the end of fascism. Lonati had already revealed his role many years before to writer and newsman Roberto Gervaso, who was writing a biography of the Duce's mistress.[2] Gervaso published Lonati's account in the book *Claretta* without any comment, taking no position whatsoever, as any serious historian would if he was unable to find any corroborating evidence to confirm the truth of what he learned.

When he handed me his manuscript at the editorial offices of the newspaper at Via Vitruvio, 43 in Milan, we agreed that I would call him to set another appointment as soon as I had finished reading it. Bruno Giovanni Lonati was a man of 73. He was a peaceful and polite person with the manners of a gentleman and a rather sad look in his eyes; he was originally from Legnano. During his entire career he had been a highly respected company manager and the author of technical books on mechanical engineering that had been translated into various languages. From 1936 to 1956 he worked at the Franco Tosi Company. In the meantime he served in the military (from 1941 to September 8, 1943) and took part in the Resistance as the commander of a partisan division made up of the Garibaldi Brigades 111, 112, and 113 operating in Milan. He was politically active and a union member in the Italian Communist party until February 1946. After that he dropped everything and moved to Turin, first as the head of a mid-sized company and later at Fiat where he also held managerial positions overseas. After 1980 he headed a large company in Bari specializing in mechanical engineering. Later still he was an industrial consultant to various companies. In brief he was a responsible person, a man with "gravitas," as they say.

Lonati's manuscript is as brief as it is dry, almost like a military report. It took only a few hours for me to read it. His story in essence is as follows.

At 4 p.m. on April 27, 1945, Lonati was in the school building on the Viale Lombardia in Milan. With his men he was interrogating some fascists who had been arrested, when Captain John appeared unexpectedly. Lonati had met him towards the middle of March.

He knew that John was a British army captain and a member of the secret services who parachuted into northern Italy but quickly went to Switzerland where he set up his own network of informers and collaborators extending over Lombardy and specifically around Como and Varese. John lived in the same boarding house as Lonati on the via Vallazze in Milan, using a false name. From there he organized his partisan activities. They were on friendly terms. John even confided the history of his family to Lonati, since he was of Italian origin. They had emigrated to England at the beginning of the century, setting up a small tailor shop in London and, later, a larger enterprise of men's clothing. The business was run by his brothers while John opted for a military career.

John came right to the point: "Take your weapons and two men you trust and come with me. My orders are to take Mussolini into custody. He's been captured on Lake Como." Lonati trusted John completely. He called Bruno and Gino, who had both been part of his "Division" for some time. This is how he described them:

> I used to drive around in a car with my trusted men. Their names as fighters were Bruno and Gino. Bruno was a few years older than I; he was very stocky and always smiling. He had a pleasant, happy-looking face; he looked like a pushover but since he was originally a peasant he was really very shrewd, practical, and dedicated. He had been a good fighter and did not possess a mean streak. Gino on the other hand was about thirty and more of a malicious type. He was thin, had dark skin and curly hair. He also had a great record as a partisan fighter and was an excellent driver.

Lonati also brought along a third partisan fighter, a very young man known for his bravery. His name was Lino. They took a .9 caliber Beretta, Sten submachine guns, hand grenades, and left in a Fiat 1100 that had been requisitioned from a doctor. They spent the night at a villa at Brunate overlooking Como, where Franco of the British Special Forces provided information. The next morn-ing, April 28, the "commando" left for Bonzanigo and the De Maria house where Luigi Canali (Captain Neri) had taken Mussolini and Claretta Petacci the night before. They got there after a shoot-out at Argegno at a barricade manned by a group of stupid partisans who had failed to recognize them. John did not hesitate and fired an entire clip at those misguided men who fired back. Lino was shot dead. Gino drove on in the bullet-riddled car.

Once they reached the De Maria house John and his men quickly disarmed, tied up, and gagged the three partisans whom Neri had posted there to guard the Duce. It was then that John finally told Lonati and his two companions their mission's objective: to seize Mussolini's secret documents before the Communists did so for Stalin and shoot the Duce and his mistress.

Unfortunately the papers were missing. Mussolini said they had been taken from him at Dongo. John began cursing; he would go and get the documents later or other members of the "Special Forces" would do so.

The fateful moment came at around 11 a.m., when Lonati shot Mussolini and John fired at Claretta Petacci. "This woman knows everything about Mussolini, as well as the contents of the papers. If we don't do it the others will anyway." The two dead bodies were hidden on the ground floor of the De Maria house. That is where Walter Audisio would find them in the afternoon and "re-shoot" them both—after taking them to the gates of the Villa Belmonte close by.

End of story.

I read and reread the text. What could I say? I think that among the "Dongologists" I am the one who is closest to accepting this story as plausible but without any kind of proof. That was the gist of my conversation with Lonati when we met again in the Via Vitruvio. Could he give me the full names of Bruno and Gino, I asked? No, he did not know them. What about a name and address for John? He couldn't because he was sworn to discretion. Were any photos taken of the executions? Yes but John took them and he, Lonati, never saw them. He did say that he would provide proof during the coming year (1995), on April 28, when the fifty-year limit would end, and when—as he kept on repeating—"the London archives will be opened." But, I answered, the archives of the Public Record Office in London *have* been open since 1975 and there is no trace of the entire matter.

I was sorry to disappoint Lonati but I could not publish anything. We parted with a kind of regret but also with mutual respect for one another. I thought about the whole story often over the next few days. Out of an old habit as a reporter I spent some time checking things out. Lonati turned out to be a true partisan commander of the Garibaldi units. I spent a day at Argegno, first at the archives and bureau of vital statistics of the municipality, and then with the parish priest (where I found nothing), then at the cemetery to find out if Lino and the other partisans killed on April 28 were buried there (but I did not find anything). Finally, I had a chat with some of the local old timers. There, I found some corroboration at last. Specifically at the "Barchetta" café where I approached some older men who remembered the short but deadly shoot-out very clearly. However, at the end of our talk—as it often happens around these parts—they politely refused to give their names and addresses. I knew that they were not lying. There really had been a firefight on the morning of April 28 at Argegno between a partisan roadblock and a car (a Fiat "1100" perhaps?) on its way to Dongo and some people were killed. I received confirmation that several hand grenades were thrown from the car. Those men were serious and it was a "commando-type" action by any standard.

I was wondering how Lonati could know this. My explanation was—if indeed he was intent upon telling a false but plausible story—that it must have been simple enough for him as it was for me to find out about that firefight. Similarly, how could he possibly invent the secret base at Brunate, above Como, in the villa where the "commando" had spent the night of April 27? It was precisely to a villa in that same location, clearly a secret base of the British Special Forces, that Captain Neri was to bring Mussolini and Claretta

Petacci. But there had been some problems and Neri had opted to fall back on the De Maria house.

What then? Still, in considering the possibility that Lonati had intelligently constructed a colossal falsehood, even that strange coincidence could be explained. Lonati could have found out about the villa at Brunate by reading the well-known book by Franco Bandini, *Vita e morte segreta di Mussolini*,[3] and adapting it to fit his imaginative account.

When Lonati's book was published that fall I answered those requesting my opinion (the dailies *Avvenire* and *Il Secolo d'Italia*) by saying: "The story is plausible but remains unsubstantiated." And I added: "Too bad. Because for years I had imagined that Mussolini died exactly that way." Here is an excerpt of the interview I gave to *Il Secolo d'Italia*, published on September 9, 1994:

> *The version by Bruno Giovanni Lonati sensationally confirms your theory that an officer of the British secret service, even though using "native help," had killed Mussolini.*
>
> Lonati's story is plausible, but unfortunately it remains uncorroborated. I always felt that the Special Forces could have been called upon to carry out the mission—to retrieve the papers and physically eliminate Mussolini and Claretta Petacci (who was in the know of all Mussolini's secrets, even the most confidential ones). There existed a vast network of Italian partisans located in key positions. I even think I have identified a few of those "anchor" persons.
>
> *For example?*
>
> For example, Captain Neri, better known as Luigi Canali, and his lover, the partisan woman Gianna, whose real name was Giuseppina Tuissi—both of them were Communists, yet both were killed by the Communist party a few days after the events at Dongo. Why? Very simple. Because they decided to obey the Special Forces rather than the orders coming from the Party (and therefore Moscow's orders). There are still people on Lake Como to this day who know about this but are afraid to talk.

You don't mean to say that the Communists can kill to this day?

No, but they can destroy people's careers, and the children, and grandchildren of those who might be tempted to talk. I know a few of them and I am pressuring them to tell me their story. They know a lot and all confirm that my thread—the "British" thread—is the right one. Yet to this day the Communists still have the power to intimidate in those parts. When I travel to the lake to talk with these people it feels as though I am suddenly in Sicily in the grip of the Mafia rather than all the way up north. No one can voice the slightest doubt that Mussolini's "executioners" were anything but those "glorious followers of Garibaldi" with a red bandanna around their necks.

Four years later this writer was able to personally experience, through a decision of the Italian Supreme Court in Milan, what could happen to anyone with those kinds of doubts who dares identify the liars by name.

2. Lonati's unpublished memoir

Two years after the publication of Lonati's book, the editor of the monthly *Storia Illustrata* gave me a long typescript he had just received: "Here, this stuff is for you," he said. There were twenty-four typed pages with handwritten corrections by Lonati. It is the chronicle of his frustrations, of the useless efforts of his more than two-year period to find proof, even of the smallest kind, that would indicate that he was telling the truth in his book. It was a very bitter and final acknowledgment that he had failed.

I read and reread. I was thinking of calling him for another face-to-face conversation, to take him through another "third degree." But to what avail? His memoir and confession already contained everything and actually nothing. Nothing that could justify a big news story, a scoop. I filed the pages away in one of my many "Mussolini-Petacci" drawers. It could come in handy if I ever decided to write a book on the "British connection," I thought.

Now that time was at hand. I retrieved those twenty-four pages entitled "An Unfinished Story." The text provided the answers to all the questions that anyone using common sense would have asked Mussolini's self-proclaimed executioner. Who were the persons with you? Are they alive or dead? Why have they never confirmed your story? Did you take any pictures at that location? Where are those pictures? Did you try talking with the British? What did they say? How did you manage with the Communists, with the "Party"? Have they ever attempted to seek revenge?

Reading those pages once more as I began writing this chapter, I could see that Lonati did what I would have done if, having made such a sensational assertion, no one had taken me seriously. I would have desperately sought ways to confirm my statements. Lonati began looking for such confirmation locally on Lake Como and getting the same feeling that for so many years I, and scores of other historians and "Dongologists," also experienced. In Lonati's words, "the old people saw things and their children are in the know but will not speak. It seems as if they have all spread the word: they refuse, don't remember, and will not answer. They know what happened but keep their mouths shut." "Could it be," asks Lonati "that the men at Mezzegra did not notice that at 6 p.m. the bodies of Mussolini and Claretta Petacci were already stiff when they were loaded on board the truck? Yet they could not have been shot less than two hours before according to the official version." And he provides the answer: "They did notice it, and said so several times to the friend who accompanied me during my research." But to Lonati they answered that they could not remember.

At some point during this unusual personal investigation around the lake Lonati learned the name of a very elderly lady. The woman had spoken confidentially to a friend that she had witnessed, at 11 a.m. on the morning of April 28, 1945, as she looked on unseen from behind a little wall around her house in the via Nuova, near Zampa, the execution of Mussolini and Claretta Petacci. It took place at the bottom of the little street going to the De Maria house. It was precisely the time and place of Lonati's story. The woman's son had been one of the youths who had loaded the bodies on the truck in the little square at Mezzegra.

Lonati listened to the narrative, delivered in a "clear and firm voice," by the lady's friend and recorded it on a cassette in front of his two companions who accompanied him as witnesses. One hour later, without the old man's knowledge, the two witnesses went to the woman's front door and asked her to confirm what she said. She denied everything. Nothing of the sort ever happened. Had the man invented everything? Was the old woman lying?

What about the British? Anyone aware, even through hearsay, of the methods and traditions of Her Majesty's Secret Service cannot escape the following dilemma: either Lonati had invented everything and therefore the matter was of no concern to them; or he was telling the truth—but since no one took him seriously he could go on living at no personal risk because world opinion was not convinced that the murder of Claretta Petacci ("by now viewed as the twentieth century's Juliet" as Lonati says) was carried out by an Englishman acting under the orders of Prime Minister Churchill.

Lonati made every possible attempt to contact the British. In 1981, when he decided to give his account to Roberto Gervaso, who was writing the biography *Claretta*, Lonati traveled to London. He went looking for John, who in 1945 had told Lonati to "remain silent for at least thirty-five years." "After that time I and my two companions, Bruno and Gino, would be free to go public with the facts." He added that "only fifty years later, in the British archives, we could obtain unimpeachable confirmation because everything was written, documented, and photographed."

In July 1981 Lonati spoke with John's brother, Mr. X, who was the manager of a large London retail store. He was told that John was in Canada. Lonati left his phone number as he tells the story:

> A few days later John called me; it was a long phone call. His Italian was a bit rusty but we understood each other rather well. He told me he was still connected to the services and had even become one of the heads. He underscored that the documents that concerned me were in good hands and confirmed

that once the fifty-year limit had passed his country's authorities would release them to me. I told him—recalling what he had told me long before in Milan—that once thirty-five years had gone by I intended to go public by telling the story to a reputable Italian scholar. John said he had no problem with that and that I could do as I wished. I told him that I would like to see him in London during the first week of August and that I would be staying at the Royal Lancaster Hotel. A few days later I left with my wife. He had given me a phone number in Coventry where I could reach him; however, the number turned out to be nonexistent. Days passed and there was no sign of John. On the following Wednesday, precisely on August 12, 1981, as we returned to the hotel we found a message from John, which I still have. It said he could not come to London and was coming to Italy at the end of August. From then on I never again had any contact with or news from him. I must say that during the entire time of our visit to London we knew that we were being followed.

In a final attempt before handing over his notes to Roberto Gervaso, Lonati paid a visit to the British consul in Milan, Mr. Thompson, on February 2, 1982, and showed him the text. As Lonati recounted: "The consul authorized me to give the notes to Gervaso for publication in his book and together we wrote the draft of a letter saying that at the fifty-year limit the British authorities would release the documents to me."

The "50-year limit from the events" was finally reached in April 1995. The book, *Quel 28 aprile* (which the historians had been expecting with some skepticism since 1982), had, by then, been published for several months. Everyone remained silent. There was no reaction, and no denial on the part of British authorities. On June 6, 1995, Lonati wrote to the British ambassador to Italy asking for the documents immediately following the execution of Mussolini and Claretta Petacci. No answer was received, only complete silence. The story obviously did not concern them at all.

The only remaining threads were Bruno, Gino, and the other former partisans of the Viale Lombardia. "At least give us the full names of Bruno and Gino, I asked Lonati that day in the office of the editor of *La Notte*, "then I will begin to believe you." His answer was that he did not know them either. At that point Massimo Donelli and I looked at each other and shrugged our shoulders. He really did not know their names and two years later he explained why in the memoir he published in the magazine *Storia Illustrata*:

In the summer of 1995, since the British had not given me the documents I had requested, I went looking for Bruno and Gino. I returned to Milan, to the Viale Lombardia where my commando was headquartered at the local social club, "Arcinova Angelo Fiocchi," named after Angelo Fiocchi, who had been shot by the fascists. I spoke with Dante Cavallari, the founder of the "Circolo," and with Giordano Fiocchi, Angelo's younger brother. I was then able to get information about Bruno, who was the son of a caretaker of a building on the Viale Lombardia and had emigrated to Brazil in 1947 since he was unable to find any work in Italy. I should say at the outset that I am not sure I had found the real Bruno, but had a strong feeling he may be the person. After some more research I found out that in 1959 he had returned to Cremona from São Paulo. I went to Cremona and discovered that since September 2, 1969, he was residing with his wife in Liguria in an apartment he owned. That was where I located him. I got his phone number from the telephone company, called, and made an appointment to meet at his home on a Sunday morning at the end of May. He was over eighty years old and I remembered him as being very stout. Even before asking whether he recognized me or not I explained the reason for my visit. He made a whole set of statements that made me suspicious. Yes, he had been at the headquarters in the Viale Lombardia but his wartime alias, he said, was not Bruno but Luigi; and furthermore he never got to use a weapon. During the days that followed I returned to the social club in the Viale Lombardia, where I was told that Bruno never had an alias as a fighter; it was simply his real name. There were no other partisans by that name. He was the only one. He never even asked me what I was seeking. All along his main response was that indeed he had been a partisan but had not seen any action.

When a frustrated Lonati once again returned to the social club he was introduced to Mario Mazzali, a partisan whose fighting name was Peppone. He confirmed that Bruno had never had an alias and told me that after Liberation he had fled Italy, which he illustrated with some very graphic gestures, clearly meaning that if Bruno had remained in Milan his life would have been at risk. I then asked Peppone" about Gino. "I'll think about it," he answered. He gave me a name and told me to come back in a few weeks. When I returned Peppone was nowhere to be found—one more person staying out of reach. Later on, Fiocchi also became elusive, and oddly enough for an eighty-year-old, I was told he was always having important meetings.

After many years Lonati reestablished his relationship with Giovanni Pesce, head of the GAP brigades in Milan, who holds the gold medal of the Resistance. Pesce is an elderly man but, as Lonati describes him, "clearheaded, bouncy, full of life, and not at all conceited." The old bad blood was forgotten. Lonati spoke of him admiringly and with sympathy, saying that he was "convinced that no one better than he knows how the operations of April 28, 1945, were carried out." The reason was that "Pesce went to Dongo after Valerio and Lampredi had left Milan but on a mission having different objectives that he would never reveal to me." Pesce was to find that those shot at Dongo and Mussolini and Claretta Petacci were indeed dead. "The accepted versions of Mussolini's death that have been published in the last few years as well as the first one by Walter Audisio, which was politically motivated, all made him laugh and I have seen him chuckle." But "he will remain silent as long as he lives." Why? "For the same old reasons, he has no ax to grind, he is living a quiet middle-class lifestyle, and finds all the historical versions acceptable as long as his name is not mentioned and that he is not placed anywhere near Giulino di Mezzegra, even though he was present that day."

Poor Bruno Giovanni Lonati. No one believed him in 1982 when Gervaso published his story in the book; no one believed him in 1994 when he published his book *Quel 28 aprile*. No one believed him as he wrote bitterly at the end of his memoir for *Storia Illustrata*: "For over thirty-five years I kept everything to myself, cutting off any relations with the men I was with at the time. Then, per our agreement, I told the truth. At the same time the British assured me that once the fifty-year time limit was up I would be given the documentation containing the proof. I was in for a bitter surprise at the fifty-year limit. Since what I had been promised was not forthcoming, I attempted to reconnect with the past, something that happened too late and was very difficult, almost impossible to do. Surely I should have started a long time before. All have become statues of stone. They all say that I look younger than my age. So be it. Now, however, my years are hitting me all at once; I can feel my life getting shorter. Mistakes and misplaced trust tend to catch up with you. At the conclusion of my book I wrote: "I certainly wouldn't do it again." Now I can add: "It would have been much better had I kept it all to myself."

3. Mystery man: the "Alpino"*

Apparently Bruno Giovanni Lonati could not (or would not) produce a single scrap of proof confirming the veracity of his story. There appears in his memoir—going even beyond his own intentions—a character he could not possibly have invented because he reappears in a very different situation that we shall examine in the next chapter, a circumstance Lonati could not be aware of. This was the "Alpino."

Who was the Alpino? He was actually a British secret agent who appears at the time of the deadly mission at Bonzanigo. Lonati

---

* Alpino: literally "Alpine man"; refers to a member of the special mountain troops of the Italian army.

was informed of his existence and his role during the overnight stay in the little house between Como and Brunate. The local British agent Franco indicated how the group could reach the house where Mussolini and Claretta Petacci had been taken: "Don't worry, I've already set things up along the way so that someone will show you how to get to the house; after Tremezzo on the right you'll find a man wearing an Alpine hat. Stop, and he'll provide you with information as to the exact location and the path or give you new information. The password is 'Let's go for a nice hike' and the answer is 'I know a nice place.'"

Lonati states in his account:

> Right outside Tremezzo we saw our man—I shall call him the Alpino from now on because he was wearing hiking boots, knickers, a green corduroy jacket, the typical Alpine hat without the feather, and he smoked a pipe. He was holding a walking stick, and was rather short, with a short mustache; he had a lively look on his face. We stopped and exchanged passwords. Then he gave the itinerary the group was to follow: "Keep going. After Azzano there's a sign on the left of the lake indicating Mezzegra. Stay on that road. You'll reach Bonzanigo and then I think you'll have to walk. The house where 'he' is should be toward the end but I don't know which one. If you see any people it's best not to ask any questions. Be very alert when you see some partisans. That's where he should be."
>
> The Alpino reappeared at the end of the mission, and again was bright, well prepared, and very helpful. At the agreed place at Tremezzo the Alpino was there waiting for us. Seeing us from afar he cut across a steep shortcut. The car could barely get through and it was a very bad road. It took us some ten minutes after many winding curves before we reached a barn. Without a word the Alpino opened one of the empty pens and waved at us to enter with the car.
>
> At that point John informed the Alpino of the mission's success and said: "We have not found the papers we were looking for; we must get busy and find out where they are." The

Alpino agreed, then told the group to stay put ("there is something to eat"). In the meantime he would get them a better car
to replace the battered one they arrived in. The Alpino went
off on his bicycle. [...] A little after 4 p.m. we heard the noise
of a car. We jumped up with our weapons and took our positions. It was the Alpino; he had exchanged his bike for a car
identical to ours except that it was black. I asked John: "Don't
tell me that this car is also a coincidence." "Not at all," John
replied; "he knows how to get things done." The Alpino came
inside the house and gave us the latest news. [...] John again
asked him about the documents. "Nothing," answered the
Alpino. "The men of the 52nd Brigade who captured him must
have the papers. There are some very sharp guys but also some
elements I don't like." "All right," said John, "make one more
attempt and let me know. We're going back to Milan and you
know where to find me." "Yes, sir!" answered the Alpino, giving us a military salute. We got in the car he had brought over.

The Alpino then disappears. No one had any information about
him, not his name, address, age, or what became of him. However,
he did not disappear permanently.

He actually made another appearance as a British secret service
agent in the matter of the death of Giuseppina Tuissi (the partisan
woman Gianna), Captain Neri's mistress. Lonati knew nothing about
that case and he knew the part played by the Alpino even less because it surfaced only after the publication of his book, *Quel 28
aprile*. The occasion was the interview by Alessandro Zanella and
this writer of "F. D.," a witness to Gianna's death. The story was
published in a Milan weekly magazine *Noi*, and it is worth citing
here in its entirety.[4]

4. *The missing link: the Alpino in the life and death of Gianna*

The following narrative came to the author and his friend and
colleague, Alessandro Zanella, from a man who shall remain anonymous as "F. D." It was only because of the assurances given by this

writer and Zanella regarding their discretion that F. D. agreed to tell his story as a direct eyewitness. He was in physical fear. In his own words: "The fear of ending up like all the people who got killed because they wanted to talk." This was how, according to his dramatic story, he came into the "life of Captain Neri's companion Gianna. Gianna was being shadowed by a mysterious Englishwoman up to the day of her death, which took place on Saturday, June 23, 1945. The woman in question was about thirty-five years of age, had direct access to the partisan leadership, and disappeared right after the murder.

In April of 1945 I was seventeen, working as a mechanic in a shop in Como that had been requisitioned by the authorities. I was good at fixing cars. Even though I did not have my license I could drive any kind of vehicle very well.

Following the events at Dongo and the capture of Mussolini's column, there was a change of command at Como—from the fascists to the partisans of the CLN. Naturally, we mechanics went over to serve the new masters. I was in charge of driving one of the cars the partisans were using; it had been part of the Mussolini convoy. All the cars were assembled in the garden of the Villa Passalacqua at Moltrasio. There were more than fifty cars with plates from all over Italy (I remember GE, BO, PV, MI, etc.); there was a Fiat 626 truck belonging to the GNR; and a few German motorcycles. I was able to start the engine of one metallic gray Lancia "Aprilia" with GE plates that the partisans on guard had authorized me to keep and asked me to use often when driving them to various locations.

I was minding my own business. There was a lot of movement during those weeks at the Villa Passalacqua because the building had been the headquarters of the Bank of Italy during the Republic and there were lots of comings and goings of civil servants, military men, and trucks to transport the valuables to places I did not know.

One day, I can't remember the precise date, but it must have been around May 10, a green Fiat "1100" came to the Villa

Passalacqua with a very important partisan commander. He was Pietro Vergani [Fabio], in command of all the Garibaldi men in Lombardy. With them was a man dressed as an "Alpino," carrying a rifle and accompanied by two women. I was immediately struck by the younger woman with black hair. She seemed to be suffering and had an intense look in her eyes; she was constantly looking around as if she needed reassurance that she could trust us or as though she was on her guard. She said her name was Gianna and wanted me to call her by that name. The other woman, whose name I remember as being Coven, or something like that, was English, around thirty-five, dressed in black with a long skirt and dark blouse; she carried a backpack. She treated Gianna with what I immediately sensed was an affected kind of familiarity; I detected in her something insincere and false. Instinctively, as it can happen to a sixteen year old, I felt my sympathies going to Gianna as I hid a kind of antagonism toward the Englishwoman. The Englishwoman was living inside the Villa Passalacqua, even though up to that point I had never seen her. The villa was very large, however, with many exits. [...] Along with Gianna, the Alpino, and the Englishwoman we went to the PCI federation office at Como in the Palazzo Terragni where Gianna was hoping to get news concerning her lover, Luigi Canali [Captain Neri], who had mysteriously disappeared on May 8. The woman named Coven went into the offices with her. Gianna came out crying; she was very distraught. They had nothing to tell her. She then asked me to drive her to Milan. I had her and the two others get into the Lancia "Aprilia" that was assigned to me and drove off.

During the trip, as I listened to what Gianna was saying (she did almost all the talking, the Alpino was only agreeing with her, and the Englishwoman said very few words in broken Italian), I formed a rather clear idea about the girl and what was bothering her. She wanted to know the truth regarding the mysterious disappearance of Neri. "I have every right to know," she said to her two traveling companions, "and you must help me." From time to time she would break down in tears and sob desperately, which I found heartbreaking. Our eyes would meet in the rearview mirror and she understood that I was also upset.

Once in Milan I pulled up in front of the Palazzo Cusani, where the Garibaldi Brigades were headquartered. I stayed in the car with the Alpino. Gianna and Coven went in. After a short time some partisans came and took the Alpino inside. Some two hours later two partisans roughly took me inside also, where a commander, whom I later identified from pictures in the newspapers as Walter Audisio, subjected me to a harsh interrogation. He wanted to know if I knew Gianna, why I had taken them there and what I knew. "Nothing," I answered. "I was only following Fabio's orders." He did not want to believe me. And in truth Fabio did not give me the order to go to Milan. It took me a long time to convince him. Then he let me go. I waited several hours more, perhaps four hours. When Gianna came back with the Alpino and Coven, I saw that she had been through an ordeal and was very distraught. I felt sorry for her. She gave the impression she was about to faint at any moment. The Englishwoman was holding her up as if she were a sleepwalker or someone in a daze, but one could clearly see that she felt no compassion for that poor girl. The Alpino was even more silent. Those two had used Gianna, just as they had used her companion earlier, and now they were abandoning her to her fate.

During the return trip Gianna recovered from her torpor. The car ran out of gas on the highway and stopped. After a long wait we saw a column of British vehicles arriving behind us. Coven firmly waved down the "Jeep" at the head of the convoy, showed her identity card to an officer who was in charge, and a few soldiers were immediately ordered to fill up our tank with gas and let us have an additional filled can for safety. We were near the Lomazzo exit where some of Gianna's relatives were living. She asked me to drive her there and gave me directions. We all felt the need to stop for a break after all the stress we had gone through in Milan. They offered us a light dinner. We all ate in silence. Gianna then couldn't stop talking about

Neri and cried. The girl spoke to me after dinner. She affectionately called me "Balilla."* I was a young kid and she trusted me. She showed me the inside of her purse where she kept a small handgun with a silver handle. "This," she said, "belonged to Claretta Petacci. Look, her initials are engraved on it. I'll give it to you," she promised. "I hate weapons. I can't look at them anymore. But you must help me find Neri."

It was very late at night when we returned to the Villa Passalacqua. The Englishwoman invited Gianna to sleep at her apartment inside the villa. The Alpino and I slept in the car.

During the next few days I went on with my work at the Villa Passalacqua with many interruptions for car trips at Gianna's request as she pursued her useless search. I was not always with Gianna, who often went out with the Englishwoman. Then for a long time I didn't see her [Gianna]. She had been arrested in Milan on Vergani's orders and was locked up in one of the Party's sections. She was then released with the strictest orders not to show up at Como. However, the girl did not obey.

She came looking for me. She was white as a sheet. She told me that she had finally found out the truth. "Balilla," she said, placing her hand on my shoulder, "now I know. They killed him! And they want to kill me, too!" I would have wished to comfort her, hug her, tell her not to despair, but I was only a frightened seventeen-year-old kid, without weapons, and in no position to do anything to help her.

I am sure that that was the last day of her life. That very evening, what I can call today quite frankly "the death squad" showed up at the Villa Passalacqua, the killers to whom the Coven woman and the Alpino handed Gianna. These were the "M" brothers, with a motorcycle that also had the partisan woman "G" on board, and another partisan called "P." It was a small group that specialized in the elimination of fascist prison-

---

* Balilla refers to the legendary teenager in Genoa who in 1740 was said to have led the revolt against the occupying Austrian army. The name was used by the Fascist party's youth movement for boys aged 8–14.

ers. The prisoners were taken from the schools at Moltrasio to the Lido and killed there. The bodies were then thrown into the lake. They would have the prisoners walk to their execution by telling them that they were being transferred to the concentration camp at the via XX Settembre.

Gianna knew them all very well and had nothing to fear from any of them since they were friendly towards her. They acted as if they were trying to lift her spirits. After talking to her in a friendly way, the three on the motorcycle left. The partisan "P," Gianna, Coven, and I remained. After a while "P" suggested we all go to Cernobbio for ice cream.

Coven said she couldn't come for some reason. Gianna and "P" got in my car. We drove in the direction of Cernobbio. It was a very dark night. When we reached the bottom of the Pizzo di Cernobbio road we saw the three on the motorcycle stopped by the side. I stopped along next to them. The two brothers pretended to be repairing a breakdown. The partisan woman "G" crossed the road and said, "The motorcycle is broken." "P" offered to have her get into the car with us. But she declined: "No I'd rather walk a little." Then she turned to Gianna and said, "Come on Gianna, come with me, let's walk." Gianna got out of the car. As soon as she did so, "P" said to me, "Let's you and I go now."

He had me pull up in front of the café that was in the building facing where the Regina Olga hotel is today. "P" ordered a beer and ice cream for me. After about fifteen minutes we heard the noise of a motorcycle. The two brothers and "G" arrived. Gianna was not with them. "G" sat down, looking nervous, and said, "She figured it out. We had to take care of her on the road and then throw her into the lake. Now she can go keep her man company." I froze. All of a sudden I understood. I began shaking like a leaf. "P" looked at me for a second, and then said, "You get out of here. You're done."

I hurried out of there, terrified. Those murderers had killed her! I could not comfort her anymore nor could she give me the pistol with the silver handle as a gift. I felt the guilt, the curse, the powerlessness of just being a young upstart. As I drove back to the Villa Passalacqua I noticed with horror a large bloodstain on the paved road very close to the low wall. That's when I began to fear for my own life. I was convinced that those people would think it over and try to kill me as well. I was on guard. I asked about Coven and the Alpino. They had suddenly disappeared and no one knew anything. However, just a few days later, at Moltrasio, there was a lot of commotion because the British prime minister, Winston Churchill, had arrived and was staying at the Villa delle Rose, known today as Villa Versace, at the start of the via Madonnina where the road climbs up to the Villa Passalacqua. I was too young at the time to make certain connections and reach some conclusions, but today I can see that Churchill's presence just steps from villa used as the headquarters by British espionage and where most probably the most explosive among Mussolini's documents had been assembled was no simple coincidence.

A few days later, still in fear for my life, I asked my partisan commander, Amos Santi, for permission to return home for family reasons. A few days later I disappeared without leaving a trace. I left the lake and went to Trent where I had a friend. I found a job. Meanwhile, the years went by, but I could never erase from my mind the memory of Gianna and her tragic end.

When the Padua trial began in 1957 regarding the theft of the Dongo gold and the related murders, including that of Gianna, I was the only one who knew the sequence of events, at least in Gianna's case, but I was too frightened to come forward. So I kept my secret during all the years that followed. Today I am an old man and I have decided to tell what I know in the hope that other people who know and saw what happened will step forward. At this point no one should fear for his life, though some killers are still alive and, as in my case, have the support of many friends and mafia-style cover among Communists and former Communists. This prompts me to avoid revealing my identity even today. However, the time may be at hand to lift the shadow that has been hovering over Como for some fifty years, called the "Lake's Curse." Too many bodies lay dead under those dark waters, and are still waiting, at least for the truth if justice cannot be done.

This is where "F. D.'s" story ends. Both this writer and Antonio Zanella agreed not to reveal the identity of the narrator out of respect for the enduring fear he continued to feel. One fact is beyond a doubt: "F.D." had never heard of Lonati. On the other hand, Lonati could never have imagined the existence of a totally unforeseen witness confirming the presence of an Italian as an *Alpino* working as an agent for the British secret services on Lake Como.

5. Maybe it was Captain Johnson

At the beginning of 2003 Bruno Giovanni Lonati agreed to appear on a television program about the mystery of Mussolini's death[5] and also agreed to take a lie detector test. He repeated the highlights of his story and again talked about the mysterious Captain John. However, the lie detector concluded that he was lying, or at least not telling the whole truth. This probably began with Captain John. Was it really Captain John or Captain Johnson? The latter was the nom de guerre of Malcolm Smith, whom we have already encountered in Chapter VI, and who was involved in the search for the Mussolini-Churchill papers. A British subject and certainly a member of the Special Forces with very important responsibilities, Malcolm Smith was born in Palermo, the son of the British consul in the Sicilian capital, and he spoke native Italian. His name had come up for the first time (amid the general indifference that the most sensational news about the Duce's death elicited from the Italian publishing and cultural establishment, conditioned by what Renzo De Felice referred to as the "vulgate" served up by the Communists[6]) in a memoir by partisan leader Francesco Magni (Francio), who was from Como and a member of the 52nd Garibaldi Brigade, published in 1985 by the Centro studi "Enrico Mattei" in Pavia in a pamphlet entitled *I ribelli della Resistenza nelle Prealpi Lombarde* [The Rebels of the Resistance in Pre-Alps Lombard,].

The following passage is the key part of the Francio memoir:

> Audisio—at about 4 p.m.—left Dongo with two cars to go to the De Maria farmhouse. With him was Michele Moretti, who knew the location. Pedro, who did not trust the "accountant" [referring to Audisio], took another car, and a Dongo partisan who was close by with him, and began following Audisio's cars from a distance. When they went up the steep incline towards the De Maria house, they stopped before the mountain path begins going up to the house itself. Some time later, Pedro also stopped and got out of the car. Suddenly he heard machine-gun fire. He then began running with his gun in his hand and right past the curve he saw Audisio and his companions with their machine guns at the ready, almost in front of the gates of the Villa Belmonte. In front of them on the ground were Mussolini and Claretta Petacci.
>
> Pedro rushed up to Claretta to feel for a pulse. She was already cold and her blood was coagulated. Mussolini was in the same condition. It was almost 5 p.m. He turned to Audisio: "What's going on?" Audisio said: "The Italian people have applied justice. Remember that. Otherwise you will wind up the same way!" Pedro left them and ran to the De Maria farmhouse. He found the three partisans who stood guard and Mrs. Lia [De Maria] bound and gagged. [...] They told him what had happened. That morning four partisans showed up at the farmhouse and using a trick they disarmed the guards, tied them up, and gagged Mrs. Lia. Then they went into the room where Mussolini and Claretta were held. From the yelling it was clear that they were looking for something and didn't find it. Then they came out with Mussolini and Claretta at about 10 a.m. and soon after we heard the gunshots. These were Johnson [Malcolm Smith], Giacomo,[7] Bruno, and another one.

Francesco Magni, who was the author of this sensational memoir, had mysteriously died on June 30, 1947, at Porlezza, where he drowned in the waters of Lake Lugano,[8] but his close relatives had kept his memoir and published it many years later in 1985 after overcoming long years of terror. Was Francio one more victim on the list of those in the know?

As for Malcolm Smith, he never did go back to England. He married Elda, a beautiful girl from Florence, and lived with her in an elegant house at Montorfano, in the hills overlooking Lake Como, where he became a regular at the "Villa d'Este" golf club. Many people attempted to get him to speak up but he would refuse with a sly smile. Today both Elda and Malcolm Smith are no longer alive and they left no children. However, when a magazine writer[9] used the Francio memoir to advance the theory that the posse of the four "executioners" that appeared in the morning was led by Captain Johnson, his recently widowed wife categorically denied the allegation: "My husband had nothing to do with the deaths of Mussolini and Claretta Petacci." Perhaps he had been mistaken for Captain John?

Partisan leaders *(clockwise from upper left):* Emilio Sereni (Communist),
Leo Valiani (Partito d'Azione), Sandro Pertini (Socialist), Luigi Longo (Communist).

Marshal Rodolfo Graziani *(left)* with local fascist
leader Vincenzo Costa in 1945.

Marcello Petacci as a student
in Rome in the late 1930s.

The Petacci family in Madrid in 1947.
Between Claretta's parents are the two sons
of Marcello Petacci, Benvenuto *(left)* and
Ferdinando. Standing in back is Myriam
Petacci, Claretta's sister.

General Raffaele Cadorna *(left)* and Walter
Audisio (Colonel Valerio) on April 30, 1945.

The main locations around Lake Como where the events of April 26–28, 1945, took place:
1. the Como Prefecture. 2. Menaggio. 3. Grandola. 4. Valle d'Intelvi. 5. Cernobbio. 6. Moltrasio.
7. Musso. 8. Dongo. 9. Colico.

Pier Luigi Bellini delle Stelle (Pedro) as a partisan leader in 1945.

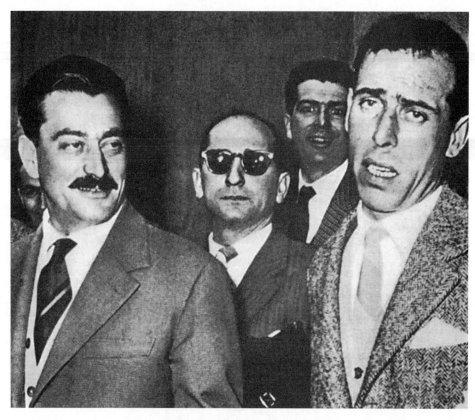

Pier Luigi Bellini delle Stelle (Pedro) (*left)* and Urbano Lazzaro (Bill) *(right)* at the Padua trial in 1957.

Michele Moretti (Pietro).

Luigi Canali (Captain Neri).

Giuseppina Tuissi (Gianna).

The De Maria house, at the foot of the steep hills,
as it appeared in 1957.

Dorina Mazzola at age nineteen when she claimed to
have witnessed Mussolini's execution from her house on
April 28, 1945.

The room in the De Maria house where
Mussolini and Claretta spent their final
night on April 27–28, 1945.

Lia De Maria in 1957. She helped Luigi
Canali (Captain Neri) by offering her house
to hold Mussolini and Claretta Petacci
during the night of April 27–28, 1945.

Dongo, April 28, 1945. The fifteen fascist leaders of the RSI who were part of Mussolini's convoy were executed by the partisans in the early afternoon. Their bodies would reach Milan in the early hours of April 29, along with those of Mussolini and Claretta Petacci loaded on the same truck.

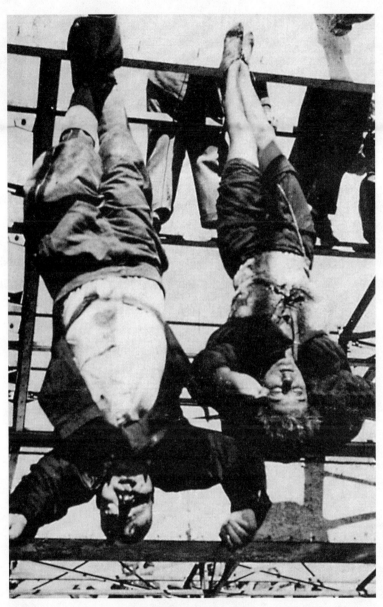

Mussolini and Claretta Petacci at the Piazzale Loreto, April 29, 1945.

Colonel Charles Poletti, head of AMGOT in Italy, speaking on the radio in Rome in 1945. *(Charles Poletti Papers, Rare Book and Manuscript Library, Columbia University.)*

OSS officers in northern Italy: Capt. Emilio Q. Daddario *(left)* and Capt. Aldo Icardi on April 30, 1945, near Milan.

Right to left: Capt. Aldo Icardi, Col. Charles Poletti, and Capt. Emilio Q. Daddario in Milan on April 29, 1945. *(Charles Poletti Papers, Rare Book and Manuscript Library, Columbia University.)*

Walter Audisio (Colonel Valerio) in his
partisan uniform in 1947.

President Harry Truman greeting Italian Premier Alcide De Gasperi in 1951.

Palmiro Togliatti, General Secretary of the PCI (Italian Communist Party).

Ferdinando Petacci, nephew of Claretta Petacci, in Milan in 2000.

Historian Renzo De Felice, shortly before his death in 1996, holding the published editions of his 8-volume unfinished Mussolini biography. He stated that he was convinced that a secret back-channel correspondence between Mussolini and Churchill did in fact exist.

Chapter XII

A VICTIM WITH TOO MUCH EVIDENCE

The story of Luigi Canali (Captain Neri) and Giuseppina Tuissi (the partisan woman Gianna) who were killed by the Communists because, after having delivered Mussolini to the British, they were against the "Great Dongo Robbery." The endless chain of deaths following those two murders that marked the collapse of fascism.

Luigi Canali (Captain Neri), the key figure in Mussolini's capture, his custody, and, above all, his being handed over to the "executioners," mysteriously disappeared on May 7, 1945. Since then he has been slowly forgotten to the point that today the public at large has never heard the name Captain Neri, even among those who are interested in the events surrounding the fall of fascism. However, a group of historians and journalists—Franco Bandini, Giorgio Pisanò, Giorgio Cavalleri, Roberto Festorazzi, and particularly Alessandro Zanella—attempted to dig deeper into the role he played. The general conclusion was that his tragic death on May 7, 1945, could be attributed to the fact that he was determined not to let the PCI (the party to which he belonged) take the Dongo treasure. We are not referring to Communist historians who explain his execution as a logistical mistake due to a Party squad in charge of summary executions which had not been informed of the cancellation of a previously issued death sentence.[1] We refer to the independent historians, according to whom Neri was first and foremost a good Italian before being a good Communist. He wanted the "Dongo treasure" he had retrieved with Gianna to go to the Italian State. That is where things stand as of now, with, however, a small but extremely important variation as we shall see—which makes Neri and Gianna appear to be even more honest than we previously thought.

This writer is indebted to Alice Canali, Neri's sister, for sharing her firsthand knowledge of her brother's character.[2] Alice Canali gave us access to scores of documents and unpublished letters her brother had written. While these do not reveal the reason for his death, they give enough insight into his personality and allow us to reconstruct the true story of the man that fate brought face to face with Benito Mussolini at the final appointment of his life.

Luigi Canali, the future head of Resistance of the Lower Lario and Lecchese areas, was born in Como on March 16, 1912, the oldest of three children. His father was from Brianza and a nurse at the local hospital. His mother, Maddalena Zanoni, was born in Brescia but raised in Mantua. This was a socialist family that joined the Communists after the Leghorn Congress of 1921 and raised their children in the ideal of freedom and justice. Luigi Canali was a healthy and strong young man who excelled at sports, especially running the hurdles. He found a job working on the cable railway at Brunate. He was very keen at improving his education and read books on religion, philosophy, and literature. He took evening courses and became an accountant. He was drafted in 1936 and sent to East Africa as a lieutenant in the army engineers.

A bundle of letters, unpublished notes, and diaries that Alice showed this writer indicate the kind of feelings a young man who had been sent to fight a war that repulsed him could feel. These are very beautiful letters and notes that deserve an entire chapter unto themselves. "You want to make me into a hero come what may," he wrote on April 22, 1936, to a lady friend. "We must be half a million men against half as many blacks who are poorly equipped and have no air force. They are dying by the tens of thousands. We are still writing casualty lists of our men by name because there are so few. And yet supposedly we are the heroes . . . Personally I feel I have made greater moral and material efforts in civilian life with no one telling me anything. Have I been lucky? Then there are 499,000 other lucky ones in East Africa!"

In another letter he writes: "The importance of discipline is obvious. However, I don't think or remember that nations have achieved much through discipline alone. Actually, I am sure that without an underlying activity in the economic, social, moral, or religious field nothing truly lasting can be created. In fact, I am convinced that without such activity discipline can only be enforced through fear or ignorance."

Then there is an answer to a little girl from Como who had written a letter to the "dear fighters": "Dear Parisina, I am sure that you have created your own idea about the war and the situation we are in, but after all, it is much better that way. Keep on referring to us as 'dear fighters' and pray for us. However, I would like to convince you of something: while we will know how to face everything quietly, we must all pray to God fervently in order to give men more common sense, enough to understand that wars are terrible and frightening and that they should be the last thing we should think about."

A family friend wrote to him from Lourdes in an attempt to transmit some of her faith to him. Luigi answered with a long beautiful ten-page letter, of which said: "Since you are fundamentally a good person (just as fundamentally as I should be a bad person) who does not think that such beautiful ideas as divinity, the revelation, and the incarnation could be the result of needs, fears, and necessities that are part of human nature, but are conceivable only as fantasies under the nightmare of the fear of death that our parents tell us as part of our traditions and therefore are true."

The young Luigi wrote about his feelings and private conflicts in a diary that his sister treasured like a sacred relic: "I don't agree that wars are inevitable, nor do I subscribe to other such theories, and find that the attitude of the religious leaders of the world is highly reprehensible. They mix the name of God with humanity's most shameful and degenerate passions."

At a different date he wrote: "There are many steps where morality could rest. For example, I can see that there is a morality that speaks of the good that one does without any expectations of material, moral, or spiritual rewards and beyond the pleasure of having accomplished it."

And finally a somewhat surprising annotation that almost sounds prophetic, dated April 27, 1936: "I am reading *The Duce's Father* by Francesco Bonavita, a lawyer and an old comrade who shared Alessandro Mussolini's ideas. I am thinking about my father, our fathers: of ourselves who are living with our eyes wide open in times that are thick with events and historic changes; what a situation! The small and almost always temporary gambles of the Duce's father remind me of the colossal one engaged in by his son: I hope to be able to 'see' him, gigantic in the face of history, morality, and humanity's greater values."

These thoughts give an idea of the standards of the twenty-four-year-old Luigi Canali. We can imagine how he had matured by September 8, 1943, seven years later when as a veteran of the retreat from Russia he returned to civilian life in Como and a job at the SIC (Società Idroelettrica Comacina).[3] He had demonstrated his bravery in Russia, saving scores of men in his unit and, as his sister recalled, "he managed to come home with the thing he treasured most: the small blue trunk filled with his books."

His commanding officer during the African campaign wrote the following words about him: "His serious, loyal, willful, and disciplined character with its moral rigor and his generosity is very well regarded by his officers and the soldiers of the rank and file. He is looked up to by those of lower rank, whom he encourages to be active, and sets them a tireless example. In every circumstance he draws out the best results. He has excellent qualities as an organizer, healthy initiative, and a practical approach. He finds solutions to every difficult situation and remains very calm in the most worrisome moments." This is the man who, following the reestablishment of fascism in northern Italy and the German invasion, gathered a group of veterans of the Russian front along with fleeing soldiers after September 8, 1943, and with them began the Resistance in the Como region. At first he went by the name of Renzo Invernizzi; then, after June 1944 (when the Germans had already put a price on his head and forced him to give up his job at SIC, which also served as his cover), he took the name that was to become popular among his comrades and feared by the enemy: Captain Neri.

He created, with many other Communists in the Como region, the 52nd Garibaldi Assault Brigade and became its commander. A second lieutenant of the royal army, Pier Bellini delle Stelle (Pedro); a Finance Guard, Urbano Lazzaro (Bill); and a laborer who also happened to be the local soccer champion, Michele Moretti (Pietro), all reported to Neri. The attacks on the enemy were growing in intensity; the western side of Lake Como was firmly held by Neri's Garibaldi men. The previously unpublished text of a flyer he had distributed in the streets of Como in reply to an offer from the fascist authorities is clear:

> Colonel Pozzoli[4] recently sent to the "Luigi Clerici" battalion of the 52nd Garibaldi Brigade a request that we surrender with our weapons, promising that we would not be punished. [...] We have thirty dead comrades to avenge. Once they have all been avenged we will negotiate, but it will be about one single issue: your unconditional surrender. Until then we will only speak the language of war with you, and require the same treatment from you because any other form of contact repulses us.

Captain Neri, therefore, had become, in the course of the tough year 1944, a legendary Resistance leader and oddly, in historical texts (especially those written by Communists), his name is never mentioned along with those of Gino Moscatelli, Aldo Gastaldi, or Arrigo Boldrini. Strangely, but rather understandably, Luigi Canali was never a faithful and uncritical executor of the Party's orders. Actually he quickly became a troublesome comrade.

His sister gave us the background:

> His disagreements with the Party already surfaced in 1944. Luigi didn't hold the future PCI member of Parliament, Fabio—Pietro Vergani, who was the Garibaldi division's commander—in very high regard. He disagreed with the PCI's decision to place, as commanders of the Garibaldi forces, high-ranking officers of the army that had disbanded on September 8. Those were officers loyal to the monarchy, with Party "political commissars" operating alongside them. Luigi didn't trust the officers who had fled on September 8, abandoning their men. He knew them well. Therefore, he refused to let the command of the Garibaldi Divisions of the Lario region, which he had created, be placed under the monarchist Colonel Umberto Morandi [Colonel Lario]. Luigi felt that was an unnatural decision, harmful to the revolutionary quality of the Garibaldi units, which after the war took the popular support that pushed them into taking up the fight against the foreigners into their political commitment.[5]

This was a deep political clash, which in a party subjected to rigid discipline such as the Communist party could only be called "deviationism." Why then had Luigi Longo and Palmiro Togliatti decided to add monarchist officers to the Communist units? The motivation was to control the army when the insurrection was to take place. A decision that the Soviet advisers requested and that failed because of Allied opposition.[6]

Therefore, having greater insights than the party chiefs, Captain Neri didn't hesitate to clash head-on with Fabio, even though it was to cost him the command of the Garibaldi forces in the Lario region and his being replaced by Colonel Morandi. Neri had to settle for the command of the 52nd Brigade.

It was at this time that he met Gianna. Petite, pretty, with large blue eyes that made her look like a doll—that was how Alice Canali remembered her—she was a GAP[7] militant from Milan. She was born on June 24, 1923, in Baggio, and had to hide in the mountains to avoid capture by the fascists.

The *Muti* fascist militia unit found out her activities (as a worker at the Milan military hospital she handed out passes to the soldiers who didn't want to return to the front lines) and had murdered her fiancé, Gianni Alippi, who was twenty-four and also a member of the 3rd GAP—one of the four men to be executed at the Viale Tibaldi on August 28, 1944. The leadership of the Garibaldi Brigades in Lombardy then sent her to be a dispatch rider for the 52nd.

In this new activity Giuseppina Tuissi took the nom de guerre of Gianna, in honor of her fiancé. At twenty-one she had already experienced pain, and had to identify the torn body of her lover at the morgue after a public execution in front of women and children.

It's hard to tell how and in what circumstances love appeared between Gianna and Neri. Luigi Canali had only been married for one year and was about to become a father. No doubt his wife would miss her husband's support when she most needed it. Certainly Neri's wife failed to see why her husband had chosen the harsh and difficult path of covert struggle. She thought she had married a quiet accountant with a steady job at the hydroelectric company. Some people even found it necessary to inform her about the young and attractive partisan female dispatch rider who often went off on risky missions with Captain Neri.

It was just before one of those missions in nearby Switzerland that Luigi Canali and Giuseppina Tuissi were captured by the Black Brigades from Como. It happened at Lezzeno, during the night of January 6–7, 1945. Some of the "small fry" who had fallen into the net told the Black Brigades about the locations of secret bases. The behavior of Neri and Gianna, when they were captured and during the days that followed (terrible days of physical and moral torture in the former Carabinieri barracks at Como-Borghi, which had been requisitioned by the Black Brigade) was at once a masterpiece of sheer guts and clever thinking. This was described in two accounts that the two young people wrote as soon as they were freed and handed back to their commanders (a copy, however, remained with their families). Luigi Canali's memoir of forty-three typed pages reads like a literary piece and a thriller at the same time. It describes in meticulous detail the tortures the Black Brigades had thought up as well as Gianna's heroic behavior as she was tortured and hit as many as one hundred times, locked up for a whole night in a phone booth with a rat, then stripped naked and raped by her jailers in front of Neri, who was forced to watch while in chains.

One after the other the top leaders of the Resistance in Como wound up under arrest. The meeting in the fascist jail between Captain Neri and Colonel Lario is described as follows:

> Colonel Lario entered the room and after quickly looking at me came to the table where Mariani and company were seated and saluted respectfully.[8] "Do you recognize this one?" asked Mariani. "Yes, that's Neri," he answered, red as a beet. I answered with a commiserating smile. [...] At first he was stammering and got confused but then he quickly gave the details, especially after he was able to describe the role of the men and the communications system similar to a "fishbone," a word that inevitably strengthened his discussions of the art of war that he indulged in. He portrayed himself as a victim of the Communists. [...] He said he agreed to take command of the group to control its actions, adding that the Communist members of the leadership were the true inspiration and decisionmakers behind the attacks, which he never had approved and in many cases prevented altogether. He said that I was the only one to provide complete reports, not just about military matters but also regarding politics. Once Colonel Lario was freed, Mariani, talking to his other comrades-in-arms, summed it up: "So basically he's the real fascist here."

In the meantime Dante Gorreri (Guglielmo), the secretary of the underground Communist party in Como, was arrested. Neri was condemned to death. "We'll shoot you at the Camerlata cemetery," they told him. One evening he could have escaped but did not follow through. This is how he described that decision:

> There was only Corbella [a member of the Black Brigade]. I made an unpardonable mistake. Corbella was an older man and I

could have overwhelmed him easily enough in my cell. But he was a "good" soldier, always looking after me with compassion. He had lent me his blanket and that night he shared his bread and cheese with me. They would have certainly punished him.

Neri managed to escape (another adventure) during the evening of January 29 by trekking through the snow. By then, strangely enough, the PCI leaders had already put the word out—since January 25—that Neri was a traitor, that he had not kept silent in the fascist prison and talked. This calumny was being spread in Milan where Paolo Vergani was in charge and not in Como where no one would have believed it. And it was in Milan still that the calumny found its sublimation in a death sentence issued in the back room of a retail shop (owned by the brother of Mario Melloni[9]) by a Communist "court," which also included Paolo Vergani,[10] Aldo Lampredi,[11] and Giovanni Pesce[12]—the top echelon of Communist Resistance. The Party had reached the decision to get rid of this embarrassing "deviationist" and issued an implacable order to the armed groups: "Kill agent provocateur Neri."

Those "judges" knew nothing about the fact that the fascists took their revenge for that setback by torturing Gianna in the extreme. They arrested Neri's mother and almost killed one of his uncles who helped him hide in Milan. They did in fact kill Eugenio Curiel—a young hero of the Resistance in Milan, the head of a university student's unit—by mistake, thinking that he was Neri, the man who constantly eluded their search. In the end they decided to free Gianna so that she could serve as bait and allow the capture of the leader of the 52nd Garibaldi Brigade, who had successfully tricked them. It was of no concern to Pietro Vergani that the Garibaldi unit fighters of the Lario region, led by Oreste Gementi (Riccardo), were in open revolt because of that infamous death sentence of Captain Neri and were demanding his immediate rehabilitation. The important issue was to get rid of that dangerous Communist who had a mind of his own.

A few reports that Captain Neri wrote for his commanding officers provide a harrowing account of those terrible weeks, and also contain some extremely valuable first-hand intelligence regarding fascist defensive positions in the Valtellina where they had set up the final "redoubt." Neri does not hesitate to complain bitterly about the "monstrous injustice" he was subjected to and attributed it to the "incompetence, laziness, and bad faith" of the leaders of the delegation from Lombardy, and Fabio in particular.

Those were the fateful days when Neri was being hunted down by fascists and Communists alike and was not at all ready to throw in the towel. He approached British agents, placing himself under their protection and at their service at the same time. He knew several Englishmen. Many villas around Lake Como belonged to wealthy English families who came during the winter before the war. Those families had left their property in the care of trusted persons who felt, now that fascism was in its death throes, that the time had come to repay that trust with friendship and loyalty. It should be kept in mind that one of the top organizers of Special Forces n. 1, the man actually responsible for the administrative side of the parachute drops of British military missions in the north, was in fact from Como, even though he was a British subject. His name was Mr. Beauky and until 1940 he owned a hotel on the lake. He had studied in Italy in the past, spoke the Como dialect to perfection, and was now a captain in His Majesty's army.

Neri returned to Como under the protection of British agents who also provided him with money and weapons. He hadn't managed to have a satisfactory airing of his grievances with Fabio after successfully dodging the fascist police. Together with Gianna, Neri was welcomed back like a brother by the men of the 52nd Garibaldi Brigade, now under the command of the very young Count Pier Bellini delle Stelle.

According to testimony given by Bill (Urbano Lazzaro) the deputy political commissar of the 52nd Brigade at the Padua trial[13] on May 4, 1957:

Neither Pedro nor I considered Neri and Gianna to be spies. [...] When they returned they were immediately sent back to the ranks. In order not to humiliate Neri in front of his comrades, who trusted him completely (since orders from above prevented us from giving him back the command of the Brigade), we named him chief of staff. I don't think this happened too often. In the Garibaldi Brigade that rank did not exist.

According to Pedro's deposition on April 21, 1947, in front of Judge Jasevoli at Como: "Neri's prestige and his authority over everyone were such that the Milan Command had to take the facts into account and the countermanding orders were received just one month before the insurrection: Neri was not to be executed because everything had been cleared."

Therefore, the fighter was fully returned to his duties as a partisan commander of unimpeachable authority and prestige by the morning of April 27, 1945, when events were to suddenly plunge him directly at the heart of Italy's history. The man who actually called for the surrender of the German convoy (led by Lieutenant Fallmeyer), negotiated with the Germans for five hours, and led them to believe that in case of a firefight their situation was hopeless (in the end he let them go ahead towards Switzerland on condition that they abandon the fascists to their fate), was Pedro, but the power behind the dramatic negotiations was really Neri. At the time the command staff of the 52nd Assault Brigade, Luigi Clerici, included four persons: Pedro, the commander; Pietro (Michele Moretti), the political commissar; his deputy Bill; and the chief of staff, Neri. The only one to combine military cleverness, experience with the willingness to take risks to outsmart a "bluff" like the one he pulled on Fallmeyer (who was led to believe that the road towards the upper part of the lake was full of partisans armed to the teeth)—the only one to outwit the Germans was still Neri.[14]

The sequence of events will show that Neri was the real moving force behind what took place until 3 p.m. on the afternoon of April 28 when Colonel Valerio, whomever he really was, suddenly appeared, snarling like a wild animal. Valerio arrived with an execution squad of Communists from the Oltrepò Pavese region and very specific orders: shoot fifteen "hierarchs" on the spot, since the dramatic show of an execution at the Piazzale Loreto had been "preempted" because Mussolini had already been killed.

From the moment Mussolini and all the fascist leaders surrendered to the partisans, Neri was the one in charge of what was to be done about the Duce and his entourage, deciding their movements and transfers. Neri decided to take Mussolini to the safety of the barracks of the Finance Guards at Germasino. He gave orders to assemble all the luggage belonging to the ministers and the suitcases full of gold, jewelry, and foreign currency found in the Alfa Romeo belonging to Prefect Gatti (the treasure known as the "Dongo gold") into a large room at the municipal building overlooking the lake—giving responsibility in writing to Gianna, the only person he trusted blindly. It was Neri who sent Gianna to Musso to bring back everything else remaining in the "Mussolini convoy" of automobiles that were already being pilfered by the local populace and the undisciplined men of Captain Davide Barbieri. Neri assembled a few employees from the Dongo municipality, placing them under Gianna's orders to write up the inventory of the confiscated goods. It was also Neri who personally demanded that the two briefcases Mussolini was carrying be brought to him—the famous briefcases containing the fateful documents.

"Take good care of those bags. They contain Italy's destiny." Those were the words Mussolini addressed to Bill right after being recognized at Dongo in the fifth truck of the Flak convoy by the partisan fighter Giuseppe Negri.[15] Bill grabbed the briefcases without giving much thought to their the importance and almost immediately handed them to the partisan Lorenzo Bianchi, who held on to them for about two hours and then gave them to the man everyone considered as being in charge during those fateful hours, Captain Neri.[16]

Captain Neri put the two briefcases in a safe place. (Where? No one would ever know.) Then he returned to handle his two illustrious prisoners. It was he, once again (and not Pedro), who made the decision during the night of April 27–28 to transfer Mussolini, with his head wrapped in bandages to avoid his being recognized, from Germasino to Brunate, above Como, to the house of someone he knew. Later on Pedro would keep on repeating that he only followed Neri's orders. What did Captain Neri have in mind that night when the two cars carrying (besides Neri himself) Mussolini, Claretta Petacci, Pedro, Gianna, Michele Moretti (Pietro) and the two partisans Lino and Sandrino took the treacherous road of the Lario region towards Como? He had one specific objective: to deliver the prisoner [Mussolini] to those who were his true friends when both Fascists and Communists were seeking to kill him; the friends who believed in him, allowing him to continue unencumbered his fight for freedom. In accordance with the terms of the peace treaty Mussolini was to be transferred alive to the victorious Allies. Luigi Canali did not want the Duce to end up in the hands of the Communists, and wished to hand him over to his British friends. They were expecting him at the house between Como and Brunate. At that precise moment Neri was far from imagining that the British had something radically different in store for Mussolini, certainly not an interrogation followed by a press conference in front of journalists and film crews from all over the world. Neri's sister told this writer on several occasions that Canali was adamantly opposed to any kind of summary justice. To quote her own words:

> The only person my brother confided in during those days was our mother, Maddalena. I was still at Mantua, involved in the anti-fascist struggle with my husband and returned to Como only after Luigi's disappearance. He told our mother, who then repeated it to me, complaining about Mussolini's violent death, which he did not favor, and that he did not want the Duce to perish like that, and certainly not Claretta Petacci, and that a regular trial would have been preferable. "Because," he said sadly to our mother, who could never forget his forlorn expression, "it's best to hear people out." In remembering those words on several occasions my mother and I thought that during those hours when Luigi was near him, my brother must have spoken at length with Mussolini and became convinced that it would have been in Italy's best interests to let the prisoner defend himself at a public trial.

Back in Moltrasio the little convoy stopped. Something had gone wrong: the motorboat that was supposed to ferry the Duce to the other side of the lake did not appear. The sound of several blasts and the flashes of the explosions could be seen in the distance at Como. While the shooting was almost certainly attributable to the victory celebration by the Garibaldi fighters firing in the air, there was also the risk that the cars could be stopped. Once again Neri made a quick decision. He was to hand over Mussolini alive to the British, was not about to run risks, and fully intended to accomplish the mission he had committed himself to. Therefore, he decided to hide Mussolini at Bonzanigo in the De Maria house. Alice Canali remembers: "Lia De Maria was almost our relative; we had shared the same wet nurse. My brother knew he could trust her and her husband completely." Once again, without asking any questions, Pedro and the others executed Neri's orders.

At about 3 a.m. on April 28 Mussolini and Claretta Petacci were resting in the bare little bedroom of the De Maria children. Leaving Lino and Sandrino to stand guard, Pedro returned to Dongo. Neri, Gianna, and Moretti went towards Como instead. Where were they going? Who were they to meet? Certainly to the headquarters of the Communist party that—as in every town in northern Italy—had occupied the fascist "Casa del Fascio." Alice Canali would never know with any certainty who her brother was meeting, with whom he spoke, or what had been said. "I can't say with whom he met at the new party headquarters," she told this writer many years later, "but what is certain is that he had a very animated discussion over there. My brother was once again acting on his own and going against the Party's plans." The reason for the dispute as we now know was the "Dongo treasure."

It was at this time that Michele Moretti, who until then had been fiercely loyal to Neri, began to distance himself from his comrade. He could see that Luigi Canali was heading for a clash with the Party and he returned to Dongo. Neri and Gianna remained in Como alone. All they could do was inform their English friends about what they knew, beginning with the location where Mussolini was being held, and everything they knew regarding the "Dongo treasure." This was how in good faith the two lovers passed on to Churchill's men exactly the kind of information they required to undertake their mission—the elimination of the Duce and his mistress—and the tools to blackmail the Communists into silence and—as they did in effect—take on the dishonorable responsibility for the murder of Claretta Petacci.

We cannot know for sure what Neri told his mother concerning that dramatic story. In all probability he must have told her many things, judging from what Alice Canali remembers: "My mother told me that Luigi confided that he was disgusted with the Communist party's behavior, because—in his words—'Those dishonest and incapable people are harming the entire movement.'"[17]

In the early afternoon of April 28 Neri and Gianna were at Dongo in time to witness the arrival of Aldo Lampredi (Guido), and then of Colonel Valerio with the execution squad led by Alfredo Mordini (Riccardo). First Lampredi and then Audisio spoke with Neri so that he would vouch for them with Pier Bellini delle Stelle, who did not trust the new arrivals. Neri knew Guido very well as Luigi Longo's right-hand man and the commander of the Garibaldi Divisions. He understood that the terrible mission that took them there under orders from the Party could not be opposed. Neri was able to pull rank on Pedro. The men of the 52nd Assault Brigade stepped aside to allow the "executioners" to operate.

That would be the last time Neri obeyed orders from the PCI. The truck used by Colonel Valerio, with its tragic shipment of dead bodies for the macabre display at the Piazzale Loreto, then left Dongo. Luigi Canali concerned himself solely with the fate of the captured "Dongo treasure," which he could not stand to see fall into the hands of the Communist party because it did not belong to the fascists but to their victims. For the moment he signed off on a temporary delivery of the "treasure" to the Como Communist Federation and had it also signed (for approval) by Pedro, Bill, and Michele Moretti. He vigorously opposed a project by some Communists to load the valuables on a truck and to fake an ambush where three partisans would be killed. The treasure would then "disappear" and the attack would be attributed to rogue fascist groups, while the PCI could grab an immense fortune without a hitch.[18]

"As long as I'm alive you won't do any such shit!" yelled Neri. He ran to comfort Gianna, who was crying at the sight of such treasure and knowing where it came from.

"There was an immense quantity of valuables: jewels, money from every nation, hundreds of millions," he told his mother a few days later, adding: "Had I not been there that stuff would have been lost. I could see from time to time that something would disappear. I didn't think I was in such awful company, mother."

During the days following the executions of the fifteen "big wigs" and of Marcello Petacci on the lakefront at Dongo, Captain Neri saw everything he had believed in crumbling around him. He was powerless by now to stop the daily massacres of the survivors of the "Mussolini convoy" who were being shot, five of them every night. In his office at the Como PCI Federation, three doors down from that of Dante Gorreri, the Party's provincial secretary, Neri could only rehash his disappointment and attempt to slow down the excesses in Como and Milan as best he could.

The tension turned into a big fight with Gorreri on May 2, 1945. According to the testimony of Onorina Garavello, a former PCI typist at the Padua trial on July 7, 1957: "Gorreri was screaming that he was the boss. Captain Neri was also screaming that finally it would become clear as to who the real traitor was. They were talking about money. Gorreri told me to go away. Later on he threatened me and wanted to know what I heard. He wanted to know if I had really understood what the true origins of the 'Dongo treasure' were." In good faith Onorina said that she had not understood that part.

It was also no secret that Luigi Canali openly accused Dante Gorreri of having "talked" when he, Gorreri, had been arrested by the Black Brigade, thereby obtaining a *safe-conduct* to go to Switzerland. Neri was determined to get to the bottom of that story. These were the kinds of persons who had accused *him* of treason! Now he would show them! Yet he still had something that the

PCI wanted very badly: the Duce's secret papers. At least he would prevent them from falling into the hands of the PCI, or the British for that matter.

Alice Canali remembers: "The evening of May 6, 1945, before going to sleep, my brother confided to mother, who felt very bad about him. She sensed that he was in danger and noticed some rough-looking types lurking outside our house. Luigi attempted to quiet her fears, revealing that he still had 'a mission to accomplish.' The next morning, he said, he would take the Duce's papers to a safe-deposit box and then he would permanently retire from politics. 'I am disgusted,' he said, then added, as though to himself, 'Obviously I can't immediately disappear. The world press will talk about these papers for a long time.' He left the house early the next morning, never to return."

On that same morning Pedro met Dionisio Gambaruto in Como. Gambaruto, known as Nicola, was the head of the so-called "people's police," which was to be dissolved by the Allies in mid-July. As Pedro testified at the Padua trial on June 13, 1957: "Gambaruto informed me that he was just waiting for written orders to execute Neri. He told me that he already had the verbal order. My impression was that Neri was already being held prisoner at that time." Pedro looked everywhere for Neri but couldn't find him. By then the commander of the 52nd Brigade didn't count anymore: real power exercised through terror was concentrated in the hands of the PCI.

While Captain Neri was being brutally murdered, Gianna was held as a prisoner of the 113th Garibaldi Brigade in Milan in the former "General Cantore" barracks on the orders of Pietro Vergani (Fabio). On May 9, the day after Neri was assassinated, Fabio called in Gianna and told her coldly that her man had been "executed by a partisan unit in the mountains carrying out the old death sentence." Now Gianna could go back home to Baggio and stay there. She was not to attempt to return to Como. The Party no longer had any use for her.

It would take more than a novel to describe the harrowing experience the young woman went through. Her only fault was to have been in love with Captain Neri and to have shared his ideals of patriotism and justice. One of her dear friends, Vincenzina Coan, received a dramatic letter from Gianna dated May 23.

Dear Vincenzina,

Unfortunately this will be a poorly written letter because I am not too steady at this time. First it was the Fascists and now my own comrades. The leaders of my party for which I lived and still live have turned me into what I am. They have dishonored me, made it impossible for me to live and deprived me of the person I held dearest and for whom I would have given my own life. I don't think I can endure this agony much longer. Even for someone as strong as I used to be, to endure these attacks on one's dignity and ideals, and to be accused of treason, when your man is executed like a traitor, when you know he lived for his ideals, is too oppressive and makes you want to die. One feels oppressed and long for death. [...] There are too many people who are debasing our party and they seek to eliminate anyone who witnesses this.

A few weeks after she sent this letter on June 19, 1945, Gianna decided to find out about Neri's death and went to Como. In her handbag she was carrying the receipt of the "treasure" that she had demanded on the morning of April 29 from the heads of the PCI when they picked up the bundles of banknotes, gold, coins, and jewelry from the house of the Venini sisters at Domàso. Even though the true origins of the "treasure" were not stated in that note, the poor woman felt she could frighten the leaders, and demand to be told the truth regarding her man's death and have him rehabilitated publicly. For four days, with Alice Canali, who arrived from Mantua, Gianna went up and down the lake front asking everyone for news about her Neri and letting it be known that she was determined to avenge his death. On the evening of June 23 she agreed to go with two "comrades" on a red motorcycle. The thugs promised to "take her to see Neri's dead body." They took her to the Pizzo di

Cernobbio instead and killed her there; then they dumped her body into the lake.

According to Alice Canali:

> The following morning my husband was as anxious as I because Gianna had not returned. He went to Party headquarters. As he was speaking with Piero Mentasti, an administrator, a man called Viazzi arrived. "Do you know what happened at the Pizzo last night? A friend of mine, Della Torre, was there with his fiancé. They saw a motorcycle arrive with two men and a girl aboard. The three went down the stairs. Then they heard a desperate cry and one pistol shot. The two men walked back up and went away. Della Torre and his girlfriend walked down and found a newspaper with bloodstains." My husband immediately understood that Gianna had been murdered. Then my husband, irate, cried out: "Careful about what you are doing, you murderer! If you dare touch my wife I'll mobilize my partisans in Mantua and we'll settle matters once and for all!" Today I know that my husband's words saved my life. Everyone in Como knew that he meant business, just as he had fought hard against the Nazi-fascists.

The deaths of Neri and Gianna were the signal of a horrible series of murders whose victims were only guilty of knowing something about the executions or were trying to find out the truth about them. The following were therefore also killed and thrown into the lake: Anna Bianchi, a typist for a short time at the headquarters of the Lince partisan group; her father Michele, who was a dedicated Communist, because he wanted to avenge his daughter; Eufrosina Fontana who had been told in confidence about the matter by Anna Bianchi; Lisa Chiappo, the former partisan dispatch rider known as Dina, who had talked under torture by the Black Brigades and automatically exonerated Neri from the false accusations of the Communist "court"; two partisans from Cinisello, Magni and Il Biondino, who were friends of Gianna; the journalist Franco De Agazio, who in November 1946 in his weekly *Il Meridiano d'Italia* began publishing the memoirs of Neri and Gianna (obtained from Neri's mother Maddalena). De Agazio was probably about to discover and publish the true origins of the so-called "treasure of the RSI."[19]

Gianna's brother, Cesare Tuissi, knew everything about the death of Mussolini and Claretta Petacci and was cut down by machine gun fire; hand grenades were lobbed at a Carabinierie NCO, Ettore Manzi, the head of the Dongo station, who had been too active and tried to save the lives of the fascist prisoners under his control. It is very probable that Manzi was the first to find the "British thread" and the true origins of the "Dongo treasure." Pedro and Bill were drawn into an ambush at Gravedona and were able to save their lives in a shoot-out.

The murder of Franco De Agazio (bravely replaced as editor of *Il Meridiano d'Italia* by his very young nephew Franco Servello, who was later to become a politician and a senator), along with the attack and brutal beating of Don Giuseppe Brusadelli, a priest, and the editor of *L'Ordine*, the Catholic daily newspaper of Como, had the desired effect: of intimidating the more aggressive newspapers that had gone too far in their revelations about the mysterious deaths on the lake. Among these, *L'Italia*, edited by Monsignor Pisoni, with the articles by Arrigo Galli, and *Il Corriere Lombardo*, founded by Edgardo Sogno[20] and edited by Angelo Magliano.

Neri's mother and sister never gave up. In multiple complaints and filings with the courts and the police department they kept on naming the instigators and perpetrators of the murders. The State prosecutor kept on ignoring them.

On November 10, 1945, the Como section of the CLN, represented by its president, Enrico Stella, and the secretary Oscar Sforni—both of them non-Communists—had filed court documents regarding the disappearance of the "treasure of the RSI." It was the beginning of an investigation, which, after many adverse episodes, ended on October 6, 1949, with a sentence by the Milan Court of Appeals of theft, extortion, and multiple homicides "against Dante Gorreri, Pietro Vergani, and twenty-eight others." The trial, however, because of innumerable motions and other technicalities, would only begin on April 29, 1957, in Padua Superior

Court. The PCI had managed to protect the two men accused of having ordered the killings, Vergani and Gorreri, by getting them elected as deputies to Parliament. On the dock and in chains there was only Maurizio Bernasconi (Mirko), the former deputy commander of the "people's police," one of the two accused of killing Gianna and who was under arrest for a number of robberies. This was how Franco Di Bella, the *Corriere della Sera* correspondent, described him at the Padua trial: "With the slanted eyes of a Chinese mandarin, a slightly hooked nose from his twenty-four years in jail, he observed the trial in a detached manner, much like an English baronet might glance at his horses in the paddock from the grandstand at the races."

Those accused of the most serious crimes did not go to trial. Two Communist members of Parliament were free and even though the goal was to find out the truth about a treasure of some five billion (as of 2004) U.S. dollars the state did not take part as the injured party.

Chief Justice Augusto Zen took a firm and honest attitude: "The fact that the fascist leaders," he dictated into the record, "did not leave all those valuables for safekeeping with Cardinal Schuster, but chose to take them along, was the reason for their death." This statement was not enough to encourage those like Cadorna who could have finally cleared the Dongo mystery but decided not to do so. Walter Audisio could say: "We partisan leaders will be the ones to hold the real trial!" And Luigi Longo could boast: "We Communists don't need to answer to anyone; we hadn't anticipated at that time that the Resistance might stand accused of anything."

It had been established that those who murdered Neri, Gianna, and all the others were also responsible for the greatest theft in Italy's history and would not be held accountable for what they had done. On July 24, 1957, one of the six jurors, Silvio Andreghetti, age 63, collapsed and was taken to the hospital. Judge Zen adjourned the trial until August 5. A few days later Andreghetti, who according to Alice Canali "was following the proceedings very closely and was very sensitive to the evolution of the case," committed suicide in the hospital or perhaps was "suicided." The trial was adjourned once again and in the sixty years since it was never reconvened.

In concluding this final chapter about the dark tragedy of Neri and Gianna, I must extend a note of thanks to Dr. Pasca Piredda, who is a truly extraordinary character in the military history of the Second World War. She was the spokesperson and close collaborator of the fascist minister of popular culture of the RSI, Fernando Mezzasoma. At one point she was "kidnapped" by three young officers of the *Decima Mas,* who took her by car one night from Salò to La Spezia and introduced her to Daria Olsuviev, the wife of Prince Junio Valerio Borghese, who appointed her on the spot head of the Prince's press office for the entire unit. The excitement of adventure and the unit attracted the very young Pasca into agreeing to become a key figure in the propaganda of the RSI.[21] Recently Pasca Piredda wrote a book about those old stories and I had the opportunity to meet with her and hear the account of those events in her own words.[22]

But as she remembered some of those adventures that had nothing to do with Mussolini's death or the "Dongo treasure," suddenly Captain Neri and Gianna appeared in her narrative.

> The partisans of the 52nd Garibaldi Brigade arrested me at 2, Piazza Fiume [in Milan] at the headquarters of the *Decima* on the afternoon of April 29 while the bodies of Mussolini and the others who had been executed were still dangling in the Piazzale Loreto. The partisans took me to the offices of Sitra, a food company located along the Naviglio Pavese canal, which had been turned into a jail, and handed me over to the jailers. There was a "people's court" inside the building with some individuals who all referred to each other by first names (I can remember some of them: Italo, Carlo, Valerio), and they were wearing red kerchiefs. I was taken to that court and upon hearing what my role was at the *Decima* they condemned me to death. The execution was to take place the next morning, April 30. I will never forget the awful night I spent in a dark cellar. Partisans had machine guns constantly pointed at me (and at a dozen others who, stuffed into a room next door, had also been condemned to death). That, in addition to the continuous humiliations we had to endure.

At dawn we were dragged outside on the bank of the Naviglio. I was walking quickly and I despised the partisans because at that instant I didn't care about anything any more, not even about dying. Suddenly a hand grabbed me by the arm: "Come with me! I have to ask you some questions!" It was a young partisan commander, about 28 to 30, good looking, who was completely different from the elements that were set to shoot us. He took me to a shack where there was a table and some chairs. A girl, a partisan as well, was sitting on one of the chairs. "I see you were Borghese's press chief," he asked. "Aren't you afraid of dying?" That was how the dialog that saved my life began. After the first few words he introduced himself. "I'm Captain Neri," he said, "and this is Gianna." "How did a girl like you get in thick with those fascist thugs?" "And you, how could you get involved with these characters who are only looking for a bloodbath?" was my response. (In the meantime we could hear machinegun fire from the partisans ending the lives of my jailmates.) Captain Neri fell silent and then, almost painfully, said: "You saw those people . . . Unfortunately the revolution has overtaken us. They tied a red kerchief around their necks and now they enjoy seeing people suffer and killing them. I only know three or four of them at the most. The others are just destroying everything. Listen, I don't want you to be killed. I'll save you."

The partisan commander grabbed the phone, dialed a number, and asked for someone with a foreign name, certainly British or American, that I didn't grasp then and there. I can't remember in any case. He asked for a jeep to be sent "because I have a person to pick up and drive to your headquarters." Less than fifteen minutes went by, enough for Captain Neri to ask me some questions about the *Decima*. Much to my amazement the door opened and two British officers asked me to follow them. They drove me to a building and set me up in a small room. I immediately understood that this was a safe house of the Intelligence Service. They were hunting down Prince Borghese and wanted me to help them. After a few days they handed me over to an OSS team and fate took its course, ending in freedom after a rather short time in prison. I never again heard from Captain Neri and Gianna. Shortly thereafter, I was summoned by General Leone Zingales, the military prosecutor of Milan who asked me about the circumstances of my meeting with Neri and whether he told me about the Dongo gold. No, he didn't tell me about it and therefore I was of no help to the general. I never forgot the man who saved my life, the Communist commander who was clearly working with the British.

Appendix I

THE TEN CLUES
TO THE "BRITISH THREAD"

1. ACCORDING to the official histories Colonel Valerio was Walter Audisio, an accountant by profession, but according to Bill (partisan commander Count Piero Bellini delle Stelle, who seized Mussolini) Valerio was actually Luigi Longo, the number two man in the PCI. To this day no one knows for sure who Colonel Valerio really was. The fact is that he reached Dongo early Saturday afternoon, April 28, 1945, and in the town's main square announced that the CLNAI ordered him to execute "Mussolini and the Salò ministers" on the spot. However, he did not obey those orders to the letter. Since he found Mussolini already dead, he simply shot the corpse. As for the others, he did not just limit his action to the "Salò ministers"—to get to the correct number (fifteen was too little) he also ordered shot an air force captain, an employee of the ministry of the interior, a newspaper man, a former Communist, and so on.

2. The order to shoot Mussolini and his ministers never existed. The CLNAI, which was the official entity representing the Bonomi government in northern Italy, had not issued a death sentence, which it legally could not do, nor even less could it issue an order for an execution. As the representative of the Socialist party within the CLNAI, Sandro Pertini, in a speech broadcast on radio at 8 p.m. on April 27 (several hours after the news that Mussolini had been captured) and rebroadcast at 1 p.m. on the following day April 28 (when Mussolini was already dead) said: "He must be handed over to a People's Court to be tried as rapidly as possible. He must and will be executed. This is what we want even though we think the firing squad will do that man too much honor: he deserves to be killed like a mangy dog." Without any references to the "mangy dog," but also calling for a "trial," statements were issued by representatives of the Partito d'Azione (Leo Valiani); by the Christian Democrats (through Achille Marazza); and by the Liberal Party (through Giustino Arpesani). Ferruccio Parri, who was still in hiding in Switzerland, was in basic agreement: "As for those who were shot on the Dongo square, and who had been selected by Valerio according to criteria I am not aware of, it seems to me that several of them did not deserve to end up that way at all." By law the CLNAI was supposed to follow the DLL (Decreto Legislativo Luogotenenziale) n. 142 of April 22, 1945, regarding "the crimes committed by Mussolini and the fascist ministers" who created the CAS—Corte d'Assise Straordinarie (Special High Courts) to judge such cases. Why would the CLNAI act differently? To revolt against the government of the Lieutenant General of the Kingdom? There was not the slightest reason for it to do so; but faced with the fait accompli, meaning the execution of Mussolini and Claretta Petacci by the British services, after some frenzied agreements with Rome, the CLNAI had to come up with the ridiculous claim after the fact, issued to the press on April 29: "The CLNAI declares that the execution of Mussolini and his accomplices which it ordered is the necessary conclusion of a moment in history that leaves our country covered with ruins that are both moral and material...," etc.

3. A book would not be enough to describe the contradictions that plagued Walter Audisio, whom the PCI presented as being Colonel Valerio, during the remaining twenty-three years of his life after April 1945.

In the memoir he dictated and published on November 18 and December 17, 1945, in *L'Unità*, he expanded on his exchange with Claretta when he denied her permission to slip on her panties. This detail, as we know, was contradicted by Lia De Maria, who was host to Mussolini and Claretta Petacci, and who revealed that Claretta had to wear her underwear because she was having her period. In Walter Audisio's book, *In nome del popolo italiano*,[1] however, the entire incident disappeared.

Some other absurd details also appear, such as Walter Audisio (Valerio) speaking to Mussolini using the familiar form even though he stated that he managed to convince the Duce that he was actually a fascist who had come to free him. The book also describes Mussolini as a trembling coward when facing his "executioner," a detail that was explicitly denied by Communist partisans such as Pietro (Michele Moretti), and Guido (Aldo Lampredi). On January 23, 1996, *L'Unità* published a report written by Guido, a PCI functionary who had given it to Armando Cossutta, who was then part of the Party leadership and a member of Parliament in 1975. According to that report it is clear that at the moment of his death Mussolini did not drool (as Audisio claimed) nor did he thunder "Viva l'Italia!" (as in Moretti's versions), but actually cried out, "Aim at my chest!" This appeared to be an inexplicable, posthumous recognition offered to Mussolini (someone they had demonized for over half a century) in the official mouthpiece of the Communist party, by a person (Lampredi) that led one to believe had not even been present at the Duce's death. This important statement was in fact dusted off (some twenty-one years after it had been made) in the midst of the disputes about the "British thread" that this writer set forth, confirmed by Professor Renzo De Felice's statements concerning the contradictions of the left-wing "vulgate."

The autopsy report written by Professor Caio Mario Cottabeni noted that there was no food present in Mussolini's stomach. This contradicts what both Walter Audisio and Lia De Maria had stated—that the prisoner had lunch at noon on April 28: milk, polenta, bread, salami, and fruit. This detail would then confirm the assumption that Mussolini couldn't have had that meal because he was already dead by that time.

4. Why did the execution of the "fifteen" at Dongo take place in front of a crowd, while that of Mussolini and Claretta Petacci was carried out in secret? In the second case, were all those living in the neighborhood sent away so no one could witness the event? Neither the PCI nor the CVL have offered an explanation.

5. There exists a three-hundred-page analysis (this writer has a copy) written by Professor Ado Alessiani, who was the forensic medical advisor of the Rome Court. Based on the analysis of the bullet trajectories and rigor mortis at the time of the autopsy, it becomes clear that the time of Mussolini's death can only be in the morning of April 28, and the shots could only have been come from above, not from below, as the case would have been if the execution had taken place in front of the gate of the Villa Belmonte.

6. It is impossible not to seriously consider the version offered by a highly regarded leader of the Resistance, Urbano Lazzaro (Bill), deputy commander of the 52nd Garibaldi Brigade and the man who captured Mussolini. In his book, *Dongo, mezzo secolo di menzogne* [Dongo, Half a Century of Lies],[2] Bill reconstructs Mussolini's death in the greatest detail, placing it in the morning of April 28 in front of the De Maria house and carried out not by Walter Audisio but by the number two man in the PCI, Luigi Longo, the commander in chief of the Garibaldi Divisions.

In his now "classic" book, *Vita e morte segreta di Mussolini*,[3] Franco Bandini was the first to write that the death of Mussolini and Claretta Petacci took place in the morning of April 28 in front of the De Maria house, while at 4:30 p.m. the two dead bodies were "re-executed" to give credence to the official version concocted in the intervening hours in the frenzied phone calls between "Valerio" and the leadership of the PCI and the CVL (Corpo Volontari della Libertà).

In 1950 the great journalist Paolo Monelli, in his historical biography, *Mussolini piccolo borghese*,[4] underscored the contradictions that made the "official" version of Mussolini's death appear implausible.

In his book *L'ora di Dongo*, Alessandro Zanella,[5] the historian from Mantua, placed the shootings of Mussolini and Claretta Petacci in the morning hours in front of the De Maria house by Captain Neri (Luigi Canali), Gianna (Giuseppina Tuissi), and their companions. He based his findings on a legal document where Gianna's brother attributed the executions themselves or responsibility for them to his sister and to Neri. This may also confirm that those who ordered or carried out the shootings were agents acting for British intelligence, as Bruno Giovanni Lonati stated openly.

According to the eyewitness account by Dorina Mazzola, as told to Giorgio Pisanò and published in his book *Gli ultimi cinque secondi di Mussolini*,[6] Mussolini and Claretta Petacci were executed on the morning of April 28 in front of the De Maria house in Bonzanigo.

In an interview given by 83-year-old Angelo Carbone to reporter Gaspare Di Sclafani, published in the weekly *Gente* of May 8, 1999 (number 19), the former partisan fighter, who was a friend of President Sandro Pertini, confirmed that he was an eyewitness and stated: "It isn't true that Claretta Petacci was killed with Mussolini in front of the gate of the Villa Belmonte. That story was a total fabrication."

7. At the ISMLI (Istituto per la storia del movimento di liberazione in Italia)[7] office in Pavia there are two recordings on audiocassettes for "future memoirs" by two members of the firing squad at Dongo—Barbieri (who had been a political commissar at Capettini) and Gardella (who later became the PCI mayor of Voghera). Those recordings are still kept secret and when this writer requested permission to listen to them, the director of the Institute, Professor Guido Guderzo, politely refused. There is also a

memoir ("to be published only after my death") written by a Como CLN member, Ferrero Valsecchi, and a similar one by Gugliemo Cantoni (the partisan Sandrino), which disappeared immediately following his death. What is there to hide after so many years?

Cantoni was left as a guard by Captain Neri at the De Maria house, along with his comrade Giuseppe Frangi (Lino), who died a few days later, killed by machine gun fire. Sandrino was allowed to live because he agreed to forget forever what he had seen and heard that morning at Bonzanigo. This is clear from the testimony given at the Padua trial of 1957 as recounted by Bill:

> Here is Sandrino once again. Along with Lino he was a sentry at the De Maria house at Bonzanigo for Mussolini and Claretta Petacci. At first he denied that Neri was present when Mussolini was executed,[8] but later he had to admit that he was there. He denied being present at the shooting and having stood guard for the two dead bodies. I felt bad for Sandrino. He lies in such a way that everyone becomes convinced that he is lying, but he knows that he is running an even bigger risk if he told the truth.

8. There is a path laced with blood linking so many of the witnesses of the events at Dongo and Bonzanigo; it also quickly leads to those family members attempting an investigation to find out what may have happened to their loved ones. In the meantime the "Dongo treasure" that disappeared was made up, for the most part, according to innumerable accounts, of the plunder by the fascist police of the valuables of the Jews who were sent to the death camps. At the same time the documents that Mussolini was carrying also disappeared.

9. Some documents made public by SS General Karl Wolff provide something more than just a trace of the actual contacts between Mussolini and Churchill during the 1944–1945 period. These are also confirmed by many eyewitnesses, providing a credible idea of their content. From phone taps of conversations and

copies of the letters from the Duce and Claretta Petacci that were in the private files of the Nazi general it clearly shows that by 1944 Churchill already identified Stalin as being the greatest danger to the West and how Churchill, was putting pressure on Mussolini for Hitler to make a greater effort on the eastern front. With the complete collapse of the Third Reich and of Italian fascism coming on the heels of the Yalta conference between the United States, England, and the USSR, British intelligence had understandable reasons to make sure that any trace of the Churchill-Mussolini contacts disappeared.

10. The death of Carlo Alberto Biggini, an RSI minister and personal friend of Mussolini (who received some of the most confidential information from the Duce), remains very mysterious. He was suddenly hospitalized at a Milan clinic for a rapidly spreading malignant tumor. There are, however, credible accounts, such as the one by Father Agostino Gemelli, contradicting that diagnosis. Biggini died alone, far from the comfort of his family, and the persons who assisted him in his dying moments later denied having any contact with him. Biggini's demise brought about the total silence regarding the documents that the Duce gave him shortly before the end. Mussolini hoped that those documents would contribute to saving his life and serve as a justification for Italy's policies at the end of the war. The documents disappeared and were useless to the Duce and his faithful minister. The threads that confirm beyond a doubt the existence of a Mussolini–Churchill correspondence after 1940 (that even include the Japanese ambassador to Rome, Shinrokuro Hidaka) lead to the briefcase that Biggini was given for safekeeping. It is in that briefcase Biggini was to hold onto that the proof of the information we have provided will be found.

Appendix II

INTERVIEW WITH LUCIANO GARIBALDI

*The weekly magazine Italia Settimanale published
an interview with this writer on February 9, 1994.*

BEGINNING with an article in *Avvenire*, the Catholic daily
newspaper gave its "imprimatur" to Father Ennio Innocenti, a Rome
theologian, who states that Mussolini went to confession and had
communion a few months before his death. Later, in a series of
articles published in the daily *La Notte*, he made the ultimate "pro-
vocative" statement that Mussolini and Claretta Petacci may not
have been killed by Communist partisans but rather by British agents
belonging to the Special Forces. Luciano Garibaldi, newsman, historian, and contributor to *L'Italia Settimanale*, the author of books
such as *Mussolini e il Professore*, and *L'altro Italiano* ("a biography of
Egardo Sogno that I am very proud of," he says, "because he is the
historical figure of contemporary Italy I have the greatest respect
for"), answers the avalanche of criticism he was subjected to in this
interview. Few people have given any credibility to the purported

religious conversion of the Duce, while most historians rejected the thesis of the dictator's executioners being "British."

Q. Garibaldi, let's start with this challenge to the historians who are stuck in descriptions dating back fifty years. What is your evidence?

GARIBALDI. First of all, the historians of the final days of fascism are not at all stuck in the falsehoods that were disseminated mainly by the Communists right after the Liberation. There have been Franco Bandini, Giorgio Pisanò, Urbano Lazzaro (the partisan Bill, who actually captured Mussolini), and finally Alessandro Zanella, all of whom were able to demonstrate in their books how the "accepted" Communist version is false from the first word to the last. As for "evidence," I have none, nor did I ever claim to have any. All I have done is to develop logical assumptions based upon the choices made by the executioner at Dongo.

Q. What were those assumptions and who was the "executioner"?

GARIBALDI. The "executioner," as Franco Bandini already discovered in 1978, was Luigi Longo, the number two man in the PCI, and his "criteria" were the result of an understandable, however pitiless, logic of vengeance: the fifteen "martyrs of the Piazzale Loreto," therefore "fifteen fascists to be shot (plus their leader, obviously, Mussolini), so that the ledger would be set straight." However, the dead bodies that were dropped on the pavement of the Piazzale Loreto were not sixteen but eighteen. The others were the Petaccis, brother and sister. Marcello Petacci was executed on the orders of Colonel Valerio, while the killing of his sister had not been either planned or ordered by the CLNAI.

Q. Wasn't Claretta Petacci accidentally killed by a volley shot from Valerio with his machine gun?

GARIBALDI. Not by Valerio! You mean by Luigi Longo, the real Valerio, who was the hardest, toughest, most military of the old fighters in the Spanish Civil War, where he was known as Comrade Gallo the commander of the Garibaldi battalions in Spain. How can anyone believe a volley going off accidentally in the excitement of the moment? What could have prompted it since those two, Mussolini and Claretta, were alone, without any weapons and she was certainly in a state of total panic?

Q. You're saying that they found Claretta dead next to the Duce's body, both of them silent forever . . .

GARIBALDI. And relieved of the valuables they were carrying that were actually neither gold nor jewels but the original letters sent by Churchill to Mussolini—up until the eve of the collapse to convince Hitler to end all resistance in the west to stop, together with the Allies, the Red hordes coming from the east.

Q. Those were the documents that were to be seized under any circumstances by the partisans?

GARIBALDI. Naturally! The Communist partisans were simply the Italian arm of the Red Army. They were acting exclusively on orders from Stalin. If Stalin had those papers he could openly accuse Churchill of double-crossing him and of trashing the Yalta agreements, and could then demand much more than the territories of Eastern Europe.

Q. So, clearly the British had a vital interest in recuperating the letters and silencing Mussolini forever.

GARIBALDI. And Claretta, who knew everything and had a copy of all the letters.

Q. But someone must have led the British to Mussolini's hiding place at the De Maria house at Giulino di Mezzegra before the arrival of the "executioners" and Luigi Longo from Milan?

GARIBALDI. It was Captain Neri, the man who had hidden them with the De Marias and who therefore had to be eliminated a few days later by the PCI, which was angry at having been beaten to the punch by the British.

Q. But Captain Neri was a Communist partisan, already condemned to death by a court-martial headed by Amerigo Clocchiati as a suspect of being a spy for the fascists.

GARIBALDI. No, Neri was a British agent. I am not the one who is saying this. It was also stated by Pedro some ten years ago. Pedro was the commander of the 52nd Garibaldi Brigade—Neri's commander—and Clocchiati had written as much in a book no one paid attention to: *Dall'antifascismo al De Profundis per il PCI.* My critics should go and read page 250: "The serious issue is that Neri was precisely the person who could deliver Mussolini to the British. Why did Neri go to Dongo? Who sent him there? What was his mission?" Neri was punished not—as Zanella argues in his book, *L'ora di Dongo*—because he shot Mussolini on his own initiative without explicit orders from the Party, but because he facilitated the arrival of the British ahead of anyone else. Furthermore, Neri was not the type to kill someone in cold blood, and a woman even less.

Q. How can you support that assertion?

GARIBALDI. I know everything about Neri. I'm a friend of his family; I've read all of his letters, his diaries, and the thoughts he wrote down. He was a clear, transparent type of man. He felt that Communism was useful for the people and at the same time he was a democrat and an absolute anti-fascist.

Q. And you Garibaldi, are you a fascist or an anti-fascist? When you offered, in the highly regarded daily *Avvenire*, the possibility of Mussolini's religious conversion, you were accused of attempting a rehabilitation of the Duce and fascism in the eyes of the people, especially the Catholics.

GARIBALDI. Following in the footsteps of my colleagues in the 1970s who in order to be hired as editors of daily newspapers had to solemnly swear that they were "laymen, democrats, and anti-fascists," I will declare that I am a Catholic, a democrat, and an a-fascist, even though I am convinced that had I been of adult age during the Resistance I would have been with the partisans—the anti-Communist partisans mind you. As for the Duce's conversion, Father Ennio Innocenti was able to prove it beyond a doubt. If some people dislike the idea of that conversion, it's because the demonization of the opponent, a technique the Communists have always mastered, lingers on.[1]

Appendix III

A PERVASIVE FEAR

1. "IMMINENT death threat."

From the report by Police Inspector Ciro Verdiani, sent to the ministry of the interior in November 1945:

> There is an imminent death threat hanging over anyone knowing too much, wanting to find out, or talking about the destination and possession of the so-called "Duce's gold."

2. "Neri" was killed because he disagreed with the destination given for the Duce's gold and threatened to reveal the facts."

From the "highly confidential" report sent on December 16, 1945, to Premier Alcide De Gasperi by the Como chief of police, Davide Grassi:

> Regarding the so-called "Duce's gold," there have been many theories, investigations, and clues. Only the arrest of Michele Moretti could probably shed some light in all that darkness if he were interrogated in a clever way; but we may legitimately

assume that either Moretti, being unable to remain at large any longer, will be made to disappear, just like Captain Neri, Gianna, Annamaria, and others who knew a lot and wanted to know a lot more about the Duce's gold; or that Moretti will provide an explanation, which will not lead to any positive results, and we shall return to darkness.

In any case it must be made clear that Moretti will necessarily have to be judged in accordance with the existing code; the indictment can only be for unlawful appropriation—damaging no one knows whom! Under such circumstances Moretti will certainly remain totally silent, given the links he has to his own Party. Even entering a verdict of guilty that would entail a short sentence, he will always hope easily avoiding telling the truth due to the code of silence that ties all the Party members, and which has also very strongly infiltrated the police forces and prison guard personnel.

[…] It is also clear, according to credible confidential information, that Neri was killed because he disagreed with the intended destination of the Duce's gold and that he threatened to reveal these facts. The killing is said to have taken place in Milan and ordered by a Communist party member called Fabio, using the excuse of an old death sentence that a partisan court had issued while still in the underground period.

It is also certain that Neri's mistress, the partisan woman Gianna, also dissented with the destination given to the Duce's gold. The order for that murder is said to have come from Fabio. The killing took place at Pizzo, between Cernobbio and Moltrasio. The executioner was Captain Lince (now at large because he was the leader of the gang of the Café Robecchi in Como) and one Maurizio Bernasconi (now in custody in the San Donnino jail in Como as deputy chief of that same gang). Bernasconi has not yet been questioned regarding his participation in the murder.

There are many other homicides and disappearances connected to the vanishing of the so-called "Duce's gold," leading us to believe that a rather vast and strong organization wishes to keep the current location of the gold itself absolutely secret.

Among those murdered there was also the partisan Lino, who was found dead at the beginning of May and portrayed as having committed suicide, while according to confidential information and because of the way the body was found, he must have been hit by a machine gun volley that caught him by surprise on the road to Dongo.

From all the information and confidential statements obtained, the events that took place and that are still unfolding; from confidential conversations with some Communist party leaders; from their silences, surprises and contradictions, we must conclude that the issue of the Duce's gold cannot be isolated, but is connected to the broader and more strictly political issues, such that even if the questions surrounding the Duce's gold and the entire underground activity connected to it were known, the highest leadership of that Party would necessarily be the targets of reaction that are difficult to predict at this time.

[...] A man called Fabio is the leader of the secret organization. [...] That organization has deeply penetrated the Como police department to include the current commander, Vinci himself, and the deputy commander, Invernizzi, who are without a doubt visiting the Russian Mission in Milan at least once a week. That organization has undoubtedly received the so-called Duce's gold.

3. "Their permanent silence was secured by their death, since they dared go too far in their bold rebellion. [...] Nothing has specifically been done regarding the complaint and the facts by the police and political authorities because of complicity and fear."

From the report sent on December 25, 1945, to Premier Alcide De Gasperi from the Prefect of Como Virgilio Bertinelli:

The issue of Mussolini's gold has turned into a political issue much discussed in the Como-Milan area. It is a bone of contention among political parties, a reason for infighting and blackmail among local leaders, an insult and a defensive move among politicians; the moral shame of the facts is not involved. A recurring theme in the press and at political rallies concerns the possible theft of the Duce's gold, which is also a figure of speech since the mass of valuables was the final spoils grabbed by the fascist and German leaders who followed him when he attempted to use the Alpine valleys to reach the coveted Swiss haven.

[...] The fascist leaders and their automobiles were stripped of everything they carried at various locations and using different methods: money, jewels, suitcases, documents.

[...] With Moretti's arrest it would be possible to follow the path and destination of the gold that, using various routes and according to our information, led to the Communist party at Como and Milan, which all those involved belong to one way or the other.

[...] The Communist party (as well as those groups of the CLN and CVL that have at every possible turn been eager to write in letters to the authorities, saying they wish to shed full light on all the facts relating to the Nazi-Fascist convoy), on the other hand, is hiding and withholding from the law those who are guilty, preventing Moretti from talking and being turned over to the authorities.

More ominously there is the death threat that has already been effectively used against elements of the Communist party that have rebelled or talked or could have done so given the opportunity, such as Captain Neri (by his real name, Luigi Canali) a Communist and his mistress Gianna (by her real name, Giuseppina Tuissi) a Communist as well, and others who have disappeared at various times, done away with by orders of the Communist party.

Captain Neri and Gianna removed the jewelry, precious stones, valuables, and luggage at Dongo and brought them to Communist party headquarters. They must have had the receipts that were issued. Death ensured their permanent silence because they went too far in bold rebellion.

Tuissi's brother filed a complaint with the Allied command at Como and then with the Royal Police Station at Milan against Fabio, a leader of the Milan Communist party as the instigator who is supposedly the pseudonym of Luigi Longo. Nothing tangible was done by anyone—at least by the political and police authorities—in response to the complaint, either due to collusion or fear. No report, not even incomplete, by any kind of official entity exists.

4. "A general propensity to remain silent." From the deposition at the Padua trial of 1957 by attorney Felice Camoni, a member of the Commission appointed by the Como CLN to investigate the disappearance of the "Dongo gold":

> We were clashing head-on with a general sense of secrecy and fear while some threatening letters also reached the Commission's offices. A man's hide at that time wasn't worth ten lire. And those who were to be interrogated fled three hundred kilometers away. Had we only had two carabinieri things would have been different.

5. "Slammed against the wall by Colonel Valerio's men." From the deposition of attorney Davide Grassi, former police chief at Como at the 1957 Padua trial:

> In that chaotic situation with Mussolini fleeing I was appointed chief of police in Como and I still don't know who picked me. My first official act was to be slammed against the wall inside my own office by Colonel Valerio's men because I had defended a former OVRA agent they had found in the courtyard and wanted to execute on the spot.
>
> JUDGE: Were you able to make any investigations at that time?
>
> GRASSI: You mean an inquiry into the disappearance of the "Dongo gold"? How could I possibly do so since I was completely surrounded by Communist policemen? The Communists were calling the shots!

Appendix IV

THE DIARIES OF CLARETTA PETACCI

Interview with Luciano Garibaldi by Mario Suttora, U.S.
correspondent of the weekly magazine Oggi, *published on March 19, 2003.*

THE MYSTERY goes deeper, and the mysteries surrounding the death of Benito Mussolini, instead of fading away, grow thicker. The new supervisor of the Italian State Archives, Maurizio Fallace, has filed a complaint with the carabinieri for the theft of the correspondence between the fascist dictator and his mistress Claretta Petacci covering the entire year 1937 of her diary. The only surviving heir to Claretta Petacci is her sixty-year-old nephew, Ferdinando, who lives in Phoenix, Arizona, who sounded the alarm in this weekly magazine in an exclusive interview about those dramatic documents. "Someone doesn't want the truth to be known," he said. Now the news that the diary and the letters had already been plundered by persons unknown is creating renewed suspicion.

Q. What is so explosive about the Mussolini-Petacci papers?

GARIBALDI. Theoretically, no one should know because for the past fifty-eight years every government has been covering it by calling it a "state secret." However, by law that should only last fifty years. Therefore, in 1995 when the time was up I asked permission to see it. But the Archive prevented me from doing so by adding another twenty-year period to protect the privacy of the persons involved. I went directly to Giorgio Napolitano, the minister of the interior at the time, asking permission to leaf through even a few pages under the vigilant eyes of the functionaries of the Archive, those concerning the months from the end of 1944 to January 1945.

Q. Why did you limit yourself that way?

GARIBALDI. Because I found out about the transcripts of the phone conversations between Mussolini and Claretta—tapped by the Germans who were checking everything. Those discussions concern secret contacts that the Duce was having with Winston Churchill's British emissaries. "I will succeed at convincing Hitler," said Mussolini to his mistress, who had become his political confidant at that dramatic time. He opened up to her because he knew by then that he could almost not trust anyone else.

Q. What did Churchill want from Mussolini?

GARIBALDI. To stop the USSR, which was advancing too quickly in Europe while the western Allies were still stopped on the Rhine.

Q. And what did you expect to discover in Claretta's secret diaries?

GARIBALDI. What she was writing—at least during the days that correspond to the phone calls the Nazis tapped. She listened to everything and during her long sleepless nights at the Villa Fiordalisio on Lake Garda she did a lot of writing. Her diaries, in fact, are enormous—some fifteen thousand pages, one thousand per diary as she confided to her sister Myriam.

Q. Why didn't Napolitano let you have access to them, since the "state secret" period had expired and your work was of a scientific-historical nature, certainly not in search of private gossip?

GARIBALDI. His answer was strange. He maintained that the archivists had already checked the diaries and hadn't found anything I was looking for.

Q. Therefore, someone has already read and studied the secret documents. And how come the year 1937 disappeared?

GARIBALDI. The letters from that year are not expected to contain any important political revelations. They most probably deal with lovers' correspondence and complaints by the mistress of someone who was still very much a ladies' man and having other romantic escapades. They may have been sold at a high price to some millionaire private collector. There are quite a few of them around the world.

Q. The commercial value of the correspondence and diary could therefore be rather high. Was that the reason her nephew Ferdinando is requesting them?

GARIBALDI. Ferdinando Petacci has every right to obtain possession as the only living heir. If they are not returned to him once the fifty-year limit comes, it would constitute theft.

Ferdinando Petacci was only three years old when the car he was traveling in with his aunt Claretta, his father Marcello, his mother, and brother was stopped at Dongo on Lake Como in April 1945. The partisans executed his father (even though he stated that he was in contact with the British—perhaps for this very reason), raped his mother, and his brother never recovered from the shock and died at a very young age. Ferdinando now lives in Arizona and is demanding that his property be returned to him, including the right to privacy. How can it be extended to the closest relatives?

However, the State Archive has different ideas. Superintendent Fallace announced: "This year, after seventy years, we will open for consultation the beginning of the papers relating to 1933." It was during the preparatory meeting for this publication that the theft was discovered. Already in 1950, when the carabinieri discovered the documents in a trunk buried in the garden of the Villa Fiordalisio by the caretaker couple Cervis (to whom Claretta had left everything before leaving Gardone), someone purged them of the most potentially embarrassing parts. On the other hand, this happened to all the documents that had anything that could embarrass the British. The documents, for example, that Mussolini handed to the trusted Japanese ambassador, Shinrokuro Hidaka: we asked for them many years ago and his answer was simply that he had handed every-thing over to his government. Naturally, the Japanese government responded that they were a state secret. The photocopies Mussolini gave to Minister Carlo Alberto Biggini have also vanished.

Q. Are we sure that proof of the Mussolini-Churchill contact exists?

GARIBALDI. One must certainly not imagine letters starting with a "Dear Winston" or "Dear Benito," but there is no doubt about contacts through emissaries. Pietro Carradori, Mussolini's orderly, told me in 2001 that he accompanied him twice at night in secret from Gargnano to Ponte Tresa on the Swiss border to those meet-ings. Even the partisans who took part in those events have be-gun—in the 1990s when they were elderly men—to break the wall of silence that has existed for half a century: Urbano Lazzaro, the famous "Commander Bill," who captured Mussolini and Marcello Petacci, has written two books. It's a pity that the Historical Insti-tute of the Resistance in Pavia will not allow the cassettes with the testimony of another deceased partisan to be listened to.

The mysteries of the Dongo gold and the execution of those partisans who rebelled against the official version continue. They shall go on for twelve years if the Italian government doesn't de-cide to lift the classification (which lasts only thirty years in the United States). And perhaps never—if another strange "theft" were to unfortunately take place.

Appendix V

The Resistance Sullied

We reproduce the most relevant parts of the interview with Urbano Lazzaro by Luciano Garibaldi in the weekly Il Borghese *on August 7, 1997. Urbano Lazzaro was the partisan commander who captured Mussolini. The title of the interview was "The Resistance Sullied by the Communists," with the tag line, "A truth interview with one of the last of the great protagonists of the Resistance still alive, Urbano Lazzaro, known as Bill, former deputy political commissar of the 52nd Garibaldi Brigade, the man who, in the early afternoon of Friday, April 27, 1945, discovered Benito Mussolini on a flak (German anti-aircraft unit) truck wearing a German military disguise to escape capture, and declared him to be under arrest in the name of the King and of the Italian People."*

LAZZARO. I met Bill at Vercelli, where he was spending part of his summer vacation with his wife. Bill was born in Vicenza and is now seventy-three. He has been living in São Paulo, Brazil, for many years where his three daughters were born. One of them is a magistrate of the Brazilian Republic and another is involved in scientific research at São Paulo University. Bill has kept his Italian nationality after having traveled half way around the world as a technician at the Snam Progetti Company, which was specialized in building oil refineries. Every year he returns on vacation with his wife in her hometown. The events he became involved in some fifty-two years ago have left their mark in his life enough for him to write three books: *Il compagno "Bill"* [Comrade "Bill"]; *Dongo mezzo secolo di menzogne* [Dongo, Half a Century of Lies] and *L'oro di Dongo* [The Dongo Gold], all of them published in Italy.

My reason for wanting to meet with Bill is rather specific, since I wanted to ask him to testify at my trial next February in the court of Milan. I am accused of stating that the Communists have told only lies about Mussolini's death. (The children of an employee who signed Benito Mussolini's death certificate, placing the time of death at an impossible hour at 4:20 p.m. on April 28, 1945, sued me for libel. It was my contention in one of my historical investigations that the death certificate was unreliable.)

Bill was candid and up front, removing all my illusions: "Don't have me coming to Italy in February when I enjoy the sunshine of Brazil. However, should you wish to know whether the Communists told the truth or lied regarding what took place at Dongo and the end of Benito Mussolini, I can answer unhesitatingly that they are lying, and shamelessly at that, as they have always lied."

I must confess that I was flabbergasted. Such a conclusion is even harsher than what I have said in my books and articles. However, Urbano Lazzaro did not mince words: "They have lied and continue to lie, beginning with the identity of author of the massacre at Dongo, the famous Colonel Valerio of the CVL, sent from Milan as the executioner of Mussolini and the members of the RSI government."

Q. Why are they lying?

LAZZARO. Because Valerio was not Walter Audisio, as we continue to tell generations of Italian pupils in the schools, but rather Luigi Longo, commanding general of the Garibaldi Brigades and at that time the number two man in the PCI after Palmiro Togliatti. By ordering the Dongo executions Longo was not following the orders of the legitimate government of His Majesty the Lieutenant

General but rather an internal decision of the PCI and therefore of the Soviet Red Army which the Communist party represented in Italy.

Q. You're aware of the seriousness of what you're saying?

LAZZARO. Fully aware. So much so that I attempted to stop Longo, meaning Colonel Valerio as soon as I understood that like an exterminating archangel he was about to shoot the guilty and the innocent alike, ticking them off with revolting mechanical indifference from the prisoner's list that I and my men had captured in the German convoy that was fleeing.

Q. How could you have stopped Longo since he arrived from Milan with a firing squad?

LAZZARO. That would have been very easy. All I had to do was to call for help from my Garibaldi men at Domaso; I actually took my motorcycle and went there to call them as soon as I understood that Longo was going to shoot the prisoners. I was a military man and a "Guardia di Finanza" (Treasury Police) and in my mind, according to my moral code, the prisoners were sacred, as in The Hague Convention. Only the Nazis were killing hostages and prisoners without a trial.

Q. Why were you unsuccessful at preventing the massacre?

LAZZARO. Unfortunately I got there too late. When from Domaso I reached Gravedona leading my men and got to Dongo, the tragedy was consummated and the truck filled with the corpses of those who had been shot had already left for Milan where it was to reach the Piazzale Loreto after loading the bodies of Mussolini and Claretta Petacci—killed that morning at Giulino di Mezzegra.

Q. Therefore, in the morning and not at 4:20 p.m., as the accepted Resistance literature proclaims that the Duce was put to the wall and executed more or less solemnly "in the name of the Italian people."

LAZZARO. Look, I was not present at Giulino di Mezzegra so I just have to go by what I was told later by my men, who were either there or had heard it from eyewitnesses. One thing is certain—the Communists have always lied about what happened at Giulino di Mezzegra.

Q. Why did you, Lazzaro, become part of the Resistance?

LAZZARO. Because you can only swear once.

Q. Can you explain this in more detail?

LAZZARO. When Mussolini was freed at the Gran Sasso and set up the RSI, our commander assembled us saying that we were to swear allegiance to the new government. All the Treasury guards were at attention on the square, ready to swear, including Colonel Malgeri, who on April 25 would go over to the partisans. I was the only one who refused to swear.

Q. Why?

LAZZARO. Because I had already sworn once before to be faithful to the King.

Q. Were you a monarchist?

LAZZARO. No, just a soldier, a man, who must deal with his own conscience.

Q. What happened?

LAZZARO. I had to run away to Switzerland to avoid arrest. I returned from there to fight the Germans and their fascist allies. That's how it was until that fateful April 27 when at Dongo we stopped the German column that was fleeing toward Switzerland.

Q. Did you ever have problems with the Communists?

LAZZARO. Yes, they tried to kill me at least seven times. But at that time it wasn't so easy. I was also armed, and rather well if I may add. Once in 1946 Togliatti came to Como for a rally. They also wanted the flag of the 52nd to be present. I refused and said: "It didn't go for De Gasperi, for Nenni, and it will not go for Togliatti." Then at the rally Togliatti told me "So you're the famous Bill, the one who caught Mussolini. You see, if you had thrown your lot in with us you'd be in Parliament next to me by now."

Q. And instead?

LAZZARO. I couldn't find a job for four years until I moved to my wife's hometown near Vercelli and found work as a laborer. Then after studying to become an oil technician I managed to be hired by the Snam Company and I emigrated overseas.

Q. What is your final view of the Resistance?

LAZZARO. An inspiring page in Italy's history. Too bad the Communists sullied it with their thirst for blood.

Glossary

Abbreviations

AMG	Allied Military Government
AMGOT	Allied Military Government in Occupied Territories
Brigate Nere	Black Brigades (fascist party military units, 1944–1945)
CLN	Committee of National Liberation
CLNAI	Committee of National Liberation of Northern Italy
DC	Christian Democratic party
Decima Flottiglia MAS	Tenth MAS Flotilla (fascist naval units)
Decima MAS	same as above
GAP	Partisan Action Group
GNR	National Republican Guard (fascist units)
Istituto Luce	Newsreel film and photographic institute of the fascist regime
MI6	British Intelligence
MOVM	Medaglia d'Oro al Valor Militare [Gold Medal for Military Valor]
MVSN	Fascist militia, 1922–1943
OSS	Office of Strategic Services (American intelligence in WWII)
OVRA	Italian secret police, 1922–1943
Partito d'Azione	Action Party (part of the resistance movement)
PCI	Italian Communist party
PFR	Republican Fascist party, 1943–1945
PNF	National Fascist party, 1923–1943
PRO	Public Record Office (British archives)
PSI	Italian Socialist party
RAR	Ridotto Alpino Repubblicano (Alpine Redoubt for the fascist last stand)

RRS	Raggruppamento Repubblicano Socialista (socialist group set up by Mussolini as a loyal opposition within the RSI)
RSI	Repubblica Sociale Italiana (Italian Social Republic), 1943–1945. Fascist regime in northern Italy
Salò	Republic of Salò (named after the town on Lake Garda)
SOE	Special Operations Executive (British wartime commando units)
SS	German military and police units

Pseudonyms

Captain Neri	Luigi Canali
Gianna	Giuseppina Tuissi
Pedro	Count Piero Bellini delle Stelle
Bill	Urbano Lazzaro
Pietro	Michele Moretti
Colonel Valerio	Walter Audisio
Fabio	Pietro Vergari
Lino	Giuseppe Frangi
Sandrino	Guglielmo Cantoni
Guido	Aldo Lampredi
Riccardo	Alfredo Mordini
Guglielmo	Dante Gorreri
Ercoli	Palmiro Togliatti
Francesco	Pietro Terzi
Nicola	Dionisio Gambaruto
Mirko	Maurizio Bernasconi
Giacomo	Bruno Giovanni Lonati
Francio	Francesco Magni

BIBLIOGRAPHY

(Principal works consulted by the author)

Amicucci, Ermanno. *I 600 giorni di Mussolini* (Rome: Faro, 1948).

Andriola, Fabio. *Appuntamento sul lago* (Milan: SugarCo, 1990).

——. *Mussolini-Churchill carteggio segreto* (Casale Monferrato: Piemme, 1998).

Anfuso, Filippo. *Rome, Berlino, Salò* (Milan: Garzanti, 1950).

Audisio, Walter. *In nome del popolo italiano* (Turin: Teti Editore, 1975).

Bandini, Franco. *Le ultime 95 ore di Mussolini* (Milan: Mondadori, 1959).

——. *Vita e morte segreta di Mussolini* (Milan: Mondadori, 1978).

Bastianini, Giuseppe. *Uomini, cose, fatti* (Rome: Vitagliano, 1959).

Battaglia, Roberto. *Storia della Resistenza italiana* (Turin: Einaudi, 1964).

Bobbio, Norberto. *Resistenza* (January 1964).

Bonavita, Francesco. *The Duce's Father.*

Bordogna, Mario. *Junio Valerio Borghese e la X Flottiglia MAS* (Mursia: Milan, 1995).

Bottari, Paolo. *All'ombra della grande ciminiera: la Cucirini Cantoni Coats* (Lucca: M.P. Fazzi Ed., 1994).

Campini, Dino. *Mussolini-Churchill: i carteggi* (Milan: Italpress, 1952).

——. *Piazzale Loreto* (Milan, 1972).

Caprara, Massimo. *Quando le Botteghe erano oscure* (Milan, 1997).

——. *PCI la storia dimenticata* (Milan, 2001).

Carradori, Pietro. *Vita Col Duce* (Luciano Garibaldi, ed.), (Milano, Effedieffe, 2001).

Cave Brown, Anthony. *The Secret War Report of the OSS* (New York, 1976).

Catalano, Franco. *Storia del CLNAI* (Milan: Bompiani, 1956).

Cavalleri, Giorgio. *Ombre sul lago* (Casale Monferrato: Piemme, 1995).

——. *Storia del Neri e della Gianna* (Como: Nodo Libri, 1991).

Chassin, L.M. *Storia militare della Seconda guerra mondiale* (Florence: Sansoni, 1964); original title: *Histoire de la deuxième guerre mondiale* (Payot: Paris, 1963).

Churchill, Winston S. *The Second World War*, 6 Vols. (London: Cassell and Co. 1948–1954; Italian translation: *La seconda guerra mondiale* (Milano: Mondadori, 1948–1954).

Chessa, Pasquale. *Rosso e Nero* (Milan: Baldini & Castoldi 1995).

Cione, Edmondo. *Storia della RSI* (Rome: Latinità, 1950).

Clark, Mark. *5.a Armata Americana: campagne d'Africa e d'Italia* (Garzanti: Milano, 1952); original title: *Calculated Risk* (New York: Harper, 1950).

Clocchiatti, Amerigo. *Dall' antifascismo al De Profundis per il PCI: testimonanze di un militante* (Verona: Edizioni del Paniere, 1991).

Collier, Richard. *Duce! The Rise and Fall of Benito Mussolini* (New York: Viking, 1971).

Corvo, Max. *The OSS in Italy 1942–1945: A Personal Memoir* (New York: Praeger, 1990).

Crapanzano, Guido e Giulianini Ermelindo. *La cartamoneta italiana* (Milano: Spirali, 2003).

Cucco, Alfredo. *Non volevamo perdere* (Bologna: Cappelli, 1950).

D'Aroma, Nino. *Mussolini segreto* (Bologna: Cappelli, 1958).

——. *Vite parallele: Churchill e Mussolini* (Rome: CEN, 1972).

Deakin, F. William. *The Brutal Friendship. Mussolini, Hitler and the Fall of Italian Fascism* (New York: Harper and Row, 1962).

De Felice, Renzo. *Rosso e Nero*, interview by Pasquale Chessa (Milan: Baldini & Castoldi, 1995).

——. *Mussolini L'Alleato: La Guerra Civile 1943–1945*, ed. by Emilio Gentile (Einaudi: Turin, 1997).

Eisenhower, Dwight D. *Crusade in Europe* (New York: Doubleday, 1948).

Faenza, Roberto and Fini, Marco. *Gli americani in Italia* (Milano: Feltrinelli, 1976).

Festorazzi, Roberto. *Mussolini-Churchill: le carte segrete* (Milano, 1998).

Franceschini, Ezio. *Concetto Marchesi* (Padova: Antenore, 1978).

Francesconi, Teodoro. *Le bande BAC in Dalmazia 1942–43* (Milano: Editrice Militare Italiana, 1992).

Galli, Lodovico. *Una vile esecuzione* (Brescia, 2001).

Garibaldi, Luciano. *L'altro Italiano. Edgardo Sogno.*

——. *La pista inglese* (Milan: Ares, 2002).

——. *Mussolini e il professore* (Milan: Mursia, 1983).

——. *Un secolo di guerre* (Vercelli: White Star, 2001); U.S. edition: *Century of War* (New York: Friedman-Fairfax, 2001).

Gervaso, Roberto. *Claretta* (Milan: Rizzoli, 1982).

Gilbert, Martin. *The First World War* (New York: H. Holt, 1994).

Hitler, Adolf. *Mein Kampf* (Milan: Bompiani, 1941).

NOTES

Introduction

1. David Stafford, *Churchill and Secret Service* (New York: Overlook, 1997).
2. Renzo De Felice, *Mussolini. La Guerra Civile 1943–1945* (Turin: Einaudi, 1997–1998).
3. François Delpla, *Churchill et les Français* (Paris: Ed. du Polygone, 2000) p. 561.
4. Winston S. Churchill, *The Second World War. Triumph and Tragedy*, (Boston: Houghton Mifflin, 1953) Vol. VI p. 529.
5. Gerhard L. Weinberg, *A World At Arms* (New York: Cambridge UP, 1995) pp. 609–611 and p. 1076, notes 67 and 68.
6. *New York Journal American*, May 18, 1947 "Secret Nazi Files Disclose Plan for Sneak Red Truce" The article mentions a conference between Hitler and his commanders held on July 17 and 18, 1943 where the Führer would have stated "…a threat by Japan that she will enter the war against Russia will help to make the latter accept the German offer of an unannounced armistice on the Eastern front to be kept secret from the Anglo-Saxons. Russia would continue to accept lend-lease materials. This political goal is worth every sacrifice."
7. Arkadi Vaksberg, *Alexandra Kollontai* (Paris: Fayard, 1996) p. 435–436.
8. Stafford, op. cit. p. 311.
9. Wilhelm Höttl, *The Secret Front* (New York: Enigma, 2003) p. 232.

Chapter I — The Mystery of C. A. Biggini

1. Dino Campini, *Mussolini-Churchill: i carteggi* (Milan: Editrice Italpress, 1952), pp. 230–231.
2. Ibid., p. 235.
3. Ibid.
4. Luciano Garibaldi, *Mussolini e il Professore—vita e diari di Carlo Alberto Biggini* (Milan: Mursia, 1983).
5. Archivio Centrale dello Stato, RSI, Segreteria Particolare del Duce, confidential correspondence, b. 76, f. 646, sf. 2, "Letters and telegrams from the Duce to Biggini."

6. Luciano Garibaldi, *Mussolini e il Professore*, passim.
7. See Aldo A. Mola, "Giellisti," Ed. Cassa di Risparmio di Cuneo, Collana Storica della Resistenza Cuneese, 3 vol., 1997.
8. Dino Grandi, a senior fascist leader, spearheaded the movement to force a vote at the meeting of the fascist Grand Council on July 25, 1943. His main instrument was to call for a vote on his "Agenda," calling for Mussolini to step aside as military leader and returning the powers of commander in chief to King Victor Emmanuel III. In effect, the "Agenda" was a move to curtail Mussolini's power and replace him. The Grand Council voted in favor of the Grandi "Agenda" by a clear majority, which included Galeazzo Ciano (Mussolini's son-in-law), who would be executed by the RSI fascists in 1944.
9. See Egidio Meneghetti, "Cronaca dell'Università di Padova," in "Mercurio," December 1945; Ezio Franceschini, "Concetto Marchesi," Antenore, Padova 1978; Norberto Bobbio, "Resistenza," January 1964.
10. See details in Chapter V of *Mussolini e il Professore*, op. cit.
11. Sandro Pertini was a key Socialist Resistance leader, later to become president of Italy.
12. See Archivio Centrale dello stato—RSI—Segreteria particolare del Duce, b.76, f.646 sf. 9, "Professori universitari."
13. Fabio Andriola, *Mussolini-Churchill: Carteggio segreto* (Casale Monferrato: Piemme, 1998).
14. The documents assembled by the author for the 1982 edition of this book are today part of the Istituto Culturale "Carlo Alberto Biggini" at La Spezia, directed by Senator Professor Gaetano Rasi.
15. Dino Campini, *Mussolini-Churchill: I carteggi*, op. cit., p. 133.
16. Peter Tompkins, *Dalle carte segrete del Duce* (Milan: Marco Tropea Editore, 2000), p. 361.
17. *Libri ribelli*, bi-yearly magazine, Biella n. 3 March 2003.

Chapter II — The Disappearing Papers of Baron Hidaka

1. Dino Campini, *Mussolini-Churchill: I carteggi*, op. cit., pp. 135–136.
2. Information given to the author in March 2003 by Professor Romano Vulpitta, a university professor in Tokyo and author of the book *Mussolini storia di un italiano* (Mussolini: The History of an Italian), published in Japan.

3. For several decades, in an effort to ridicule Mussolini and fascism, the films of the Istituto Luce were shown in movie houses and on television at double the normal speed so that both Mussolini and his entourage looked like robots.
4. Nino D'Aroma, *Vite parallele: Churchill e Mussolini* (Parallel Lives: Churchill and Mussolini), (Rome: CEN, 1962).
5. Published by Editrice Faro, Rome, 1948.
6. Alberto Mellini Ponce de Leon, *Guerra diplomatica a Salò* (Diplomatic Warfare at Salò), (Bologna: Cappelli, 1950), p. 12.
7. Ibid. p. 25.
8. Filippo Anfuso, *Roma-Berlino-Salò* (Rome-Berlin-Salò), (Milan: Garzanti, 1950), p. 493.
9. Op. cit.
10. *Il Borghese*, a weekly magazine, and *Roma*, a daily newspaper published in Naples, are both right wing.
11. Interview with Brian Sullivan by Lucia Annunziata in *Corriere della Sera*, July 2, 1944.
12. Osamu Tezuka, *Adolf* (Spanish translation [Barcelona: Planeta de Agostini, 2000]).
13. Luciano Garibaldi, *Mussolini e il Professore*, op. cit., p. 194.

Chapter III — Mussolini and the War

1. From the interview with Shirokuro Hidaka by Italian historian and journalist Piero Buscaroli, July 6, 1966.
2. Note in Carlo Alberto Biggini's *Diaries*; in Luciano Garibaldi, *Mussolini e il Professore*, op. cit., p. 299.
3. Luciano Garibaldi, *Mussolini e il Professore*, op. cit., p. 133.
4. In Milan in April 2003.
5. Author's note.
6. Giuseppe Bastianini, *Uomini, cose, fatti* Rome, 1959.
7. Article published in *Il Giornale*, dated October 22, 1995, of the conversation between S. Hidaka and P. Buscaroli of July 6, 1966.
8. These are: Dino Campini, *Mussolini-Churchill: I carteggi, op. cit.* (Milan, 1952) and *Piazzale Loreto* (Milan, 1972); Franco Bandini, *Le ultime 95 ore di Mussolini* (Mussolini's Final 95 hours), (Milan, 1959), and *Vita e morte segreta di Mussolini* (Mussolini's Life and Secret Death), (Milan, 1978); Alessandro Zanella, *L'ora di Dongo* (The Hour at Dongo) (Milan,

1993); Fabio Andrida, *Appuntamento sul lago* (Appointment on the Lake), (Milan, 1990) and *Mussolini-Churchill carteggio segreto* (Casale Monferrato, 1996); Arrigo Petacco, *Dear Benito, caro Winston* (Milan, 1985); Giorgio Cavalleri, *Ombre sul lago* (Shadows on the Lake), (Casale Monferrato, 1995); Roberto Festorazzi, *Mussolini-Churchill: le carte segrete* (Mussolini-Churchill: The Secret Papers), (Milan, 1998).

9. In the Italian *Il Borgese* on April 30, 2000.

Chapter IV — The Eyewitnesses Tell the Story

1. From his book *Decima flottiglia nostra* (Our Tenth Flotilla), (Milan: Mursia, 1986). The passage is part of a chapter regarding the relations of the Decima and the authorities in the south.

2. The island is the property of the Beretta family, the well-known arms manufacturers, who impartially supplied fascists and partisans having good relations with everyone as is customary for arms merchants.

3. Frigate Captain Carlo Fecia di Cossato committed suicide in 1944, protesting against a decree by the Bonomi government that abolished the pledge of allegiance to the King by officers, obligating him to sink German U-Boats after having sunk British submarines.

4. The occurrence was confirmed to this author by Mario Bordogna, author of the important book, *Junio Valerio Borghese e la Xa Flottiglia Mas* (Milan: Mursia, 1995).

5. Wife of Commander Borghese, of Russian origin, and working closely with her husband.

6. Raffaele De Courten was the minister of the navy of the government of King Victor Emmanuel III and had guaranteed full cooperation between the men of the Decima in the south and those in the north.

7. Decima officers in the south but still ready to fight under Prince Borghese.

8. The objective was to protect the rights of that territory and of the Italian population from Tito's plans for annexation.

9. This author has received credible confirmation of Nesi's account by former officers of the Decima Mas among them Mario Bordogna.

10. This account is from the book, *Vita col Duce* (Life with the Duce), (Milan: Editore FdF, 2001), edited by Luciano Garibaldi, part of the chapter entitled "Those British Characters!"

11. F. M. Barracu was the undersecretary to the President of the Council of Ministers of the RSI and had been decorated with the Gold Medal for military valor.

12. Quinto Navarra, Mussolini's usher and driver, author, after the war, of a book of memoirs, *Memorie del commesso di Mussolini*, introduction by Indro Montanelli (Milan: Longanesi, 1983).

13. Secret contacts were underway between SS General Karl Wolff, head of the German police forces in Italy and Allen Dulles of the OSS in Bern, Switzerland, for the surrender of 800,000 German troops in Italy.

14. See Edmondo Cione, *Storia della RSI* (Rome, 1951).

15. State Department dispatch to the U.S. embassy in Rome dated March 12, 1945, reporting Drew Pearson's revelation on radio in the U.S. See Roberto Faenza and Marco Fini, *Gli Americani in Italia* (Milan: Feltrinelli, 1976).

16. Published by Rusconi (Milan, 1993), pp. 48–50.

Chapter V — The Phone Taps as Evidence

1. Ricciotti Lazzero, *Il sacco d'Italia: razzie, e stragi tedesche nella Repubblica di Salò* (The Theft of Italy: German Depredations and Murders in the Republic of Salò), preface by Simon Wiesenthal (Milan: Mondadori, 1994).

2. It is clearly obvious that the efforts of the Duce to convince Hitler to his point of view—meaning to put all their efforts against the Russians and stop the counteroffensive in the west. The despot in Berlin, however, was still convinced that his sword could cut on "both sides" of the blade and therefore continued to fight on two fronts.

3. Mussolini felt he could pressure Churchill at least as long as he had the documents.

4. A clear allusion to the direct contacts between Mussolini and Churchill.

5. The sentence shows that Claretta was cognizant of every political issue in the State, even the most delicate ones.

6. The identity of the mysterious "man from Milan" will be discussed further ahead. See references to Tommaso David.

7. An obvious allusion to the CLNAI and the government in the south.

8. Luciano Garibaldi, *Century of War* (Friedman-Fairfax, 2001), introduction by Wolf Blitzer of CNN.

9. Riccardo Lazzeri speaks perfect German and served as the interpreter for the author's meetings with Karl Wolff in 1983. Lazzeri later wrote two books about the RSI.

10. Nicola Bombacci was a companion of the young Mussolini from Romagna and a participant in his early subversive struggles. Bombacci was one of the founders of the Italian Communist party. He joined the Duce because of the RSI's strong socialist program. He fled with Mussolini from Milan and was executed by the partisans at Dongo.

11. The decoration was awarded in June 1943 with the following statement: "Motivated by a great love of country, he volunteered even though he was sixty-seven years old. Leading a unit of volunteers he had created and trained, he operated in a particularly delicate area. In the course of violent combat against strong rebel bands, he inflicted severe casualties amid their ranks and blunted their offensive. Later, having found out the glorious end of a son who was stationed in the same area, he refused to leave his assignment, and after paying his respects, he returned to his volunteers and took command of a large and complex unit continuing to fight. During an important action he was wounded in the chest and remained among his men until the successful end of the operation. A sparkling example of Roman virtue." Gospa Srimska (Balkania) December 8, 1942.

12. Published by Editrice Militare (Italiana, 1992), pp. 32–35.

13. G. Guareschi was sued for having published a letter signed by De Gasperi that was found to be a forgery wherein the future prime minister had requested that the Allies bomb an area of Rome. De Gasperi died in 1954, a few months after Guareschi was sentenced to one year in prison, which the writer chose to actually spend in jail as a sign of protest.

Chapter VI — Mussolini on Lake Lugano and Churchill on Lake Garda

1. Ermanno Amicucci, *I 600 giorni di Mussolini,* op. cit, p. 269. Amicucci was the director of the *Corriere della Sera* and followed Mussolini's convoy. He was one of the few fascists to save his own life, having understood the trap Mussolini was falling into.

2. Edmondo Cione, *Storia della Repubblica Sociale Italiana,* op. cit. "The reason for the incredible slowness of the trip from Como to the Valtellina

will never be explained on a route that you can manage in two hours on a bicycle."

3. Ermanno Amicucci, op. cit., p. 269.

4. Paolo Bottari, *All'ombra della grande ciminiera: la Cucirini Cantoni Coats*, Maria Pacini Fazzi, ed. (Lucca, 1994), p. 245.

5. Giuseppe Vitale, *Il Rotary club in 75 anni di vicende Italiane*, ed. (Rotary Internazionale, distretto 2030, 1999).

6. E. Amicucci, op. cit., p. 270.

7. Ibid., p. 274.

8. This is the opinion in the well-known book by Erich Kuby,*Il tradimento tedesco* (The German Betrayal), (Milan: Rizzoli, 1987).

9. E. Cione, op. cit. p. 372.

10. Ibid.

11. Pietro Carradori, *Vita col Duce*, op. cit., p. 83.

12. Arrigo Petacco, *Dear Benito, caro Winston*, op. cit., p. 47.

13. Ibid., p. 63

14. *Il Giornale di Brescia*, January 2, 2001.

15. Palmiro Togliatti was General Secretary of the PCI (Partito Comunista Italiano) [Italian Communist party].

16. Massimo Caprara essay written for the original edition of *La Pista Inglese* by Luciano Garibaldi, 2000.

17. Dante Gorreri, partisan commander and Communist party leader at Como.

18. The major was obviously informed about the "mission."

19. Urbano Lazzaro, *Dongo, mezzo secolo di menzogne* (Dongo: Half a Century of Lies), (Milan: Mondadori, 1993), p. 131.

20. On August 28, 2004, the *Times* gave the story a full page written by Richard Owen with an interview of Christopher Woods, an expert on SOE operations in Italy, who took exception to Lonati's account, saying that it was a total fabrication.

21. The publication of Enrico De Toma's documents and narrative began with the April 29, 1945, issue of the weekly *OGGI* under a headline reading "Let's Open Mussolini's Briefcase." The publication of the series was suddenly interrupted after four installments by a very lame explanation by editor Edilio Rusconi, who wrote the final article: "No further material will be published to avoid unpleasant disputes with important public figures."

22. There were other sensational examples of this kind of expert forgery, such as the Hitler diaries that were sold to the German magazine

Der Spiegel and published in the UK by Rupert Murdoch's tabloids for three million dollars; or the alleged Mussolini diaries, complete—with an excellent imitation of the Duce's handwriting—by the mother-and-daughter team of Panvini-Rosati in Vercelli.

23. Naturally at that point some commentators claimed that British intelligence had pressured the Italian government to hush everything up and blackmailed De Toma: "Either you deny everything, keep the money and disappear or we'll take you out." But this kind of plot belongs to pulp fiction rather than the history books.

Chapter VII —The Big Lie: Dongo

1. Published in Italy as *Storia della Repubblica di Salò* (Turin: Einaudi, 1963).
2. F. William Deakin, *The Brutal Friendship. Mussolini, Hitler and the Fall of Italian Fascism* (New York: Harper and Row, 1962), p. 816.
3. Denis Mack Smith, *Mussolini. A Biography* (New York: Knopf, 1982), p. 319.
4. Sandro Pertini of the Socialist party and Leo Valiani of the Partito d'Azione were members of the insurrection committee that took credit for shooting Mussolini.
5. Luigi Longo (*alias* Gallo), former commander of the Communist International Brigades in Spain and head of partisan Garibaldi division. Palmiro Togliatti (*alias* Ercoli), general secretary of the Italian Communist party, member of the Bonomi government, and overall leader of the Comintern (Communist International).
6. Richard Collier, *Duce! The Rise and Fall of Benito Mussolini* (New York: Viking, 1971), p. 320.
7. Richard Collier, op. cit., p. 341.
8. General Raffaele Cadorna was head of the CVL (Corpo Volontari della Libertà), of which Audisio and Lampredi were the Communist members.
9. Richard Collier, op, cit., pp. 352-4.
10. Chassin, *Histoire de la seconde guerre mondiale* (Paris: Payot, 1963).
11. Winston S. Churchill, *The Second World War*, 6 volumes, 1948–1954, (Boston: Houghton Mifflin Co., 1953), vol. 6, p. 528.
12. Inaccurate. Mussolini was aiming at joining the bulk of German troops concentrated at Merano in the Alto Adige (South Tyrol).

13. Actually a force of 300 heavily armed men.
14. Significant point, since the official version states that responsibility for Mussolini's execution did not belong to the Communists alone but by the entire CLNAI (Comitato di Liberazione Nazionale Alta Italia), the legitimate representative of the Bonomi government.
15. Gianfranco Vené, *La condanna di Mussolini* (Milan: Fabbri, 1973).
16. They represented the Liberal party, the Christian Democrats, the Socialist party, the Communist party, and the Partito d'Azione.
17. Franco Bandini, *Vita e morte segreta di Mussolini* (The Life and Secret Death of Mussolini), (Milan: Mondadori, 1978); Giorgio Pisanò, *Gli ultimi 5 secondi di Mussolini* (Mussolini's Final 5 Seconds), (Milan: Il Saggiatore, 1996).
18. Paolo Monelli, *Mussolini piccolo borghese* (Mussolini, a Petty Bourgeois), (Milan: Garzanti, 1959), p. 363.
19. Myriam Petacci, *Chi ama è perduto: mia sorella Claretta* (Who Loves is Lost: My Sister Claretta), (Trento: Reverdito, 1988).
20. Giorgio Cavalleri, *Ombre sul lago* (Shadows on the Lake), (Casale Monferrato: Piemme, 1995), p. 70.
21. GAP—Gruppo di Azione Proletaria (Proletarian Action Group)— anti-Nazi terror cells of the Communist party.
22. Bruno Giovanni Lonati, *Quel 28 aprile. Mussolini e Claretta: la verità* (That April 28th. Mussolini and Claretta: The Truth), (Milan: Mursia, 1994).

Chapter VIII — Plundering the Gold Stolen From the Jews

1. Interview in *Il Messaggero*, Rome, August 31, 2001.
2. Mario Scelba, a leading Christian Democrat, was minister of the interior in the De Gasperi government.
3. Chronicle of the trial by Franco Di Bella, *Corriere della Sera*, June 6, 1957.
4. See Guido Crapanzano and Ermelindo Giulianini, *La cartamoneta italiana: Corpus notarum pecuniarum Italiae* (Milan: Edizioni Spirali, 2002).
5. Ibid. See the chapter "Banca d'Italia: Repubblica Sociale Italiana."
6. Real name: Michele Moretti.
7. Some rough-looking characters were beginning to take the luggage inside the cars of the people under arrest.

8. According to an unpublished eyewitness account taken by this author on June 16, 2003, the valuables were moved in the late afternoon of April 28 (after the executions) to the villa of the sisters Teresa and Luisa Venini at Domàso. Their nephew, Bartolomeo Venini, who was eighteen at the time and part of the Resistance, remembers that the house of his aunts was picked by Neri and Pedro at the suggestion of Alois Hoffman, a Swiss citizen and friend of the partisans. The house was felt to be safer than the Domàso branch of the Cassa di Risparmio Bank, which at the time could be robbed and attacked at any moment. The Venini sisters were told to give everything to a person who would come with a paper authorizing the pick up of the treasure. "This happened," as Bartolomeo Venini remembered, "at dawn on April 29, when a little after 4 a.m. a group of partisans came to his aunt's house and, after producing the papers bearing the stamp of the Como PCI, proceeded to load everything on a car to take it to its final destination.

9. Quinto Navarra, *Memorie del commesso di Mussolini* (Milan: Longanesi, 1983), p. 286.

10. Alessandro Zanella, *L'ora di Dongo,* op. cit., p. 91.

11. Tamburini was disliked by the Germans and fired on June 19, 1944, as demanded by SS General Karl Wolff. Later, to avenge the dismissal of Buffarini-Guidi Wolff, ordered Tamburini's arrest together with Eugenio Apollonio, a functionary at the ministry of the interior and a member of the Duce's secretariat. Both men were deported to Dachau concentration camp.

12. Police order number 5 issued by the ministry of the interior, published on November 30, 1943.

13. We should not forget that the "Red Squad" of the PCI murdered Franco De Agazio a few days after the start of the second of his brave investigation—this one about the mysterious death of Captain Neri.

14. Meaning the Intelligence Service or MI6.

15. Pedro (Pier Bellini delle Stelle); Neri (Luigi Canali); Francesco (Pietro Terzini); Gatti (Michele Moretti); Gianna (Giuseppina Tuissi).

16. Massimo Caprara, *Quando le Botteghe erano oscure* (Milan, 1997), and *PCI la storia dimenticata* (Milan, 2001).

Chapter IX — How the British Beat the Americans

1. Roberto Faenza and Marco Fini, *Gli Americani in Italia* (Milan: Feltrinelli, 1976), p. 14.
2. Ibid., p. 15.
3. Ibid., p. 23.
4. Erich Kuby, *Il tradimento Tedesco* (The German Betrayal), (Milan: Rizzoli, 1983).
5. Luigi Imperatore, *I giorni dell'odio* (Days of Hate), (Rome: Ciarrapico, 1981).
6. "Fallmeyer from time to time is portrayed by those present at the time a lieutenant, a captain or a lieutenant colonel, but these contradictions are only on the surface. Lieutenant Fallmeyer was just a mask. Who was beneath that mask? Who was this Lieutenant Fallmeyer, whom no reporter or historian was able to track down after the war? He surely was someone who could impart any kind of order to Birzer and see it followed. He certainly must have been a high ranking officer, perhaps a lieutenant colonel, who had to have absolutely impeccable credentials; otherwise one cannot understand why an officer of the SS, such as Birzer (who was carrying out such an important mission), could decide, under the influence of someone of the same rank in the Wehrmacht (and who was in logistics as no less an officer as Fallmeyer officially said he was) Mussolini's fate in a few minutes. Fallmeyer's authority had to be such as to cover Birzer completely. This also explains the dry report written by Birzer following a request by none other than Wolff some five years later in 1950, when the worsening of the Cold War could increase the fear of veering off of western policies." Luigi Imperatore, *I giorni dell'odio*, op. cit., pp. 163–164.
7. Dwight D. Eisenhower, *Crusade in Europe*.
8. Aldo Icardi, *Master Spy* (Pittsburgh, 1954).
9. Alessandro Zanella, *L'ora di Dongo*, op. cit., p. 433.
10. Max Corvo, *The OSS in Italy 1942–1945: A Personal Memoir* (New York: Praeger, 1990).
11. Alessandro Zanella, *L'ora di Dongo*, op. cit., pp. 433–434.
12. Ermanno Amicucci, op. cit., pp. 276–277.
13. These were the fascist units that had followed the order issued on the radio by Alessandro Pavolini, head of the Fascist Republican party

(PFR), and converged to Como. However, the will to fight had by now weakened severely in all those units.

14. Vito was the son of Mussolini's brother Arnaldo; Vanni Teodorani was Vito's son-in-law. Both were Mussolini's nephews.

15. Alessandro Zanella, *L'ora di Dongo*, op. cit., p. 295.

16. Ibid., p. 244.

17. *Why was Mussolini Executed?* Vanni Teodorani was the first one to suspect a British involvement in the killing of the Duce.

18. Statement given by Pino Romualdi to Alessandro Zanella on February 19, 1988, and quoted in *L'ora di Dongo*, op. cit., p. 290.

19. Peter Tompkins, *Dalle carte segrete del Duce* (Milan: Marco Tropea, 2001), p. 351.

20. Peter Tompkins, *L'altra Resistenza* (Milan: Rizzoli, 1955).

21. Peter Tompkins, *Una spia a Roma* (Milan: 21 Saggiatore, 2002).

Chapter X — Claretta Petacci and the Mystery of Her Diaries

1. Pasquale Chessa, *Rosso e Nero* (Milan: Baldini e Castoldi, 1995).

2. Quoted in Luigi Salvatorelli and Giovanni Mira *Storia d'Italia nel periodo fascista* (Turin: Einaudi, 1957), It is also a well-known fact that the personal friendship between Churchill and Mussolini resulted in the British political leader's contributing articles to the Duce's daily newspaper, *Il Popolo d'Italia*, and in Churchill's constant support for the pro-Italian stance of British foreign secretary, Sir Samuel Hoare, who was forced to resign (because of his sympathetic attitude towards fascism in 1936 in the midst of the period of sanctions against Italy because of the war with Ethiopia), and was replaced by Anthony Eden, a staunch enemy of Italy and Mussolini. It is of interest to note how Samuel Hoare, who had been head of the British secret service in Italy in 1917, was to fight the wave of defeatism among Italian public opinion after the rout at Caporetto by heavily financing *Il Popolo d'Italia*, that began a violent campaign against the "traitors to the homeland." See Martin Gilbert, *The First World War* (New York: H. Holt, 1994).

3. The continued silence of those in charge of the archives of the Italian State (ministries of cultural affairs and of the interior) that ignore the recent requests by Ferdinando Petacci (the last legitimate heir of the estate of his aunt Claretta) who, from Arizona where he cur-

rently resides, has asked the attorney, Ubaldo Giuliani-Balestrino, professor of criminal law at the University of Turin, to request the return of his aunt Claretta's papers, since the fifty-year period covering "State Secrets" has now passed. It has been ascertained that some functionaries of the State Archives have decided excerpts of the Petacci papers by the Archives themselves. "This would be a speculation that would be damaging to the legitimate heir." Was the reply from Prof. Giuliani-Balestrino. In the meantime the Archive, in a bizarre and suspicious-sounding way, informed the police in March 2003 that letters received by Clara Petacci in 1937 had mysteriously disappeared. The Archive director stated: "The entire year 1937 is missing."

4. She was sent by Cavour to Paris in 1854 to compel Emperor Napoleon III, by becoming his mistress (thanks to her beauty), to throw his support to the Kingdom of Sardinia against Austria during the Second War of Independence.

5. Mistress of the younger Mussolini, author of the famous book, *Dux*. Being Jewish, she fled to South America and then to the United States because of the 1938 racial laws.

6. This was a sensational statement repeated by the entire press at the time and it could imply that the content of Claretta's diaries was compromising for Great Britain. When the author and his colleague, Alessandro Zanella, received the reply that the papers contained nothing of the sort, it could also mean that in the meantime they have been tampered with.

7. Myriam Petacci, *Chi ama è perduto: mia sorella Claretta,* op. cit., p. 346.

8. "Benghino" was Benvenuto, her favorite little nephew, the oldest son of Marcello Petacci, Claretta's brother who was six and half years old; the second boy, Ferdinando, was only three years old. [Author's note.]

9. Myriam Petacci, op. cit., p. 346.

10. *Newsweek* published a story by Mario Suttora about Ferdinando Petacci in the May 19, 2003, issue with the following biographical sketch of Claretta's nephew: "Ferdinando himself made a brilliant career as an executive in a French multinational company in Europe and South America. He moved to the United States with his sons, divorced, set up a catering service in California, then slipped onto a downward path. He lost his last job in a restaurant in Colorado a few months ago." Now he lives in a trailer.

11. Conversation with this writer, April 15, 2003.
12. Myriam Petacci, op. cit., p. 395.

Chapter XI — An Executioner Without Proof

1. As all other evening papers, *La Notte* has since ceased publication.
2. Roberto Gervaso, *Claretta* (Milan: Rizzoli, 1982).
3. Franco Bandini, op. cit.
4. *Noi,* February 15, 1995 (Alfredo Rossi editor), weekly published by Mondadori.
5. "Enigma," Rai, 3 January 31, 2003, at 8:50 p.m.
6. Renzo De Felice, the greatest historian of fascism, accepted the hypothesis this writer first made in 1994. De Felice died prematurely on May 25, 1996, not having had the time to engage in deeper research.
7. "Giacomo" was the nom de guerre of Bruno Giovanni Lonati.
8. Article by Fabrizio Castellini in the weekly *Epoca,* June 30, 1996.
9. Fabrizio Castellini in *Epoca,* art. cit.

Chapter XII — A Victim With Too Much Evidence

1. This was the death sentence issued by a Communist revolutionary court in February 1945 against Neri after he escaped from the fascists who had captured him in Como. According to the improvised and misinformed judges Neri went free because he gave away the hiding place of several comrades.
2. Alice Canali, with her husband Armando Grigioni, also a partisan commander, was in Mantua and not with her brother during the Como events.
3. During the war he was promoted to the rank of captain in the corps of engineers and fought bravely. See Giorgio Cavalleri, *Storia del Neri e della Gianna* (Como: Nodo Libri, 1991).
4. Colonel Pozzoli was the Questore (police chief) of Como during the RSI and was executed by the Communists after Liberation.
5. Statement made to the author.
6. The attempt did take place on May 28, 1945, when the CVL (Comando Volontari della Libertà) in Milan held a meeting where General Trabucchi, commander in Turin, asked that the Army be disbanded (the CIL—Corpo Italiano di Liberazione) and replaced by partisan

units. Cadorna, Ferruccio Parri, and Luigi Longo flew to Rome but did not succeed. The Americans let it be known that they would have opposed such an attempt with force of arms.

7. GAP: *Gruppo d'Azione Patriottica*, the covert units of the PCI.

8. Captain Enrico Mariani was in command of the fascist Black Brigade.

9. Mario Melloni became an editorial columnist at *L'Unità* after the war, signing his writings as "Fortebraccio."

10. Neri's sworn enemy, as noted earlier.

11. Lampredi was to play a leading role in the Dongo affair and was, throughout the "mission," Colonel Valerio's shadow.

12. Vigorous enforcer of the PCI orders in Turin and later Milan still alive at this writing. According to Bruno Giovanni Lonati, he was well aware of the Dongo secrets but would never reveal them.

13. The inconclusive trial was the result of the 1957 indictment of the partisan leaders on Lake Como regarding the disappearance of the "Dongo treasure" and a whole series of murders connected to it.

14. According to the well-known assumption of the "German betrayal," Fallmeyer had, in any case, already decided—obeying the orders he had received—to hand Mussolini over to the partisans.

15. But according to an unpublished eyewitness account given to this writer by a priest, Don Franco Broggi, in June 2003, Mussolini, in a German soldier's coat and laying down on a seat as though he were sleeping, was pointed out by gestures and eloquent glances to the partisan Negri by the other soldiers seated inside the truck. Don Broggi, who was born in Dongo and is today a chaplain of the Casa Pilascini at Gravedona, was an 18-year-old seminarian at the time and lived through the Dongo events, mingling with the crowd the entire day of April 27, 1945.

16. At the Padua trial Lorenzo Bianchi, who was called as a witness, proved to be rather reticent. He was to state, contradicting his own deposition, that he had handled the briefcases "no more than ten minutes," had checked the contents, and did not remember to whom he then handed them. During the deposition he had stated, however, that he had quickly leafed through the files and saw one of them marked with Churchill's name.

17. In a recent interview Alice Canali also remembered her mother's cautionary warning to her son a few hours before his disappearance, "Don't say it Luigi, don't say it!" as the woman begged, referring to his taking part in Mussolini's execution. But that cry appears to be

more plausible since it referred to the need to keep the "Dongo treasure" a secret that could never be revealed (see Roberto Festorazzi, "The Terrible Secrets of Captain Neri," *Il Messaggero*, May 21, 2003).

18. Eyewitness account by Pierino Dell'Era at the Padua trial. See Urbano Lazzaro, *L'Oro di Dongo* (Milan: Mondadori, 1995), p. 176.

19. In conversations with this writer Alice Canali strongly underscored the honesty and courage of Franco De Agazio. She remembered how her mother, Maddalena, while she provided the journalist with the documentation he was seeking, was careful to caution him by saying: "Be careful, there is real danger in this." But De Agazio responded: "I am not afraid." A few weeks later, on March 14, 1947, he was silenced forever because of his dissent by a "death squad" of the "Red Squad," a murder squad working for the Communists.

20. Edgardo Sogno was the legendary "Comander Franchi" of the monarchist Resistance.

21. See Ricciotti Lazzero, *La Decima Mas* (Milan: Rizzoli, 1984).

22. Pasca Piredda, *L'Ufficio stampa e propaganda della X Flottiglia MAS* (Bologna: Lo Scarabeo, 2003).

Appendix I — Ten Clues to the British Thread

1. Walter Audisio, *In nome del popolo italiano* (In the Name of the Italian People), (Turin: Teti Editore, 1975).
2. Urbano Lazzaro, op. cit.
3. Franco Bandini, op. cit.
4. Paolo Monelli, op. cit.
5. Alessandro Zanella, op. cit.
6. Giorgio Pisanò, op. cit.
7. Institute for the History of the Liberation Movement in Italy.
8. According to the "vulgate."

Appendix II — Interview with Luciano Garibaldi

1. Amerigo Clocchiatti, *Dall' antifascismo al De Profundis per il PCI: testimonanze di un militante* (From Anti-fascism to Post-mortem for the PCI: Memoir of a Rank and File Soldier), (Verona: Edizioni del Paniere, 1991).

INDEX

Canali, Alice   164, 168, 176–77, 179–81, 183, 228–30

Canali, Luigi (Captain Neri)   43, 69, 86, 88, 90, 92–3, 99–101, 104, 107–09, 123, 142–44, 153–55, 157, 163–64, 166–86, 191–92, 196–99, 201, 224, 228–29

Canali, Maddalena   108–09

Candrilli, Giancarlo   44–5

Candrilli, Manlio   44

Cantoni, Gugliemo (Sandrino)   85, 192

Cappuccio, Deputy Chief   65

Caprara, Massimo   xxii, 66–8, 108

Carissimi-Priori, Luigi   28–30

Carradori, Pietro   xxi, 35, 38, 54, 63, 102–04, 206

Casalinuovo, Col. Vito   41, 91

Castelli (secretary)   61

Catalano, Franco   78–9, 84

Cavallari, Dante   149

Cavalleri, Giorgio   89, 163

Caviglia (sailor)   36

Celio, Renato   121–22

Cella, Gian-Riccardo   43, 97

Cervis, Carlo and Caterina   134–35, 205

Cesarotti (driver)   38

Chassin, Gen. I. M.   77

Chiappo, Lisa   181

Churchill, Lady Clementine   67

Churchill, Winston   x, xiv–vii, xxi–xxii, 9–14, 19, 22, 27–38, 40–4, 47–50, 52–5, 61, 63–8, 76, 78, 93, 107, 113, 122–23, 127, 130–32, 147, 159–60, 177, 192–93, 196, 204, 206, 219, 226, 229

Cianca, Alberto   115

Ciano, Edda   112

Ciano, Galeazzo   110–12

Cione, Edmondo   xxi, 8, 41, 62–3

Clark, Gen. Mark W.   117

Coan, Vincenzina   109, 180

Collier, Richard   74–6

Coppola, Goffredo   91, 96

Corbella   170

Corvo, Max   116–17, 119

Cossutta, Armando   189

Cottabeni, Prof. Caio Mario   189

Coven (agent)   155–59

Crapanzano, Guido   99

Craveri, Raimondo   116

Croce, Benedetto   7, 117

Cucco, Alfredo   xxi, 41

Cummings, Herbert   110

Curiel, Eugenio   171

Daddario, Capt. Emilio Q.   76, 119–120

Dal Verme, Luchino   83

DAlessandro, Thomas   114

DAmico, Domenico   132

DAnnunzio, Gabriele   133–34

Daquanno, Ernesto   91, 96

Darlan, Admiral François   x

DAroma, Nino   xxi, 15–6, 42, 54

David, Tommaso   46, 56–7, 122

De Agazio, Franco   106, 181–82, 224, 230

De Angelis, Maj. Cosimo Maria   122

De Carli, Prof. Mario (C. A. Biggini)   1, 11

De Felice, Renzo   xi, xx, 20, 22, 84, 86, 128–29, 160, 189, 228

De Gasperi, Alcide   9–10, 57, 64, 72, 98, 198, 200, 210, 220

De Maria, Lia   161, 176, 189–90

De Pilato, Ugo   132

De Rossi, Andrea   65

De Ruggiero, Guido   7

Deakin, F. W.   74

Dean, Charles   20

Della Torre   181

Photographic Credits

For the photographs in this book, Enigma Books wishes to thank:

Luciano Garibaldi, the author, and *Studio Garibaldi*; Paolo Pisanò for the *Archivio Pisanò* images; the Tony De Santoli collection; the Butler Library at Columbia University and the Charles Poletti Collection; and the Max Corvo Collection.